FU S

S

PS Y

Alan S. Kornspan, EdD

University of Akron

Kornspan, Alan S., 1969-
    Fundamentals of sport and exercise psychology / Alan S. Kornspan.
        p. ; cm. -- (Human Kinetics' fundamentals of sport and exercise science series)
    Includes bibliographical references and index.
    ISBN-13: 978-0-7360-7447-6 (soft cover)
    ISBN-10: 0-7360-7447-3 (soft cover)
    1. Sports--Psychological aspects. 2. Exercise--Psychological
aspects. I. Title.
    [DNLM: 1. Sports--psychology. 2. Athletic Injuries--psychology. 3.
Exercise--psychology. 4. Sports Medicine--methods. QT 260 K84F 2009]
    GV706.4.K667 2009
    796.01--dc22

                                                2008049091

ISBN-10: 0-7360-7447-3 (print)   ISBN-10: 0-7360-8463-0 (Adobe PDF)
ISBN-13: 978-0-7360-7447-6 (print)   ISBN-13: 978-0-7360-8463-5 (Adobe PDF)

Figures 2.1, 3.2, 3.3, 5.1, 7.3, and 9.1 are reprinted, by permission, from R. Weinberg and S. Gould, 2007, *Foundations of sport and exercise psychology,* 4th ed. (Champaign, IL: Human Kinetics).

Figure 7.1 is from R.D. Comstock et al., 2006, "Sports related injuries among high school athletes—United States, 2005-06," *MMWR Weekly* 55(38): 1037-1040. Available: http://www.cdc.gov/mmwr/preview/mmwrhtml/mm5538a1.htm.

Figure 7.2 is reprinted, by permission, from R. Weinberg and S. Gould, 2007, *Foundations of sport and exercise psychology,* 4th ed. (Champaign, IL: Human Kinetics), 297; Adapted, by permission, from M. Andersen and J. Williams, 1988, "A model of stress and athletic injury: Prediction and prevention," *Journal of Sport and Exercise Psychology* 10(3): 297.

Figure 8.1 is reprinted, by permission, from R.D. Morgan et al., 2005, *Life after graduate school: Insider's advice from new psychologists* (East Sussex, UK: Psychology Press), 277.

Figure 9.2 is reprinted, by permission, from R. Dishman, R. Washburn, and G. Heath, 2004, *Physical activity epidemiology* (Champaign, IL: Human Kinetics), 393.

The Web addresses cited in this text were current as of November 2008, unless otherwise noted.

Acquisitions Editor: Myles Schrag; **Developmental Editor:** Christine M. Drews; **Assistant Editor:** Katherine Maurer; **Copyeditor:** Jan Feeney; **Proofreader:** Anne Rogers; **Indexer:** Craig Brown; **Permission Manager:** Dalene Reeder; **Graphic Designer:** Bob Reuther; **Graphic Artist:** Yvonne Griffith; **Cover Designer:** Bob Reuther; **Photos (interior):** © Human Kinetics, unless otherwise noted; **Photo Asset Manager:** Laura Fitch; **Visual Production Assistant:** Joyce Brumfield; **Photo Production Manager:** Jason Allen; **Art Manager:** Kelly Hendren; **Associate Art Manager:** Alan L. Wilborn; **Illustrator:** Alan L. Wilborn; **Printer:** McNaughton & Gunn

Printed in the United States of America   10 9 8 7 6 5 4 3 2 1

Human Kinetics
Web site: www.HumanKinetics.com

United States: Human Kinetics, P.O. Box 5076, Champaign, IL 61825-5076
800-747-4457, e-mail: humank@hkusa.com

Canada: Human Kinetics, 475 Devonshire Road Unit 100, Windsor, ON N8Y 2L5
800-465-7301 (in Canada only), e-mail: info@hkcanada.com

Europe: Human Kinetics, 107 Bradford Road, Stanningley, Leeds LS28 6AT, United Kingdom
+44 (0) 113 255 5665, e-mail: hk@hkeurope.com

Australia: Human Kinetics, 57A Price Avenue, Lower Mitcham, South Australia 5062
08 8372 0999, e-mail: info@hkaustralia.com

New Zealand: Human Kinetics, Division of Sports Distributors NZ Ltd., P.O. Box 300 226 Albany North Shore City, Auckland
0064 9 448 1207, e-mail: info@humankinetics.co.nz

In memory of my mother, Shirley A. Kornspan, who showed me the importance of always trying to be positive and kind.

Contents

Series Preface **vii** ▪ Preface **ix** ▪ Acknowledgments **xi**

PART I   **WELCOME TO SPORT AND EXERCISE PSYCHOLOGY** 1

CHAPTER 1   **What Is Sport and Exercise Psychology?** 3
Origins in Psychology, Physical Education, and Sports Medicine 5
Psychology of Sport: 1900 to 1920 6
Psychology of Sport: 1920s and 1930s. 7
Psychology of Sport: 1940s to 1960s 8
Psychology of Sport: 1970s to 1990s 10
Current Status of the Field of Sport and Exercise Psychology. 11
Professional Practice Issues in Sport and Exercise Psychology 17
The Short of It. 18

CHAPTER 2   **What Can I Do With Sport and Exercise Psychology?**. 19
Academic Path 22
Professional Path 24
Other Paths Incorporating Sport and Exercise Psychology 32
The Short of It. 35

PART II   **GOALS OF SPORT AND EXERCISE PSYCHOLOGY** 37

CHAPTER 3   **Enhancing the Performance of Individual Athletes** 39
Cognitive-Behavioral Model of Sport Consultation 41
Where Does Mental Training Occur? 43
What Mental Training Skills Are Taught to Athletes? 43
Research Support for Teaching Mental Skills to Athletes 51
Who Provides Performance-Enhancement Services to Athletes? 52
The Short of It. 54

CHAPTER 4   **Enhancing the Performance of Teams** 55
Overview of Team Building. 57
Where Does Team Building Occur? 60
What Team-Building Activities Are Taught to Athletes? 62
Research Support for Teaching Team Building. 63
Who Provides Team-Building Services to Athletes?. 64
The Short of It. 65

CHAPTER 5   **Creating a Positive Sport Environment**
Leadership, Motivation, and Communication 67
Importance of Creating a Positive Sport Environment. 69
Where Do Coaches Learn to Create a Positive Environment? 72
What Methods Do Consultants Teach to Coaches? 73
Research Support for Providing a Positive Sport Environment 76
Who Provides Consulting on Positive Sport Environments? 76
The Short of It. 79

CHAPTER 6 Assessing Athletes' Mental Skills **81**

Overview of Assessment for Sport Organizations and Teams 82
Where Do Assessments Occur? 84
How Is Assessment Used in Sport Psychology? 84
Issues in Psychological Testing 88
Research Support for Using Assessments With Athletes 89
Who Provides Psychological Testing Services? 89
The Short of It 90

CHAPTER 7 Caring for Athletes
General Well-Being and Recovery From Injury **91**

What Is Psychology of Rehabilitation From Athletic Injury? 92
How Do Athletes Respond to Injury? 94
Referrals to Sport Psychologists 95
What Interventions Are Provided to Injured Athletes? 96
Research Support for Injury Counseling 99
Who Provides Sport Psychology and
      Counseling Services to Injured Athletes? 99
What Are the Unique Developmental Concerns of Athletes? 100
Where Are Personal Development Services Provided and Who Provides Them? 101
Research Support for Personal Development Services 108
The Short of It 108

CHAPTER 8 Helping Athletes With Mental Health Issues
A Clinical Approach **109**

What Is Clinical Sport Psychology? 111
Responsibilities of a Clinical or Counseling Sport Psychologist 112
Where Does Clinical Sport Psychology Take Place? 112
What Occurs in Clinical Sport Psychology? 112
Mental Health Issues Treated by Clinical Sport Psychologists 114
Research Support for Clinical Sport Psychology Services 117
Who Provides Clinical Sport Psychology Services? 118
The Short of It 119

CHAPTER 9 Using Psychology to Encourage
Involvement in Exercise and Fitness **121**

What Is Exercise Psychology? 123
Where Does Exercise Psychology Take Place? 124
What Services Are Provided in Exercise Psychology? 125
What Interventions Are Used in the Exercise Process? 126
Research Support for Exercise Psychology Services 128
Who Provides Exercise Psychology Services? 128
The Short of It 131

Epilogue: The Future of Sport and Exercise Psychology **133**

Appendix A: Learn More About Sport and Exercise Psychology **137**

Appendix B: Implementing Sport and Exercise Psychology in the Real World **141**

References **151**

Author Index **169**

Subject Index **173**

About the Author **179**

Series Preface

The sport sciences have matured impressively over the past 40 years. Subdisciplines in kinesiology have established their own rigorous paths of research, and physical education in its many forms is now an accepted discipline in higher education. Our need now is not only for comprehensive resources that contain all the knowledge that the field has acquired, but also for resources that summarize the foundations of each of the sport sciences for the variety of people who make use of that information today. Understanding the basic topics, goals, and applications of the subdisciplines in kinesiology is critical for students and professionals in many walks of life. Human Kinetics has developed the Fundamentals of Sport and Exercise Science series with these needs in mind.

This and the other books in the series will not provide you with all the in-depth knowledge required for earning an advanced degree or for opening a practice in this subject area. This book will not make you an expert on the subject. What this book will do is give you an excellent grounding in the key themes, terms, history, and status of the subject in both the academic and professional worlds. You can use this grounding as a jumping-off point for studying more in-depth resources and for generating questions for more experienced people in the field. We've even included an annotated list of additional resources for you to consult as you continue your journey.

You might be using this book to help you improve your professional skills or to assess the potential job market. You might want to learn about a new subject, supplement a textbook, or introduce a colleague or client to this exciting subject area. In any of these cases, this book will be your guide to the basics of this subject. It is succinct, informative, and entertaining. You will begin the book with many questions, and you will surely finish it with many more questions. But they will be more thoughtful, complex, substantive questions. We hope that you will use this book to help the sport sciences, and this subject in particular, continue to prosper for another generation.

Key to Icons

Look for the giant quotation marks, which set off noteworthy quotes from researchers and professionals in the field.

Psychology Insights include quirky or surprising "Did you know?" types of information.

Success Stories highlight influential individuals in the field. Through these sidebars, you will learn how researchers and professionals apply their knowledge of the subject to their work, and you'll be able to explore possible career paths in the field.

Preface

Fundamentals of Sport and Exercise Psychology is a resource for those just beginning to learn about the field as well as for those who want to refresh and update their knowledge. You might be a high school student or a university undergraduate student wanting to know more about the field of sport and exercise psychology and its related professions. Or perhaps you're studying psychology or sport science and are wondering how you can combine these two passions into a rewarding career. Maybe you're a university instructor or advisor answering students' questions about how they can apply their training to the field of sport and exercise psychology. This book will aid you in your work in any of these situations.

Fundamentals of Sport and Exercise Psychology is one of the first books to present information on the academic and professional fields of sport and exercise psychology. You will learn about the training involved in these disciplines, the services provided by sport psychology professionals, how and where professionals are currently applying their training, and the possibilities for the future of applied sport psychology practice.

Sport psychology professionals are now obtaining full-time jobs applying sport psychology in the field and working as university professors. Additionally, sport psychology professionals are working in university athletic departments as sport psychologists. Sport psychologists and mental training consultants are also working with organizations and national governing bodies that provide psychological services to Olympic-level athletes. Exercise psychologists are finding many opportunities to help people become and stay physically active as society becomes more aware of the benefits of physical activity.

Part I introduces the field of sport and exercise psychology. Chapter 1 provides a brief history of the field and explains what sport psychologists do. Chapter 2 presents the various career paths and job opportunities in the field.

Part II (chapters 3 through 9) focuses on the issues that are most commonly discussed in sport and exercise psychology, such as helping athletes improve performance, and proceeds to less commonly discussed issues, such as personal development, mental health issues, and exercise psychology. Interventions with individual athletes are discussed in chapter 3, and then group interventions, including team building and helping coaches create positive environments in order for athletes to excel, are covered in chapters 4 and 5. Chapter 6 focuses on assessment of athletes' mental skills. Chapter 7 explains the personal developmental aspects of sport psychology that enhance the well-being of athletes, including athletic injury and psychosocial development. Chapter 8 covers clinical sport psychology, and chapter 9 focuses on the topic of applied exercise psychology.

Available as
an E-BOOK at
www.HumanKinetics.com

A major focus of this text is the applied aspects of sport psychology. The Success Stories in each chapter explore how knowledge of sport and exercise psychology is applied by athletes, coaches, and sport psychologists, including mental training consultants. Psychology Insights offer interesting facts or reflections from people in the field. The many quotes throughout the chapters provide a flavor of the field from practicing sport and exercise psychologists.

Sport and exercise psychology is an ever-evolving field. At the time of this writing (fall of 2008), the information and corresponding references reflected the current status of the field. However, that very likely will change. The fluid, shifting nature of the field means that many of the Internet sources cited won't exist when you read the book, and the information likely will have changed.

This book provides you with much of the background information you need in order to pursue future studies in the field of sport and exercise psychology, and my hope is that it will motivate you to continue learning more about the field.

Acknowledgments

First, I would like to thank my wife, Lisa, and my children, Spencer, Zachary, and Justin, for their unconditional support and understanding while I was working on this manuscript.

I would like to thank my dad, Donald Kornspan, for believing in my pursuit of a career in the study of sport and exercise psychology. Also, I would like to thank my siblings, Rick Kornspan and Susan Levy, for encouraging my academic pursuits throughout the years, and my in-laws, Murray and Marianne Weisman, for their support. Additionally, I would like to thank my mentors, Dr. Ed Etzel and Dr. Andy Ostrow, for the excellent instruction and guidance they provided me while I was a doctoral student at West Virginia University.

Finally, I would like to thank Myles Schrag, Chris Drews, and Kate Maurer for their excellent work, diligence, and guidance in the editorial process of producing this book.

I PART

Welcome to Sport and Exercise Psychology

Part I of *Fundamentals of Sport and Exercise Psychology* presents an overview of sport and exercise psychology and the types of professional opportunities that exist in the field. Chapter 1 explains how the field developed from three main areas: psychology, physical education, and sports medicine. The various roles of sport and exercise psychologists and the current status of the field are discussed. Chapter 1 also includes specific resources in which students and practitioners can find more information about the field.

Many people are just beginning to learn about the field of sport and exercise psychology, and there is a growing interest in career opportunities. Students as well as counselors and instructors are interested in how training in sport and exercise psychology can be applied. Chapter 2 focuses on career paths in sport and exercise psychology. Many individuals trained in sport and exercise psychology are working in jobs outside of traditional faculty positions in higher education. The text presents an overview of the opportunities that sport psychology consultants have available to them. Specific jobs and settings for sport psychology work are discussed.

CHAPTER 1

What Is Sport and Exercise Psychology?

In this chapter, you will learn the following:

✓ What the field of sport and exercise psychology involves and what sport and exercise psychologists do

✓ How the field of sport and exercise psychology developed from three main disciplines: psychology, physical education, and sports medicine

✓ The current status of sport and exercise psychology and specific resources in which you can find much more information about the field

"90 percent of the game is half mental."

Yogi Berra

Roy "Doc" Halladay was drafted by the Toronto Blue Jays in 1995. After having initial success (he almost threw a no-hitter in his second start), he started to perform poorly, and by 2000 he went 4-7 with an ERA of 10.64. Halladay was subsequently sent to the minor leagues. As Halladay received help with his physical mechanics, he eventually returned to the majors. However, upon arriving back to the majors, he still had doubts about his abilities, which he believed affected his performance. Said Halladay, "You always have these thoughts creeping into your head, a picture of how things might not work out. . . . That's the biggest challenge sometimes is getting rid of those mental pictures and putting positive things in there. If you can get away from that and avoid that, in any part of your life, it makes a huge difference" (Wood, 2005, para. 26). After Halladay's return to the majors, he began working with mental training consultant Harvey Dorfman. Dorfman provided Halladay with readings and helped him develop a more positive outlook toward performance. After improving through his physical and mental training, Halladay went on to many successful seasons. In fact, Halladay won the American League's Cy Young Award in 2003. In discussing the importance of both physical and mental training, Halladay said, "If you're talking about Mel and Harvey, I honestly don't think I could've gotten it done without either of them" (Wood, 2005, para. 28). Roy Halladay reads Dorfman's *The Mental ABC's of Pitching* seven or eight times a year (Slinger, 2007).

Sport and exercise psychology is a field focused on the study of people and their behavior in sport and exercise (Weinberg & Gould, 2007). One focus of **sport psychology** is to teach athletes the mental skills to enhance their physical performance. This aspect of the field is illustrated in the previous story of the mental training consulting that Harvey Dorfman provided for Roy Halladay. A second focus of sport psychology is to teach coaches to create a positive environment for their athletes by leading and communicating with them. Another aspect of the study of athletes' behavior involves enhancing their psychological development by teaching life skills and providing counseling and clinical diagnoses. **Exercise psychology** focuses on the

sport psychology—The study of people and their behavior in sport.

exercise psychology—The study of people and their behavior in exercise, especially in terms of helping the general population become more physically active and adhere to daily physical activity.

practice of providing support to the general p[...]
become more physically active and adhere to [...]

Origins in Psychology, Phys[...] and Sports Medi[...]

The scientific study of the field of psycholog[...]
helm Wundt started the first experimenta[...]
Leipzig, Germany, in 1879. In that period the [...]
was organizing in the United States. Willia[...]
physical educator, organized the Associati[...]
Physical Education, and the association held its first conference.
Both the fields of psychology and physical education were experiencing
transitions during their development. Psychology was moving from a
focus on philosophy to a focus on using laboratory research to understand
behavior. Physical education was moving from a focus on exercise to a
focus on teaching sport skill and instruction. It would not be long until
individuals from these fields would begin to collaborate.

In the early 1890s psychologists and physical educators began to work
together. William James taught a psychology class for the students in
the physical training school at Harvard University. Luther Gulick, who
taught at the YMCA training school in Springfield, Massachusetts, was
also interested in the applications of psychology to sport and physical
education. See the sidebar to learn how Gulick influenced James Naismith, and the sport of basketball was born.

In addition to James and Gulick, influential physical educators and
psychologists of the late 1800s began to collaborate in conducting psychological research applied to sport and in presenting information at
conferences. Possibly one of the first studies to gain attention from the
media was conducted by E.W. Scripture and his colleagues at the Yale Psychology Laboratory (Kornspan, 2007a). Scripture was interested in determining whether the reaction time and discrimination time of expert fencers were different than those of novice fencers. He was aided in these studies by W.G. Anderson. At around the same time as Scripture was completing his studies at Yale University, G.W. Fitz was con-ducting reaction-time studies of

Psychology Insight

During the fall of 1891, Luther
Gulick taught a psychology class
in which James Naismith was a
student. In this seminar, Gulick
challenged the students to think
about creating a game that could
be played indoors during winter
months. This seminar inspired
Naismith to develop the sport of
basketball (Naismith, 1941).

[...]onference
on applications of
psychology to the
field of physical
education and sport.

1895
E.W. Scripture
publishes "Thinking,
Feeling, Doing,"
which has many
examples of how
sport and physical
activity can be studied
psychologically. The
field of sport is part of
the new psychology.

1897
Pierre de Coubertin
organizes an Olympic
Congress at Le Havre,
France, that discusses
on "Psychology of
Exercise."

1900-1919

1900
E.W. Scripture
presents "Psychology
of Physical Education"
at the American
Physical Education
Conference.

1913
An Olympic Congress
on sport psychology
and physiology is
held in Lausanne,
Switzerland.

1913
Harry K. Wolfe,
professor of
psychology at
the University of
Nebraska, proposes
the development of
a laboratory devoted
to the study of
the psychology of
football.

athletes. This period of psychology can be seen as an application of the "new psychology," which focused on precise quantitative measurement rather than on one's own philosophical opinion to sport (Kornspan, 2007a). Using quantitative measurements from the 1897 bicycle racing season, Norman Triplett studied the social psychology of cyclists. He was interested in determining whether cyclists achieved faster times while riding alone or while competing against other cyclists (Triplett, 1898).

As the field of sport psychology was developing in the United States, sport psychology was gaining international interest as well in what was soon to be seen as the field of sports medicine. Pierre de Coubertin, who organized the modern Olympic Games, did not want the Games to be only about watching sporting events. He wanted to include an educational component (Kornspan, 2007b). Coubertin's interest in sport education spurred one of the first Olympic educational congresses to hold a discussion of psychology at Le Havre, France, in 1897. The theme was sport hygiene and pedagogy, and a section of the congress was devoted to the psychology of exercise.

Psychology of Sport: 1900 to 1920

Pierre de Coubertin also organized a 1913 Olympic Congress in Lausanne, Switzerland, that focused on the psychological and physiological aspects of sport. Through this congress, he wanted to encourage the medical community to consider the psychological aspects of sport and exercise because he thought that the medical profession was focusing too much attention on the physiological aspects of sport and exercise (Kornspan, 2007b).

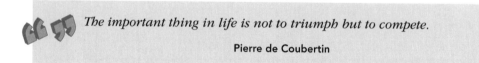

The important thing in life is not to triumph but to compete.

Pierre de Coubertin

The sport psychology Olympic Congress held in May of 1913 was attended by more than 400 people from around the world. Most of the congress focused on the psychological aspects of sport, a topic that at that time was very philosophically oriented. Many of the presentations featured personal accounts of how psychology influenced people in sport and exercise, but studies related to the scientific aspects of sport psychology were presented as well (Kornspan, 2007b). One presentation by Dr. Jean Philippe called for sport to be scientifically studied in the psychology laboratory. In fact, Dr. Philippe cited Scripture's work in his conference presentation. Interestingly, many in attendance at this first sport psychology congress believed that there was not enough scientific research to back up the claims of the individuals giving presentations (Kornspan, 2007b). Thus, one could see the influence of the new psychology, which would move from an introspective view to one of using research to support the science of the field.

During the early 1900s the application of psychology to sport was discussed in Olympic Congresses, books, and media outlets. A.G. Spalding discussed how experimental psychology could be used to influence the sport of baseball (Marshall, 1910). Additionally, a renowned psychology professor at the University of Nebraska, Harry K. Wolfe, proposed starting an American football psychology laboratory (Brannon, 1913).

Psychology of Sport: 1920s and 1930s

Coleman Griffith was one of the most well-known individuals in the study of psychological aspects of sport. Griffith began his studies informally as a doctoral student as early as 1918 at the University of Illinois (Gould & Pick, 1995). After Griffith became a professor at Illinois, he continued his work with the university's head American football coach Bob Zuppke, who was also interested in psychology. Griffith became part of Zuppke's faculty advisory staff during the 1921 football season ("Psychologist to Aid Selection of Illini Athletes," 1922). During that period, Griffith became an instructor in the University of Illinois coaching school, where he began to teach a course on the psychology of athletics.

Other psychologists and physical educators were interested in studying psychology and applying it to sport during this period. Much of the work focused on the use of testing and how testing psychological variables could aid coaches. At the 1925 American Psychological Association conference, Charles Homer Bean presented information about using psychological testing to help predict athletic performance (Bean, 1927). Walter Miles was conducting research with Pop Warner at Stanford University on the reaction times of American football linemen (Baugh & Benjamin, 2006). John Lawther, a professor of psychology and a basketball coach, was conducting reaction-time studies with athletes in the 1930s ("Big Athletes Alert," 1931). Along with these researchers, psychologists and coaches were beginning to collaborate to make practical coaching decisions to aid in the testing and selection of athletes for teams (Campbell, 1930).

Psychology Insight

Paul Brown, Hall of Fame football coach, began collaborating with psychologists while he was coaching at Massillon High School in Massillon, Ohio, during the late 1930s (Kornspan, 2006). He had Robert Henderson and Ross Stagner administer reaction-time tests, personality tests, and an intelligence test to athletes who were trying out for the football team. Brown became known as the first to bring intelligence testing to professional football. Today the Wonderlic Personnel Test, a 12-minute, 50-question intelligence test, is given to all potential National Football League Draft picks.

1920-1939

■ **1920**
Carl Diem starts first laboratory focused on the study of sport psychology in Germany.

■ **1921**
Coleman Griffith appointed to Robert Zuppke's staff as part of the faculty advisory committee to the football team.

■ **1922**
Griffith begins to teach sport psychology class as part of the athletic coaching/physical education major at the University of Illinois.

■ **1925**
A.Z. Puni starts sport psychology laboratory in Leningrad.

■ **1925**
Griffith starts the Athletic Research Laboratory at the University of Illinois.

■ **1928**
Coleman Griffith writes of his influence in bringing the subject of psychology of athletics to universities.

■ **1938**
Coleman Griffith and Jack Sterret are hired as consultants by the Chicago Cubs.

1940-1969

■ **1940**
Clinical psychologist Dorothy Yates begins to work with boxers at San Jose State College, and Richard Paynter begins to apply psychology with Long Island University football team coached by Clair Bee.

■ **1942**
Bud Winter, San Jose State College track coach, organizes a committee to conduct research at the U.S. Navy Pre-Flight School to analyze the effects of relaxation training on the enhancement of athletic activities.

■ **1942 or 1943**
Franklin Henry and Anna Espenschade begin teaching a course related to the psychology of sport.

(continued)

Throughout the world, the field of sports medicine recognized the contribution that psychology could make to the understanding of sport. In 1928, the influence of Pierre de Coubertin undoubtedly led the first sports medicine organization, the International Federation of Sports Medicine, to make one of its main purposes the study of the psychological aspects of sport. By 1958, renowned University of Iowa research professor Charles H. McCloy described in his article "What Is Sports Medicine?" numerous psychological studies that had been conducted in the area of sports medicine since the early 1920s.

During the 1920s and 1930s, the applied aspects of the psychology of sport focused on how the psychologist could aid the coach with the use of psychological testing of athletes. Many of the tests focused on reaction time; however, some psychologists were also promoting and using intelligence tests and personality tests in their consultations with athletes and coaches.

Psychology of Sport: 1940s to 1960s

The focus of psychology applied to sport from the 1920s through the 1930s appears to have been on psychological testing, but the 1940s and 1950s started to see a move toward teaching athletes psychological skills to help them improve performance. By the 1940s **interventions** were developed to help athletes relax under pressure. Dorothy Yates, a clinical psychology professor at San Jose State College (now San Jose State University), conducted research with coach DeWitt Portal to determine whether psychology could improve the athletic performance of boxers. Yates and Portal found that the interventions were effective. Thus, Yates began to teach a psychology class for athletes and aviators and began to meet individually with the boxers for consulting sessions. Yates taught the boxers how to use an intervention that she termed the relaxation set method (Kornspan & MacCracken, 2001), which is similar to using progressive relaxation paired with positive affirmations.

intervention—A method for improving mental skills. Examples are goal setting, mental imagery, positive self-talk, concentration, relaxation, and preperformance routines.

The psychology of athletics was also studied during World War II at the Del Monte Pre-Flight School in Del Monte, California. Bud Winter, a track coach at San Jose State College, collaborated with Edmund Jacobson and Dorothy Yates in testing a relaxation intervention with naval aviators. The project showed how relaxation skills definitively improved performance in athletic skills (Winter, 1981).

The popularity of psychological interventions was growing worldwide in the 1940s and 1950s. The use of psychological interventions received attention in Australia, where Olympic swimming coach Forbes Carlisle was introducing hypnosis to his swimmers ("Aussie Swim Coach," 1957). Similarly, a *New York Times* article reported that Russia was introducing hypnosis to their athletes as a performance-enhancement intervention ("Russia Eyes Hypnotism in Sport," 1957). In Toronto, Canada, Lloyd Percival started Sports College, an educational institution that provided information about sports and fitness and conducted research on relaxation. Sports College produced radio and television shows and published books, manuals, and brochures (Canada's Sports Hall of Fame, n.d.). This led to the publication of Percival's book *Relaxation Is Easy*. Additionally, conferences focused on the psychology of sport were sponsored by the Bureau of Sport Pedagogy (Kornspan, 2007b) in 1944 and 1949.

Toward the end of the 1940s, David F. Tracy suggested to the St. Louis Browns baseball team that he could help them improve performance through the use of psychological skills and hypnosis (Kornspan & MacCracken, 2003). The St. Louis Browns hired Tracy to teach hypnosis, relaxation, visualization, and positive affirmations to the athletes during spring training. This situation brought unprecedented attention to the use of psychology and specifically hypnosis in the field of athletic performance. Tracy (1951) wrote about his work in the book *The Psychologist at Bat*. In addition to working with the St. Louis Browns, Tracy worked with a university basketball team and consulted with the New York Rangers hockey team (Kornspan & MacCracken, 2003).

During the 1950s, more coaches and psychologists began to use hypnosis to help athletes improve physical performance. Individuals such as Warren Johnson, Franklin Henry, and Anna Espenschade were promoting the use of various psychological interventions with athletes. These individuals also headed graduate programs that would produce leaders in the field of sport psychology from the 1960s to the present day. Warren Johnson conducted research studies on hypnosis (Kornspan & MacCracken, 2003), and Henry and Espenschade (Fales, 1952) were chronicled in media outlets showing how psychology could be applied to sport.

The use of psychological interventions with athletes during this time would not be without controversy. The Council of Mental Health from the American Medical Association formed a committee in conjunction with the Committee on the Medical Aspects of Sport that assessed the use of hypnosis for athletic performance (Kornspan & MacCracken, 2003). The committee created a report detailing their thoughts on how hypnosis should be used for athletic performance. Generally, this report suggested that using hypnosis in sport was not good sportsmanship and that using hypnosis to improve the performance of an athlete was not healthy. However, the committee believed that there were times when hypnosis could be used to help athletes with health issues, as long as the hypnosis was not related to enhancing sport performance (Kornspan & MacCracken, 2003).

As interest in the psychology of sport continued to grow worldwide, a group of sports medicine professionals organized the first World Congress of Sport Psychology, hosted by the International Society of Sport Psychology (ISSP) in 1965 in Rome, Italy (Silva, 2002). In 1967, a group of

1940-1969
(continued)

1944
Congress on the Pedagogy and Psychology of Sport is held in honor of the 50th anniversary of the Olympic Games.

1949
International Congress of Physiology and Psychology in Sports is held in Lausanne, Switzerland.

1950
David F. Tracy is hired by the St. Louis Browns to provide hypnosis and psychology training to the baseball players for the Browns and their minor league teams.

1956
First All Union Conference on Psychology of Sport, held in the Soviet Union.

1965
First World Congress of Sport Psychology, organized by the International Society of Sport Psychology.

1966
Bruce Ogilvie and Thomas Tutko publish "Problem Athletes and How to Handle Them."

1969
European Federation of Sport Psychology is founded.

1970-1999

1970
First sport psychology journal is published: the *International Journal of Sport Psychology*.

1983
United States Olympic Committee defines sport psychology.

1984
The British Association of Sport and Exercise and Science is founded.

1986
Division 47 of the American Psychological Association is created.

(continued)

⭐ **SUCCESS STORY**

Bud Winter, Former Head Track and Field Coach at San Jose State University

Lloyd "Bud" Winter was a track (athletics) coach at San Jose State University for 35 years. In the early 1940s, he was a close friend of boxing coach DeWitt Portal. Winter learned that Portal's top-ranked boxing team had started consulting with Dr. Dorothy H. Yates, a clinical psychology professor from the psychology department. The boxing team had much success in working with Dr. Yates (Riley, 1943). She taught the boxing team how to use the relaxation set method, which involves the use of positive affirmations, to get in the right frame of mind before competition (Kornspan & MacCracken, 2001). Winter was interested in how psychology could be applied to track and field, so he began to attend Dr. Yates' psychology class for athletes and aviators. However, Winter entered the navy before he was able to have Yates work with his team. But Winter brought Yates onto a committee in the navy that studied the use of relaxation on athletic skills of cadets training at the Navy Pre-Flight School. Winter (1981) considered the research on the use of relaxation with athletes a huge success, and it helped shape his coaching. Winter would go on to a successful career as a track and field coach, coaching many Olympians and world-record holders. In the 1960s he consulted with Dr. Bruce Ogilvie, a professor at San Jose State University and a pioneer in the field of sport psychology (Ragni, 1989). Winter wrote about the importance of relaxation in athletics in his 1981 book *Relax and Win*.

---

individuals created the first sport psychology organization in North America, the North American Society for the Psychology of Sport and Physical Activity (NASPSPA), and then hosted the second World Congress of Sport Psychology in Washington, D.C., in 1968.

Psychology of Sport: 1970s to 1990s

The field of sport psychology has grown a great deal since the late 1960s. In the 1970s, only a few master's and doctoral programs were training students specifically in the field of sport psychology, and those programs focused on the academic and research aspects. However, psychologists were starting private practices related to consulting with athletes. The United States Olympic Committee was a leader in organizing the field of applied sport psychology. Richard Suinn began working with Olympic athletes in the early 1970s, and Dorothy Harris began working with the United States Olympic Committee to enhance athletes' performances. Also, psychologists and sport science professionals began consulting with professional sport teams. In the 1980s it became increasingly more common in the United States to hear about successful athletes and coaches working with sport psychologists. As a result, from the 1980s onward there has been much positive press about the field of sport psychology. Many athletes openly attribute their improved performance to their work with sport psychology consultants.

The 1990s saw a continued focus on the development of the profession of sport psychology. As the field of sport psychology gained more attention, more students became interested in attending graduate school. As more students entered graduate programs, professional organizations took a greater interest in what happened to graduates of these programs after they entered the job market (Andersen, Williams, Aldridge, & Taylor, 1997). Also, discussion of professionalization issues continued throughout the world. In the United States, the Association for the Advancement of Applied Sport Psychology (now the Association for Applied Sport Psychology) instituted a program to certify consultants through its organization (Silva, 2002).

Since the late 1970s, one of the major changes in the field of sport psychology is the addition of a focus on research in exercise psychology. As the epidemic of obesity increases throughout the world, a major problem seems to be physical inactivity. We are now seeing opportunities in which knowledge of exercise psychology can be applied in full-time employment settings.

Current Status of the Field of Sport and Exercise Psychology

As explored in this chapter, the field of sport and exercise psychology has evolved from the early years, in which psychologists and physical educators were beginning to collaborate, to the 1940s, when psychologists and coaches conducted psychological testing to help coaches with team selection, and onward, where we see professionals help athletes learn psychological skills to improve performance. Since the 1960s the field has slowly become more popular with students and in the sports world. Thus, one common question regards the current status of the field of sport and exercise psychology. Sport psychology is now becoming well established as a scientific discipline in universities. Most sport psychology professionals who focus on academic teaching and research appear to be working in university sport-related departments such as sport and exercise science, kinesiology, and physical and health education. It also appears that more individuals trained in the field of sport psychology are beginning to teach and conduct research in general psychology departments at universities. Many professionals who receive training in sport psychology go on to work for academic departments, such as sport and exercise science and physical education. Additionally, these professors who teach sport and exercise psychology often spend time consulting with athletes at the high school, university, and professional levels and help exercisers adhere to daily physical activity.

1970-1999
(continued)

1986
The Association for the Advancement of Applied Sport Psychology (AAASP) is founded.

1987
The Sport Psychology Bulletin Board is started by Michael Sachs of Temple University.

1988
British Association of Sport Sciences Register for Accredited Sport Psychologists is founded.

1991
AAASP certification is established.

1991
Board of Sport Psychologists is organized as part of the Australian Sport Psychology Society.

1996
Australian Psychological Society College of Sport Psychologists Competencies are published.

1999
Athletic Insight: The Online Journal of Sport Psychology, the first peer-reviewed sport psychology online journal, begins publication.

2000 AND BEYOND

2005
British Psychological Society establishes accreditation for MSc programs in sport and exercise psychology.

2006
The Canadian Sport Psychology Association is founded, having evolved from the former Canadian Mental Training Registry.

2007
The British Psychological Society establishes the terminology of the chartered sport and exercise psychologist.

What Are Sport Psychologists Studying and Teaching?

The field of sport and exercise psychology is becoming increasingly diverse. The field can be divided into performance enhancement, personal development, clinical and counseling issues, and exercise psychology. The following sections explain these areas of sport and exercise psychology.

Performance Enhancement   The field of sport psychology has been interested in the use of psychological skills to help athletes improve athletic performance. After assessing an athlete, a sport psychology practitioner can implement an intervention in order to help an athlete improve specific mental skills. Interventions can then be evaluated to determine whether the psychological skills taught to the athlete enhance performance or enhance enjoyment of the sport. This area of sport psychology is often referred to as mental skills training, and table 1.1 contrasts mental training consulting with clinical sport psychology.

> *There is a lot of pressure put on me, but I don't put a lot of pressure on myself. I feel if I play my game, it will take care of itself.*
>
> **Lebron James**

Typically, researchers and practitioners have studied and applied various psychological skills to improve performance. For example, skills such as goal setting, mental imagery, positive self-talk, concentration, relaxation, and preperformance routines are taught to athletes to help them train mentally in addition to training physically, tactically, and technically for their sports. Often these skills are initially taught to athletes in a group setting and then athletes will meet individually with a consultant to acquire these skills and then practice them in both practice and competition. Coaches also consult with mental training consultants and learn how

TABLE 1.1   Mental Training Consulting vs. Clinical Sport Psychology

Characteristic	Mental training consultant	Clinical sport psychologist
Training	Master's or doctorate in sport and exercise science; certification through a sport psychology organization	Training in clinical or counseling psychology; licensed or registered to practice
Clients	Athletes, coaches, sport organizations, or other performers	Athletes or the general population
Goals	Enhance the mental skills of athletes	Help athletes deal with various clinical issues
Examples of problems this professional would address	Concentration issues; how to become more mentally tough; strategies for athletes who perform well in practice, but not in competition	Clinical issues such as substance abuse, depression, and eating disorders

to use these skills in managing their own performances as coaches. More detailed information about these skills is provided in chapters 3, 4, and 5.

Helping athletes enhance performance also involves topics in psychology of coaching that can be taught to parents, coaches, and athletes. This area of performance enhancement is most related to the social psychology of sport. Such topics include communication, team building, leadership training, and creating a positive environment for sport participants.

Personal Development of Athletes Another area of sport psychology that is starting to be discussed and researched more in the literature is helping to improve the academic, career, personal, and life skills of the athletes consultants work with. Sport psychologists are studying how the athletic role relates to issues of academics, careers, and interpersonal relationships. Also, sport psychologists are beginning to study and understand how to help athletes become better prepared to deal with issues such as retirement from athletics. One way that sport psychologists and practitioners are helping athletes improve these areas of their lives is through the teaching of positive life skills. Practitioners who apply these skills are beginning to work with high school athletes and university student-athletes.

Clinical and Counseling Issues A third area of practice and teaching in sport psychology involves helping athletes deal with **clinical and counseling issues,** such as eating disorders, depression, substance abuse, gambling, crisis situations, grief, and marital and relationship problems. Traditionally this has not been a major focus of sport psychology. However, as the field of sport psychology has developed, many practitioners have written about the need for these types of services. Often sport psychology consultants will note that while they are with an athlete in a performance-enhancement session, the athlete will bring up a more serious problem that is related to a counseling or clinical sport psychology issue (Kornspan & Lerner, 2005). The mental health issues of athletes have received much attention from sport leaders and the media in recent years.

> **clinical and counseling issues—** Off-the-field problems, such as eating disorders, depression, substance abuse, and relationship problems, for which athletes seek assistance.

In fact, the National Collegiate Athletic Association (NCAA) has provided information in a sizable handbook on their Web site titled *Managing Student-Athletes' Mental Health Issues.* The NCAA's leadership in the study of and focus on the mental health issues of student-athletes has led psychologists to meet in order to discuss the mental health issues of athletes (Hosick, 2005a). Professional sport organizations are also focused on helping their athletes with clinical and counseling issues. The National Football League (NFL) has a player development program in which each NFL team has a player development director ("Player Development," 2008). One of the roles of the player development director is to encourage the use of counseling for athletes and their families to help with various issues that they may be dealing with. Throughout the world more sport organizations are beginning to focus on helping athletes with clinical and counseling issues. For example, the Australian Sports Commission, a Canadian national training center, and the English Institute of Sport have begun to provide services and networks to help their athletes deal with clinical and counseling issues.

> *A student-athlete's "mental health" may be viewed as secondary to physical health; however, it is every bit as important for healthy performance.*
>
> **Ron A. Thompson and Roberta T. Sherman** (2007)

In addition to sport organizations focusing on mental health issues, journals and books have addressed the clinical aspects of sport psychology. For example, Frank Gardner and Zella Moore published *Clinical Sport Psychology* (2006). In 2007, the *Journal of Clinical Sport Psychology* began publication with Frank Gardner as the editor.

Exercise Psychology In addition to working with athletes, the field of sport and exercise psychology has looked to increase exercise adherence and satisfaction of the general population. Many psychological interventions, such as self-monitoring and goal setting, help people adhere to exercise programs and live more physically active lives. This area of exercise psychology has become a main focus of the field of applied sport psychology. Thus, the *Journal of Sport Psychology* has changed its name to the *Journal of Sport and Exercise Psychology*. More books focusing on exercise psychology began to be published in the 1990s and early 2000s, such as Willis and Campbell's *Exercise Psychology* (1992) and Lox, Martin Ginis, and Petruzzello's *The Psychology of Exercise: Integrating Theory and Practice* (2006).

Professional Organizations in Sport Psychology

Sport psychology has a long history and is focused on various aspects such as performance enhancement for individual athletes, the team, and the coaching staff; clinical and counseling issues of athletes; development of life skills for athletes; and the development of a physically active lifestyle for the general population. Several professional organizations exist to guide the profession of sport psychology, and these organizations help to advance the field and provide clear guidance on employment opportunities, professional training, and professional practice issues.

One of the first sport psychology organizations that began to organize the field of sport psychology worldwide was the International Society of Sport Psychology (ISSP), which has been in existence since 1965. Information about the organization can be found at www.issponline.org. The North American Society for the Psychology of Sport and Physical Activity (NASPSPA) was created in the late 1960s; for many years it was the only professional sport psychology organization in the United States. In the mid-1980s two sport psychology organizations formed that focused on the applied aspects of sport and exercise psychology: the Association for Applied Sport Psychology (AASP) and the American Psychological Association, Division 47, Exercise and Sport Psychology (APA Division 47). These professional organizations are excellent sources for students and professionals to learn about the current status of the field of sport psychology. Both organizations provide a yearly conference where students can go to presentations and learn about current issues in the field of sport psychology. Also, both organizations provide Web sites that contain information about current professional news in the field and the organizations' current newsletters. There are many more sport psychology organizations throughout the world.

ORGANIZATIONS FOR SPORT AND EXERCISE PSYCHOLOGY

Asia

Korean Society of Sport Psychology
http://ksa.sports.re.kr/kssp/eng_introduction1.php

Australia

Australian Psychological Society, College of Sport Psychologists
www.groups.psychology.org.au/csp

Canada

Canadian Society for Psychomotor Learning and Sport Psychology (CSPLSP)
www.scapps.org

Canadian Sport Psychology Association
www.en.cspa-acps.ca/index.html

Canadian Psychological Association—Sport and Exercise Psychology Section
www.cpa.ca/sections/sportandexercisepsychology

Europe

British Association of Sport and Exercise Sciences
www.bases.org.uk/newsite/psychology.asp

British Psychological Society—Division of Sport and Exercise Psychology
www.bps.org.uk/spex/spex_home.cfm

European Federation of Sport Psychology
www.fepsac.com

United States

Association for Applied Sport Psychology
http://appliedsportpsych.org

American Psychological Association, Division 47, Exercise and Sport Psychology
www.apa.org/divisions/div47

Students make up a large part of the Association for Applied Sport Psychology (AASP). Of particular note for students who want to get involved in the field of sport psychology and are planning on going to graduate school in the field is the graduate student fair offered by AASP. Also, AASP offers a student section on their Web site, which addresses various issues important to students. Students can find much information about the field of sport and exercise psychology by going to professional Web sites and attending professional conferences.

What Is the Future of the Field?

Clearly the field of sport and exercise psychology is growing. Williams and Straub (2006) pointed out that in the 1990s and 2000s opportunities to conduct sport psychology consulting increased. Showing an example of the growth of opportunities in the field, in 2004 the University of Oklahoma athletic department added a sport psychologist to their staff after a survey of their student-athletes suggested that they wanted more specific sport-based counseling services (Murphy, 2006). Additionally, the number of consultants who are certified by the Association for Applied Sport Psychology continues to grow. Currently there are 217 consultants certified by AASP ("Find a Certified Consultant," 2008). In the UK, the British Association of Sport and Exercise Sciences lists 140 individuals as accredited with a specialization as a sport psychologist ("Consultant Finder," 2008).

> *Prior to the 2000 Sydney Games, only one sport psychologist was on the [United States] Olympic staff and attended the Games. This year [2008], the U.S. Olympic Committee is sending five full-time psychologists and several national governing bodies (NGB) are also sending sport psychologists or consultants to be at the Games assisting athletes and coaches.*
>
> **Dr. Jim Bauman**, senior sport psychologist, U.S. Olympic Committee (2008, p. 4)

However, Williams and Straub also pointed out that a low percentage of students (i.e., 20 percent) who graduated between 1994 and 1999 were employed as full-time performance-enhancement consultants. But it was still more than the previous tracking studies have found. (It is also important to remember that there are many more types of opportunities available outside of being a professor that do not involve consulting in performance enhancement.) Williams and Straub (2006) believe the field of sport psychology will continue to grow a great deal. They also believe that more individuals will continue to seek the services of mental training consultants. Weinberg and Gould (2007) also believe that more people are looking to gain knowledge in teaching psychological skills to athletes.

As the field is growing and more people are hearing and learning about sport psychology, more people are entering the field. This spurs a need to develop standards of what people should know in order to practice sport psychology.

Professional Practice Issues in Sport and Exercise Psychology

One of the first organizations to address the knowledge base of those practicing in the field of sport psychology in the United States was the Association for Applied Sport Psychology. In 1992, this organization began to offer certification for consultants (Silva, 2002), which provided the requirements for practicing and teaching mental training to athletes. The AASP-certified consultant certification does not require the type of training that one would need in order to provide clinical or counseling services to athletes. However, with a continuing focus on providing services and helping those who want to work full time with athletes, there appears to be more of a focus on training students to earn AASP certification and also to be trained to provide clinical and counseling services to athletes and sport organizations.

> *Those individuals who want to assume a role in sport and exercise psychology consulting will have to understand not only sport and exercise science but aspects of counseling and clinical psychology as well.*
>
> **Robert S. Weinberg and Daniel Gould** (2007, p. 18)

As the number of students who want to practice sport psychology consulting has increased, graduate programs are being developed to provide students with the proper training. Throughout the world, the field of sport psychology has continued to increase professional standards, as shown in an article in the *International Journal of Sport and Exercise Psychology* titled "Training and Selection of Sport Psychologists: An International Review" (Morris, Alfermann, Lintunen, & Hall, 2003). In the United States, one can obtain certification as an AASP-certified consultant and as a licensed counselor or licensed psychologist. To become a licensed counselor or a licensed psychologist in the United States, a person has to pass a licensure test in the state in which he or she intends to practice.

Since the mid-1990s, a few programs have been developed that provide students with multidisciplinary training for sport psychology. Many models of graduate training exist:

- A master's degree in sport psychology and counseling. A dual degree would enable a student to obtain a state license in counseling and also become certified by AASP as a consultant.
- A doctoral degree in sport psychology. This could involve counseling training (i.e., a master's degree in counseling) while completing the doctoral degree.
- A doctoral degree in counseling psychology with a minor or emphasis in sport psychology.

- Counseling or clinical psychology training at the doctoral level and elective courses to meet AASP certification criteria. Students in these situations can then find sites in which they can complete predoctoral internship hours related to working with athletes. In clinical psychology and counseling psychology training, students complete one year of practice as part of their program. This is called the predoctoral internship. Some predoctoral internships allow counseling psychology students to become trained in providing sport psychology services to university student-athletes.

The *Directory of Graduate Programs in Applied Sport Psychology* (Burke, Sachs, Fry, & Schweighardt, 2008) has a listing of predoctoral internships that provide sport psychology training. Also, clinical or counseling psychologists may be able to find supervised postdoctoral opportunities to learn how to provide sport psychology services to athletes.

Proper educational training is still a source of debate in the field of sport and exercise psychology. Training in performance-enhancement services, counseling services, and clinical services is the best preparation for students who aim to work full time in an applied sport psychology setting. However, if the goal is to teach and conduct research in a sport science department or to provide services in athletic advising, becoming trained to provide clinical or counseling services to athletes may not be necessary.

The Short of It

- Sport psychology developed from a combination of psychology, physical education, and sports medicine and became a full-fledged field of study in the 1960s.
- Today, sport psychology focuses on performance enhancement, psychosocial development, and clinical issues.
- The field has expanded to include exercise psychology, which focuses on helping people incorporate daily physical activity into a healthy lifestyle.
- The International Society of Sport Psychology (ISSP) began in 1965. Since then, many other organizations, including the Association for Applied Sport Psychology (AASP), have been formed.
- Many combinations of training are available to students interested in the field of sport and exercise psychology. In general, students might consider seeking schooling in mental training for athletes and undergo training to provide clinical and counseling services.

What Can I Do With Sport and Exercise Psychology?

In this chapter, you will learn the following:

✓ The types of training required for an academic position in the field of sport and exercise psychology

✓ The types of professional positions that people trained in sport and exercise psychology are working in outside of traditional higher-education settings

✓ Where mental skills training consultants and sport and exercise psychologists work and what types of applied jobs they do

✓ Nontraditional and emerging positions that incorporate sport and exercise psychology

> "I can honestly say I love what I do.... The things I like the most about my job are the day-to-day interactions I have with coaches and student-athletes and the quality of relationships that have evolved over the years."
>
> **Dave Yukelson**, Pennsylvania State University ("Sport Psychology: Getting Focused," sidebar, 2007).

How do I become a sport psychologist? Do I need a master's degree? Do I need a **doctoral degree**? Where do I find out about graduate programs that will help me to meet my career goals in sport psychology? What will I be studying? When I finish, what jobs will be available to me? These are just a few of the questions that students ask themselves when considering a career in sport or exercise psychology. This chapter provides answers to these questions.

Dr. Chris Carr began his career in sport psychology as a doctoral student at Ball State University in Muncie, Indiana, where he studied counseling psychology and minored in sport psychology. While completing his doctoral studies, Dr. Carr had the opportunity to work at the U.S. Olympic Training Center as a research assistant under the guidance of Dr. Shane Murphy, the U.S. Olympic Committee's first full-time sport psychologist. After completing his doctoral work, Dr. Carr served as the sport psychologist for Washington State University, as psychologist and sport psychology consultant at Arizona State University, and the psychologist for athletics at Ohio State University. Additionally, Dr. Carr provided consulting to professional teams such as the Kansas City Royals, Columbus Crew, and Arizona Cardinals. He also provided consulting services to USA Diving, the national governing body for the sport of diving. Currently, Dr. Carr is a sport and performance psychologist for St. Vincent Hospital in Indianapolis, Indiana. Carr (2007, p. 1) says, "I am convinced that a multidisciplinary training (a combination of psychology and exercise sciences) is the most applicable path to become a sport psychologist." Dr. Carr's academic and career path demonstrates some of the opportunities available to students in sport and exercise psychology.

doctoral degree—The highest level of academic training.

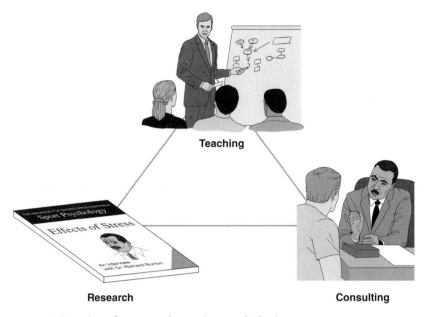

Teaching

Research

Consulting

FIGURE 2.1 **The roles of sport and exercise psychologists.**

Reprinted, by permission, from Weinberg and Gould 2007.

Generally, two types of jobs exist in sport psychology. One might be considered an academic path, involving the roles of teaching and research; the other might be viewed as a professional path, or an employment opportunity in which one plans to practice sport psychology or a related field through consulting with athletes, coaches, and sport organizations (see figure 2.1). Williams and Straub (2006) suggest that the academic market is strong for people seeking work in teaching sport psychology. The increasingly strong academic job market in sport psychology over the past two decades has increased tremendously because those in sport science departments understand what type of contributions sport psychology professionals can make in the training of other allied professionals, such as exercise physiologists, strength and conditioning specialists, physical educators, and athletic trainers. In all of these professions, course work in sport psychology can be helpful.

In contrast to jobs in sport and exercise science departments, fewer jobs have been created for teaching sport psychology in general psychology departments. Most sport psychology jobs in academia are in sport and exercise science and physical education departments. This is important to understand since it could affect your choice of doctoral programs. For example, if you want to teach sport psychology, it may be beneficial to obtain a doctoral degree specific to sport psychology from a sport and exercise science or physical education department. Based on Williams and Scherzer's (2003) graduate tracking survey, most doctoral-level graduates are obtaining employment in academic settings (Cox, 2007).

In addition to the academic path, there are emerging opportunities to practice sport psychology in full-time positions in various settings. Unfortunately, no data exist that indicate exactly how many professionals are working in full-time consulting positions. However, opportunities to provide consulting services are becoming more prevalent; these services are provided in sport academies, university athletic departments and counseling centers, community athletic centers, and private practices. Professional sports teams and individual sport agents also employ sport psychology professionals.

Various jobs in the fitness industry and in life skills training for athletes incorporate aspects of sport psychology. People who have training in sport and exercise psychology often pursue work in coaching or coaching education and in sports medicine. Some professionals apply sport psychology training to other fields. For example, individuals with training in sport psychology apply these concepts when working with surgeons, business executives, and musicians.

Academic Path

The academic path in sport psychology is very clear. This path is for those who know that they would like to be an instructor at a university. There are many options for those who obtain master's and doctoral degrees in sport psychology.

Training Required and Typical Career Path

Teaching in a university setting in sport psychology (i.e., becoming an assistant professor) requires a doctoral degree. A person taking this path may obtain a master's degree in sport psychology, which usually takes one to two years. Many students choose to complete a master's thesis to prepare them to conduct research; these programs usually take two years to complete. Nonthesis programs often take only one year. After completing a master's degree in sport psychology, a student would then usually enter a specific doctoral program in sport psychology to be trained to conduct research and to teach sport psychology. Programs training students to teach and conduct research usually provide the opportunity to obtain AASP certification and possibly training in **counseling** so that the future professors would also be able to provide consulting as part of their services to the university and community. Most people who are planning on teaching sport psychology go through a doctoral program in sport and exercise science since that is where most of the jobs in teaching sport psychology are. A few academic positions have been created in sport psychology that are in psychology departments, but these do not seem to be the norm.

counseling—Helping people with issues related to personal development.

tenure—A status of indefinite employment, often awarded to college instructors.

After obtaining a doctoral degree, a person usually seeks full-time employment in an academic setting. Some people begin careers in adjunct positions, which involve part-time teaching of various sport and exercise science classes. After they obtain full-time employment, sport psychology professionals usually begin as instructors or as assistant professors. If a person begins as an assistant professor, he or she is usually in a **tenure**-track position; tenure can take about seven years to achieve ("Teachers—Postsecondary," 2007). Usually faculty members are provided

CAREERS IN SPORT AND EXERCISE PSYCHOLOGY*

Academic Positions

- Instructor of sport and exercise psychology at a university
- Sport psychologist for a university athletic department
- Psychologist at a counseling center and sport psychology consultant for the athletic department
- Director of sport psychology for a university-based performance-enhancement center

Independent Consulting or Practice

- Mental training consultant or sport psychologist for a professional sport organization
- Sport psychologist in private practice
- Mental training consultant or sport psychologist for a professional sport agent
- Mental training consultant in private practice
- Mental training consultant or sport psychologist for an Olympic training center
- Mental training consultant at a sport academy
- Psychologist or counselor for a sports medicine clinic or hospital department
- Coach educator

Athlete Development

- Academic coach
- Athlete liaison officer
- Athletic counselor
- Athlete career and education advisor
- Director of athlete lifestyle services
- Director of player development for a professional sports team or league
- Life skills educator for a youth sport and development organization
- Performance lifestyle coordinator for a national governing body
- Performance lifestyle advisor for a national governing body
- Performance lifestyle coordinator for a professional sport league or organization
- Life services manager
- Life services coordinator
- Professional sport welfare officer
- Player development manager

Exercise Psychology

- Active living consultant
- Director of a community program devoted to increasing physical activity
- Physical activity and healthy lifestyle facilitator
- Physical activity consultant
- Physical activity counselor
- Wellness coach
- Program coordinator
- Exercise interventionist

*Because these are job titles, some of these positions involve similar responsibilities.

with a lengthy document detailing the criteria in teaching, research, and service that need to be fulfilled in order to earn promotion and tenure. After receiving tenure, sport psychology professors are usually promoted to a rank of associate professor, and some work toward being promoted to full professor. Some sport psychology professors decide to leave full-time teaching positions and pursue university administration positions, such as chair of a department, assistant dean or dean, or provost.

One trend is the hiring of part-time or non-tenure-track faculty to teach in higher education ("Teachers—Postsecondary," 2007). This can be good and bad. On a good note, there may be more opportunities for individuals to combine a consulting practice with part-time teaching in sport psychology. Additionally, if individuals have non-tenure-track positions, the focus of the job may be teaching, so they have more time to focus on applied sport psychology consultation.

Those with master's degrees can obtain college and university positions as well. Usually people with master's degrees are able to teach at two-year community colleges. These positions may not be focused on only teaching sport psychology courses.

Duties of Sport Psychology Professors

The job of a professor at a university is considered a very satisfying position. Sport psychology professors teach, conduct research, and provide service to the university community. Sport psychology professors may teach a variety of sport psychology classes depending on whether they are teaching only at the undergraduate level, only at the graduate level, or at both the undergraduate and graduate levels. Specific courses that sport psychology professors teach are introduction to sport psychology, social psychology of sport, psychology of performance enhancement, psychology of athletic injury, exercise psychology, and sport psychometrics (the application of measurement to sport psychology). Additionally, sport psychology professors supervise and instruct sport psychology practicum and sport psychology internships. In addition to teaching classes, sport psychology professors usually advise undergraduate and graduate students and serve on master's thesis and dissertation committees. Professors also conduct their own research and do scholarly writing. They may also provide services to the university by serving on departmental and university committees as well as collaborating with the community. For example, some professors may serve on local community boards or provide consulting to local school districts. Some professors provide mental training consulting to the university athletic department. Many professors serve on committees and provide other services to professional associations.

Professional Path

The training for a professional-path position may be different from that of an academic position. Although the education required for providing sport psychology services is still being debated, students should seek out interdisciplinary training if they plan to provide sport psychology services to athletes, coaches, and sport organizations. It might be optimal for a student seeking a professional-path position to be trained specifically in sport psychology by meeting AASP certification standards and to become a licensed counselor or licensed psychologist along the way. Many countries have licensure laws for psychology; therefore only individuals legally allowed to practice psychology are able to refer to themselves as psychologists. In the United States, only a licensed psychologist can legally refer to herself or himself as a sport psychologist when providing services to the general public. Additionally, only those trained in counseling and sport psychology and who are licensed counselors (not licensed psychologists) would be able to call themselves sport counselors. A person who is trained in sport psychology, is practicing in a professional service position, and is certified by AASP but is not licensed could be called only an AASP-certified consultant. Many who are trained to practice sport psychology but are not licensed refer to themselves as mental skills training consultants or performance-enhancement consultants.

Students who are planning a professional career in sport psychology should obtain field experience in applied sport psychology (i.e., work directly with athletes) in their master's or doctoral work. AASP requires at least 400 hours of supervised applied experience for certification as an AASP-certified consultant. Individuals with only a master's degree and the necessary course work can also obtain the AASP certification, but they need to first gain provisional status; after completing 300 more hours (for a total of 700 hours) they can then receive full AASP certification status ("Become a Certified Consultant," 2007).

A certification similar to AASP exists in New Zealand, where a person can obtain an accreditation as a mental skills trainer ("Equivalence," n.d.). In Japan, a person can obtain certification as an approved mental training instructor (Morris, Alfermann, Lintunen, & Hall, 2003). In the UK, a person can become an accredited sport and exercise psychologist with training in sport and exercise science through the British Association of Sport and Exercise Sciences (BASES) and can become a chartered sport and exercise psychologist if trained in psychology through the British Psychological Society (BPS) ("Qualifications and Training Routes," 2007).

In the United States, those who pursue licensure in psychology usually complete 1,500 to 2,000 hours of supervised work (Ramsay, 2005). Those who plan to practice sport psychology and become licensed psychologists may or may not complete those 1,500 to 2,000 hours of postdoctoral experience by working directly with athletes. To work as a psychologist in Australia, a person must be registered in the territory or state in which he or she is practicing ("Working as a Psychologist," 2008). Australian sport psychology programs are accredited by the Australian Psychology Accreditation Council (APAC). In most of the 32 nations that are part of the European Federation of Psychologists' Associations, both the title of psychologist and the practice are regulated. In Canada, psychologists must be licensed in order to practice ("Why See a Regulated Professional?" 2008). Those looking to practice in New Zealand also must be registered ("Registration," 2006). For a complete discussion of international professional qualifications and training in sport psychology, see Morris, Alfermann, Lintunen, and Hall (2003).

Jobs in Sport Academies

Some individuals who are pursuing professional sport psychology careers outside of academia are obtaining employment in providing mental skills training for athletes. One setting for such employment is a **sport academy** (Harwood, 2008).

Sport academies are becoming more prevalent throughout the world. One of the most famous sport academies, IMG, plans to open an elite training facility in Dubai, United Arab Emirates. In the UK, the Talented Athlete Scholarship Scheme (TASS) helps athletes ages 16 to 19 balance the demands of sport training and also continue to pursue their education. The program provides a sport psychology–specific component and lifestyle support. Harwood (2008) describes his work in implementing a sport psychology program with an English professional soccer academy. He explains that much of his work consulting with the athletes was to educate them about sport psychology and to teach them how to use a logbook to review matches that they participated in. Harwood also describes his work consulting with coaches on the development of a positive environment. The ACE Cricket Academy in Australia provides sport psychology services as well.

sport academy—A school that provides both academic education and sport training for its students.

student-athlete—A person who trains and competes in sport while attending high school or a university.

internship—An applied experience in which a student gains real-world work experience.

In some residential sport academies, students live at a school year-round and practice and train for their specific sports. At the age of 13 or 14 athletes who want to reach the elite level in a sport may choose to attend a sport school in which they spend half the day attending classes and the other half of the day training for their sports. At these types of facilities **student-athletes** work with mental training consultants, strength and conditioning specialists, and professional sport instructors and coaches.

The IMG academies have a mental conditioning staff of five mental conditioning consultants ("Mental Conditioning: Coaches," 2008). The staff provides both group and individualized mental training sessions in at least 15 areas. In addition to providing services to resident athletes, the staff provides mental conditioning programming to teams at off-site locations or teams that come to the academy for on-site mental conditioning. The IMG academies also offer **internship** opportunities for students to provide mental training to athletes under the guidance of the staff (Fletcher & Bisig, 2006). This is important because as more students are trained as interns in these settings, more full-time jobs in sport academies will be developed.

Another sport academy that provides mental training to student-athletes is the Hank Haney International Junior Golf Academy (IJGA) located in Hilton Head, South Carolina. This academy is similar to the IMG academy: Student-athletes reside, go to school, and train at the academy. The IJGA's director of mental training works with student-athletes on a weekly basis, providing them with workshops, group seminars, and individual consultation. Athletes are taught techniques in goal setting, imagery, communication skills, leadership skills, management of emotions, and concentration skills ("Mental and Physical Training," 2008). Sutton Tennis Academy in the UK is another sport academy with mental training consultants on staff.

Jobs in University Sports

One area of sport psychology that has the potential to expand is the provision of services to university student-athletes. In the past two decades more professionals have been hired on full-time, part-time, and consulting bases to provide sport psychology or mental training to athletic departments (Kornspan & Duve, 2006). Some professionals work half-time providing sport psychology services to athletic departments and also work as faculty members directing graduate programs in sport psychology.

> *I've always felt that [sport psychology] was an important element. We want to be a holistic model of an athletics department, and we wanted to and needed to include sport psychology in that model.*
>
> **Mike Gentry,** Virginia Tech assistant athletic director for athletic performance ("Athletic Performance: Sport Psychology," 2007, p. 117)

University Athletic Departments   Of interest at the university level is the need for individuals who can provide counseling services as well as mental training services to athletic departments. For example, Carter (2005), Bennett (as cited in "Athletic Performance: Sport Psychology," 2007), and Moore (as cited in Winerman, 2005) explain their work as consultants providing services in university settings. Nicki Moore's role as a psychologist for the athletic department at the University of Oklahoma at Norman is a combination of counseling and sport psychology (Winerman, 2005). Gary Bennett coordinates sport psychology services for the Virginia Tech athletic department. He averages 20 individual sessions per week with student-athletes to provide counseling and mental training. He also consults with teams on a weekly basis; they learn strategies on team building, communication, and performance enhancement ("Athletic Performance: Sport Psychology," 2007).

The University of Tennessee and Penn State University are schools that provide sport psychology services through their athletic departments. The University of Tennessee has a director of mental training; that person's staff includes a mental training consultant and one mental training graduate assistant ("Staff

Psychology Insight

An area of increasing interest is that of providing off-the-field counseling to student-athletes. Nicki Moore, a counselor and sport psychologist at the University of Oklahoma at Norman, said, "I think my position emerged because our athletics director and associate athletics director here recognized that there were a lot of counseling needs that weren't being met through traditional means" (Winerman, 2005, para. 6). Gary Bennett, a sport psychologist at Virginia Tech, said, "We try to address all the various factors that affect student-athletes' performance on and off the field.... We believe we can help athletes perform better by addressing those concerns" ("Athletic Performance: Sport Psychology," 2007, p. 117).

Dr. Dave Yukelson and several former student-athletes at Penn State University.
Courtesy of Dave Yukelson.

Directory," 2008). At Penn State University, Dr. Dave Yukelson coordinates sport psychology and mental training services for all 29 varsity athletic teams. Yukelson describes his work as follows:

> Interested in psychological factors associated with performance excellence in sport and life, I provide counseling and support to our student-athletes and coaches in the areas of motivation and goal setting, mental preparation and focusing strategies for managing peak performance under pressure, confidence and mental toughness, leadership and team cohesion, and issues pertaining to interpersonal communication skills and student-athlete development. ("Sport Psychology: Getting Focused," 2007, sidebar)

More and more professionals are providing mental skills training and sport psychology services at universities. Dr. Sam Maniar, a psychologist with the Plastics Research and Development Corporation (PRADCO) and formerly a sport psychologist at Ohio State University, compares the increase in sport psychologists working with university teams to the surge of strength and conditioning specialists during the mid-1980s. Maniar is hopeful that in the upcoming years more teams will have mental training consultants working with them (Murphy, 2006). However, there are still only a limited number of full-time opportunities to practice sport psychology and mental training in athletic departments. More part-time consulting opportunities are available in university athletic departments. Kornspan and Duve (2006) find that athletic directors see sport psychology as beneficial. Also, Kornspan, Shimokawa,

Duve, and Pinheiro (2007) found that 14 Division IA schools had a sport psychology consultant listed in their athletic department directory.

University Counseling Centers   University counseling staff outside of athletic departments are beginning to provide sport psychology services, but it is unclear how many universities have such services. Since the fall of 2000, the University of California at Davis has provided sport psychology services for student-athletes through their university counseling center. Staff work closely with the athletic department at the university. Sport psychology services in the counseling center include counseling, performance enhancement, team building, life skills development, and group educational services ("Sport Consulting and Psychological Counseling for Student Athletes," 2007).

Professionals who provide sport psychology services for student-athletes most likely do so as a part of their job providing psychological services to students in the general university community. U.S. schools with counseling centers that provide sport psychology services to athletes are Florida Atlantic University, Kansas State University, the University of Akron, and the College of William and Mary.

At the counseling center at Florida Atlantic University, Dr. Richard Rini has created a pilot program for student-athletes called Sports Optimal Performance Training. Kansas State University offers sport-specific performance-enhancement services through their counseling center. They also have a CHAMPS (Counseling to Help Athletes Maximize Personal Success) newsletter that provides information about sport psychology services ("Performance Enhancement and Applied Sport Psychology," 2007).

Although the exact number of professionals providing sport psychology services in university counseling centers is not known, a few counseling centers are providing internships for both predoctoral and **postdoctoral training** in sport psychology. This is wonderful training experience for those looking to practice full-time as a sport psychologist for a university athletic department, practice sport psychology as part of a private practice, or practice in a university counseling center. In addition to predoctoral internship opportunities, postdoctoral sport psychology opportunities are being developed that provide the job experience to move into a sport psychology position. The

> **postdoctoral training**—After completion of a doctoral degree, applied experience that continues to focus on training.

University of Oklahoma athletics department also offers a postdoctoral fellowship through their PROS (Psychological Resources for OU Student-Athletes) program. The University of Southern California offers postdoc opportunities in university mental health and sport psychology. The postdoctoral intern provides clinical services to student-athletes at the counseling center and also provides consultation and outreach services to the University of Southern California athletic department ("Post-Doctoral Fellowship Program," 2007).

Students interested in predoctoral and postdoctoral opportunities can search the Association of Psychology Postdoctoral and Internship Centers online directory at www.appic.org/directory/4_1_directory_online.asp to see which universities list sport psychology as an area of specialization. Information about postdoctoral internships is provided for both the United States and Canada. Opportunities to gain the necessary supervised experience internationally can also be found in the UK and Australia. In Australia, students can become registered sport psychologists by completing six years of training at the university level followed by an additional two years of supervised experience ("APS College of Sport Psychologists: About Us," 2008). Students can become accredited sport and exercise psychologists in Britain after completing a master's degree in sport and exercise psychology and three years of supervised experience (Niven & Owens, 2008).

Athletic Centers Providing Services to Students and Community   Individuals are also beginning to provide sport psychology services through other departments on university campuses. Professionals in these settings provide sport psychology services both to students at the university and to the residents of local communities. Three examples are the Boston University Athletic Enhancement Center, the University of Pittsburgh Medical Center, and the UC Davis Sports Medicine Center.

The Boston University Athletic Enhancement Center is part of its College of Education. This center provides people in the Boston area with the knowledge and training to improve physically and mentally and to prevent injuries. The staff consists of a strength and conditioning specialist and a center coordinator and sport psychology coach. The enhancement center also offers workshops that facilitate team building ("BU Athletic Enhancement Center," 2007).

Another university providing mental training services outside of its athletic department and counseling center is the University of Pittsburgh Medical Center. The director of mental training serves people of various ages, but she has focused much of her work on providing mental training services to high school athletes and teams. Another type of service offered is lectures on sport psychology to parents of high school student-athletes (Linn, 2004). Similarly, the University of California, Davis, Sports Medicine Center provides sport psychology services related to helping individuals enhance sport performance, rehabilitate from athletic injury, and deal with various personal issues.

Jobs in Professional Sports

Some sport psychology professionals who work in sport academies and university settings also provide services to professional athletes. And some sport psychology professionals are hired as full-time staff by pro sport teams. Other individuals work as part-time consultants to professional sports teams.

Two teams that have hired professionals to provide mental training services to players are the Boston Red Sox and the New York Yankees. Chad Bohling was hired as the director of optimal performance for the New York Yankees (Curry, 2005). The Boston Red

Psychology Insight

Baseball player and manager Yogi Berra is well known for his witty quotes. One of his most famous about baseball is "90 percent of the game is half mental." Yogi Berra meant that success in baseball required both mental and physical balance. Berra said, "Funny, baseball seems more physical than ever now—everyone lifts weights and all the guys are much bigger and stronger. But the mental part may be more important. Now you see teams with their own psychologists and players going to hypnotists" (Berra & Kaplan, 2001, p. 58).

Sox have hired two people to provide mental skills training to their athletes: Don Kalkstein and Bob Tewksbury. Tewksbury discussed his role in providing mental skills training to the Red Sox organization:

> My primary role is to help all players with the Red Sox minor league system perform to the best of their abilities. That work entails several aspects depending on the area of performance the player feels he needs work on. Those areas can include working on better pre-game, in game, and post-game routines; learning how to relax more while at the plate, on the mound, or in the field; how to deal with negative thoughts; how to improve concentration; or helping players establish proper goals. It could be helping counsel a player with personal or interpersonal issues away from the field which may be affecting a player's performance. (Laurila, 2007 para. 5)

⭐ SUCCESS STORY

Jeff Bond, General Manager of Learning and Development, Richmond Football Club

Jeff Bond began his career studying physical education at the University of Melbourne. After some years as a physical education teacher, he decided to go into the field of sport psychology. He obtained undergraduate degrees in psychology and then his master's degree in sport psychology from the University of Alberta in 1979. After receiving his master's degree, Bond became registered to practice psychology in Australia in 1981. After spending a while in private practice, Bond took the position as head of the Sport Psychology Division for the Australian Institute of Sport (AIS), where he spent the next 22 years. Bond left that position in 2004 and went into private consulting. In his role working for the AIS, Bond was the first sport psychologist appointed by Australia for the Summer Olympics, in Los Angeles in 1984, and also the first sport psychologist appointed for the Winter Olympics, in Calgary in 1988 (Terry, 2005). In total, Bond has held appointments as a sport psychologist at nine Olympic Games. Bond received much media attention when one of the athletes he worked with won Wimbledon ("Tigers in Major Development Boost," 2007).

After privately consulting, Bond has now begun a new role as the general manager of learning and development for the Richmond Football Club. In hiring Jeff Bond, Steven Wright, the CEO for the Richmond Football Club, said, "In years gone by, clubs solely focused on the physical development of the players. These days the areas of development and training at AFL clubs are so much more complex. It's about helping make the players mentally stronger and better able to perform to their optimum at the game's elite level both on and off the field, as well as assuring that our staff is working to its maximum potential. We could not think of anyone better than Jeff Bond to fill this key position" ("Tigers in Major Development Boost," 2007, para. 11).

Additional professional sport teams and organizations throughout the world that use the services of mental training consultants are the Pittsburgh Pirates (Major League Baseball), AC Milan (Italian professional soccer), the Brisbane Lions (Australian professional rugby), the Richmond Centenary (Australian Football League), and the Ladies European Professional Golf Tour.

One other model of providing mental skills training for professional athletes is as a consultant for a sport agency. Although not many professionals are employed full-time by sport agents to provide services for professional athletes, the *Dallas Morning News* reported that three performance-enhancement counselors have worked for the Scott Boras Corporation (Grant, 2005). One of these performance-enhancement counselors is Harvey Dorfman, a well-known mental training consultant for professional baseball players.

Jobs in Private Practice

Some mental training consultants and sport psychologists go into private practice, but little is known about how many individuals make a living providing sport psychology services in that setting. Lesyk (1998) has written in detail about becoming a sport psychologist in private practice. Additionally, Taylor (2008) has written an article about private practice in sport psychology, which is titled "Prepare to Succeed: Private Consulting in Applied Sport Psychology."

Suggestions from sport psychologists in private practice explain what students can expect from the profession. These authors have noted various issues, such as how to set up and build the practice, strategies for bringing in enough money to pay the rent or mortgage, and the need to do a broader set of work including managing business affairs, that should be thought of as one moves into becoming a mental skills training consultant or sport psychologist in private practice. Taylor (2008) suggests that using a retainer fee can be helpful in achieving financial goals and in providing the athlete with the best possible care and consulting.

Other Paths Incorporating Sport and Exercise Psychology

Related jobs incorporate sport and exercise psychology knowledge. One area where individuals with sport and exercise knowledge can provide their expertise is in jobs related to the promotion of physical activity. Jobs related to providing support services for athletes and coaching education also incorporate knowledge learned in the field of sport and exercise psychology.

Physical Activity Advising and Consulting

A variety of physical activity consulting positions are starting to emerge throughout the world. One type of position that is becoming more common is that of wellness coach. These individuals help people adhere to and maintain exercise programs and also help people change their behavior to achieve a more physically active and healthy lifestyle (Sarnataro, 2005). Because many government agencies throughout the world are focused on trying to help people become more physically active in order to reduce obesity, people are being hired by both governmental and private agencies as active living consultants, physical activity counselors, physical activity consultants, and physical activity advisors. Generally, these individuals work with the general population to help provide support and motivation to begin and adhere to a daily physical activity program (Fortier, Tulloch, & Hogg, 2006).

Athletic Counseling

Some people choose to use their training in sport and exercise psychology to work in the field of academic support services for student-athletes (Petitpas & Buntrock, 1995). Individuals with training in sport psychology and practical experience are suited for positions as CHAMPS/Life Skills coordinators or assistant coordinators, directors of academic services for student-athletes, and academic athletic advisors. (CHAMPS is an acronym for Challenging Athletes' Minds for Personal Success.) The CHAMPS program began in 1991 and focuses on enhancing the development of student-athletes while they are participating in university athletics ("Welcome to the NCAA CHAMPS/Life Skills Program," 2008).

At the professional level, some sport teams and leagues have individuals who serve as directors of player development, who coordinate a department that provides athletes with various types of services related to development of life skills, such as degree completion, career development, financial education, and helping players cope with stress and find assistance when necessary ("Packers Player Development," 2007). The National Football League has created player development offices, and each team is also required to have a player development specialist. A player development director may meet weekly with players who have been dealing with off-the-field issues, and in some cases athletes may be required to meet with the player development director (Kuharsky, 2007). Also, player development directors coordinate transition programs for those just beginning their work as professional athletes (Kegley, 2007).

Another emerging position is that of academic success coach for high school student-athletes. The Houston (Texas) School District has advertised to hire over 20 full-time academic coaches for high school student-athletes ("Academic Coaches," 2008). This is a similar type of job to providing academic support services at the university level. These positions were started by individuals at Springfield College in Massachusetts through the National Football Foundation. The National Football Foundation created a program called Play It Smart. They have been recruiting qualified individuals to be part-time academic coaches for high school student-athletes throughout the United States. Since the early 2000s this program has created over 159 positions for academic coaches for high school student-athletes ("Schools and Academic Coaches," 2008). Most academic coach positions for high school student-athletes are still part-time (20-hour-per-week) positions. Major responsibilities of academic coaches are providing mentoring and coaching to the athletes and also working closely with school counselors ("Academic Coaches," 2008).

Coaching and Coaching Education

Another option among careers that incorporate sport psychology is the field of coaching. Many people receive their start in coaching by obtaining a graduate assistantship to coach at the university level. Many students have an interest in understanding the mental aspects of sport and how to better lead and communicate with athletes and thus have chosen sport psychology as a specialty area to study for their master's degrees. Some university coaches also have gone on to receive their doctoral degrees in sport psychology. Mike Babcock, coach of the Detroit Red Wings, studied sport psychology in graduate school (Wyshynski, 2007).

> *There is a growing trend for the value of having a master's degree for becoming an Olympic or university coach in Canada and the U.S.*
>
> **Gordon Bloom** (Wyshynski, 2007, para. 6).

Other ways of incorporating sport and exercise knowledge into a career include being involved in youth developmental sport and life skills programs, which focus on enhancing the psychological development of young people through a sport-based program (Petitpas, Cornelius, Van Raalte & Jones, 2005). An example is the First Tee program, which incorporates a life skills curriculum into the teaching of golf.

The nonprofit organization Get Psyched for Sports also teaches life skills through youth sport. One of the main roles of this organization is to teach a curriculum in sport psychology to young athletes in school settings ("What We Do," 2007). Some organizations focus on training coaches to interact with and create positive environments for athletes. One example is the Positive Coaching Alliance.

Applying Sport Psychology to Other Industries

Williams and Straub (2006) have suggested that many more opportunities may become available for people who have an interest in applying their sport psychology skills to other domains in which enhancing performance is important. Such positions are available at the United States Military Academy at West Point, New York, and in other military and business settings (McClurg, 2006).

Individuals in sport psychology have begun presenting information on mental skills training to business executives. Williams and Straub (2006, p. 11) stated, "With only minimal additional training and preparation, who is better qualified than sport psychology consultants to do such coaching?" Students who have an interest in applying sport psychology skills that they learn in graduate school may be interested in becoming part of the Performance Excellence Movement (PEM), which is part of the Association for Applied Sport Psychology. Information about this group is available at http://aaasponline.org/students/pem.

Sports medicine clinics and hospitals are other settings in which those with training in sport psychology are providing services. Brewer (1998) predicted that opportunities for psychologists to provide services in sports medicine clinics would continue to expand; he suggested two main areas in which sports medicine professionals may provide services: preventing athletic injury and helping clients rehabilitate from an athletic injury. A few sports medicine centers and clinics hire sport psychologists on a full-time, part-time, or consulting basis.

Sport Psychiatry

A sport psychiatrist requires a medical degree and training in psychiatry. Morse (2008) published an article titled "What a Sport Psychiatrist Does." Sport psychiatrists treat athletes with various disturbances, such as attention-deficit/hyperactivity disorder (ADHD), eating disorders, depression, anxiety, and addictions. Sport psychiatrists can work with athletes from a different perspective than a mental training consultant or a sport psychologist. They apply psychiatry to sport through the use of a biopsychosocial model of practice ("Welcome," 2008). Sport psychiatrists are able to help athletes who have psychiatric disorders. For more information about the field of sport psychiatry, see the International Society for Sport Psychiatry Web site at www.theissp.com.

The Short of It

- Many graduates in sport and exercise psychology follow an academic path in which they obtain a graduate degree in sport and exercise psychology and teach and conduct research in a university setting.
- A professional path in sport and exercise psychology has begun to emerge, and some students are now pursuing jobs in applied sport psychology after completing training in sport and exercise psychology.
- Settings for applied sport psychology jobs include university athletic departments, sport academies, university counseling centers, university sports medicine clinics, professional sport teams, sport agencies, and private practice.
- Some individuals trained in sport and exercise psychology are beginning to obtain jobs in the fields of coaching education, athletic counseling, youth sport life skills development, physical activity counseling, and community physical activity promotion.

II

Goals of Sport and Exercise Psychology

Part II provides an introduction to the knowledge base in the field of sport and exercise psychology. The chapters in this part build on those in part I by showing how practitioners in the field apply their knowledge and training in their work with athletes, coaches, and people who want to start or continue exercising.

Chapters 3, 4, and 5 focus on educational sport psychology. The field of sport psychology can help athletes, coaches, and sport organizations enhance the performance of individual athletes and teams. Chapter 3 describes the mental skills of successful athletes, the importance of task-oriented motivation in achieving success, and the importance of controlling anxiety and arousal. This chapter lays the groundwork for what sport psychologists do. Chapter 4 discusses techniques for enhancing the cohesion of sport teams. The main theories of team building and how coaches and sport psychologists help athletes through that process are presented. Chapter 5 explains how sport psychologists educate coaches, parents, and administrators on creating a positive sport environment. Chapter 6 focuses on assessment of athletes' mental skills for performance enhancement.

Because coaches, administrators, and sport psychologists have begun to realize how sport can affect athletes' personal development, there has been a greater focus on the academic, career, and personal concerns of athletes. Chapter 7 introduces the psychological aspects of sport injuries and how sport psychologists can help athletes cope with their injuries and recover. The chapter also discusses how sport psychology professionals are involved in creating personal development programs and services for athletes. Chapter 8 focuses on services that clinical sport psychologists provide to athletes. Chapter 9 focuses on exercise psychology. Traditionally, the sport and exercise psychology profession has focused on helping athletes improve performance. However, consultants and exercise and wellness professionals have become interested in helping the general population begin exercising and maintain physical activity throughout their lifetime. Chapter 9 details the services and interventions that these practitioners provide to clients.

Enhancing the Performance of Individual Athletes

© Sam Greenwood/Getty Images

In this chapter, you will learn the following:

✓ What mental skills training is and the main philosophies that form the basis of performance-enhancement psychology

✓ The mental skills used by successful athletes, and how these skills help athletes focus on the task at hand and control their anxiety and arousal

✓ The settings and professionals involved in providing mental skills training to athletes

✓ Why athletes work on mental training and the specific mental skills that are taught to athletes

✓ The research that supports teaching these skills to athletes

> "Given the expectations and popularity of professional and amateur sports today, addressing the mental aspects of competition is becoming essential for athletes looking to optimize their performance and enjoyment of sport."
>
> **Dr. Aimee Kimball**, UPMC Center for Sports Medicine ("UPMC Sports Center Hires 'Mental Trainer,'" 2004)

It was December of 2006, and Zach Johnson wanted to be one of the best golfers in the world. Johnson decided to take seven weeks off from playing tournament golf to stay home and prepare for the upcoming season. He had not taken much time off in his career (Holmes, 2007). During his time off from the PGA Tour, Johnson worked with his mental skills training consultant, Morris Pickens (Holmes, 2007). Johnson worked on all parts of his game, but he put extra emphasis on his mental approach to golf. Johnson said the following:

In the past I really put too much focus into each shot, or too much merit into every shot. I was too focused on "Okay, if I birdie this hole, I can do this" or "If I make this putt, I can move up here." Now my focus is more on the process and the routine of each shot rather than the outcome. As a result I see my outcomes tighten up and be a lot better. In other words, I don't care where [an individual shot] goes. I'm going to give it 110 percent—every putt especially—but if I make it or miss it, I'll do the same thing again on the next one. (Holmes, 2007, para. 9-10)

As a result of his time off and his work with Morris Pickens, Johnson won the PGA Tour Major, the Masters golf tournament, in April of 2007. Johnson believed that Pickens was able to help him learn to relax under pressure when things were not going well and then focus on the next shot ("AT&T Classic: Zach Johnson," 2007).

Mental training consultants help athletes improve their mental skills so that they can enhance their physical performance. Psychologists and mental skills training consultants have been working with athletes since the 1940s using **cognitive-behavioral skills** to improve physical performance in sport.

cognitive-behavioral skills— Skills that focus on how thoughts and imagery relate to behavior.

Cognitive-Behavioral Model of Sport Consultation

The cognitive-behavioral model of sport psychology examines how thoughts influence thinking and behavior. Albert Ellis developed the ABC model, which shows how thoughts influence behavior (Ellis, 1962, 1994). In this model, A is a situation and C is a response. But does the situation cause the response, or is there something in between that athletes have control over so that A, the event, does not have to cause a specific response by the athlete? Ellis believed that there is a B in between the A and the C that allows athletes a choice of how they want to respond to a certain situation. See figure 3.1 for an illustration of this process. Mental skills coaches can teach techniques that help athletes control their thoughts and their images so that they can excel in practice and competition.

This type of training that helps athletes control their thoughts and images and relax and concentrate under pressure has become known as psychological skills training and is seen as an educational and positive way of helping people enhance performance. Zach Johnson learned and practiced the skill of playing one golf shot at a time so that he was focused on the process of the shot rather than focused on the outcome. Thus, Johnson learned not to worry about his score on a particular hole, but he focused on his routine and then accepted the results of each shot regardless of the outcome. This is one of the main outcomes of mental training for athletes: trying to get the athlete to focus on controlling his own effort and not worry about what he cannot control.

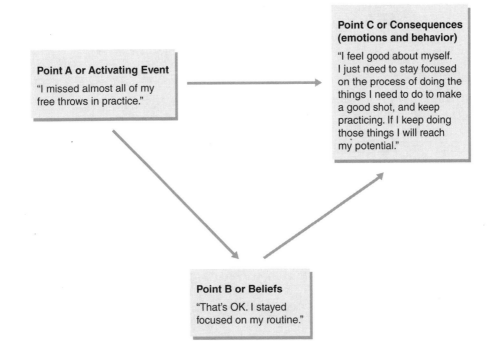

FIGURE 3.1 An example of the ABC model at work.

flow—A mental state in which athletes optimally function automatically and feel as if they cannot do anything wrong.

To help athletes get to the point of focusing on the process, not the outcome, sport psychologists and mental training specialists teach athletes various psychological skills that result in an athlete's ability to play in the zone, or the **flow** state, and not worry about the outcome. Their goal is to be focused only on making the effort to perform optimally. Mental training is just one component of an athlete's training for optimal performance. It is important to

---

⭐ SUCCESS STORY

Dr. John M. Silva, Professor Emeritus, Sport Psychology, the University of North Carolina at Chapel Hill

Courtesy of John Silva.

What does it take to kick field goals in the National Football League at the age of 46? One person who knows is elite field goal kicker Morten Andersen. Andersen consulted with Dr. John M. Silva for several years (M. Andersen, 2002).

John M. Silva has consulted with collegiate, Olympic, and professional athletes for over 30 years. He received his bachelor's and master's degrees from the University of Connecticut and his PhD in sport psychology from the University of Maryland. After starting his career as an assistant professor at the University of Wisconsin, Dr. Silva became a professor at the University of North Carolina at Chapel Hill, where he directed a graduate program in sport psychology and coached the Carolina Team Handball Club, leading the team to three consecutive U.S.A. Team Handball Collegiate National Championships. Two of the athletes he coached in the Carolina Team Handball Club made the U.S. Olympic handball team in 1996.

As a professor at the University of North Carolina, Silva saw the need for applied sport psychology to grow and thrive. He founded the Association for the Advancement of Applied Sport Psychology in 1986 and was the president of the organization at its first conference that year. Throughout the years Silva has been an influential contributor to the field for his students, other professionals, and the athletes he has coached in handball and on the mental game of sport (Silva & Stevens, 2002).

With the help of Dr. Silva, Morten Andersen learned a cognitive-behavioral approach to success in field goal kicking by charting all of his kicks (M. Andersen, 2002; Stinson, 2006) not only in competition but in practice as well. In addition to keeping track of his mental and physical performance in practice, Andersen recorded both mental and physical variables related to performance in competition. He prepared by keeping track of specific mental training advice, including a mental preparation schedule for the week, and identified specific goals and mental preparations for each game. Obviously, Andersen did not take mental training for granted. He holds records for scoring in the most consecutive games and for the most field goals made over 50 yards (Stinson, 2006).

remember that athletes train physically, technically, and tactically as well as mentally. In each one of these areas, coaches should help athletes go through an evaluation process to determine where the athlete is, where she wants to go, and how a consultant can help her achieve her goals. After implementing a plan in each of these areas, coaches and consultants can assess the athlete's progress to determine whether improvement is taking place.

Often athletes at lower levels of competition can get by with just being physically better than their competitors, but as athletes reach higher levels of physical performance, physical talent alone does not usually help them reach their potential (United States Olympic Committee, 2002). In their personality pyramid, Deaner and Silva (2002) show that as athletes move to higher levels of competition, mental training and psychological characteristics become much more important. To be successful at the highest levels, an athlete needs to be mentally tough, yet it is not easy to practice mental training.

Where Does Mental Training Occur?

When athletes are convinced of the importance of mental skills training, they begin that type of training while continuing to train physically, technically, and tactically. As noted in chapter 2, the teaching of mental skills to athletes is done in various settings by various people. The training might occur with the team or individual athletes during practice sessions, or the training may be provided off-site by consultants from private practice, private facilities, or universities.

Referring to seeking mental training services, Kellen Kulbacki, a baseball player at James Madison University, said, "Hearing from athletes in the pros, I know A-Rod has one [a mental training consultant], it was an opportunity that I needed to check out to see if it helped my game at all" (Murphy, 2006, para. 9). Kulbacki continued, "If I give [sport psychology] a shot and pick up a few pointers, I can have the mental edge as an athlete throughout the season" (para. 10).

Jill Briles-Hinton, coach for the women's golf team at the University of Florida and the 2008 SEC Golf Coach of the Year, values teaching athletes the mental game of golf and thus provides her team with mental training consultants. She said, "Humans have a tendency to listen to the experts" (Zimmerman, 2007, para. 3). Briles-Hinton brought in Dr. Deborah Graham to provide a two-day mental training seminar to the golf team. The team also has access to a mental training consultant throughout the season.

What Mental Training Skills Are Taught to Athletes?

Consultants educate athletes about mental training skills and then help them acquire and practice these skills (Martens, 1987). Sport psychology professionals teach five main mental skills to athletes: goal setting, imagery, relaxation, concentration, and self-talk.

Psychology Insight

"If you don't know where you're going, you might not get there," said Yogi Berra (Berra & Kaplan, 2001, p. 53). Berra suggested that it is important for athletes to have a plan so that they are confident in their abilities to achieve their goals. Having a plan allowed Berra to be committed to his goals of achieving success in baseball.

Goal Setting

Goal setting is one of the most important skills taught to athletes in order to help them achieve optimal performance. The goal-setting process helps athletes understand where they are currently and also where they want to go. A mental skills training consultant or sport psychologist can teach an athlete how to set systematic goals that are focused on the process and performance rather than focused on the outcome of competition.

Leith (2003) distinguishes between subjective goals and objective goals. Subjective goals are not related to a specific performance in sport; these may be related to just going out and trying one's best. Objective goals are based on an athlete's performance. For example, an objective goal of decreasing time by 2 seconds in the 50-meter freestyle event is focused on what needs to be done in order to become more successful at a specific sport. This specific objective goal would then help the athlete be more focused on the task at hand in order to improve technical and tactical skills.

Leith (2003) also distinguishes between outcome, performance, and process goals. **Outcome goals** are related to winning and losing or specific results of a competition. These differ from performance and process goals. **Performance goals** are related to various statistics that can help a person improve at what she is trying to do. For example, a golfer may analyze her game and realize that she has to hit more greens in regulation. Thus a performance goal for the season may be to improve from hitting 50 percent of the greens in regulation to hitting 60 percent of the greens in regulation.

In addition to outcome goals and performance goals, a very important type of goal for athletes to set are process goals. **Process goals** are related to performance goals; they are what the athlete should focus on while performing a sport skill. For example, in addition to setting a performance goal of increasing the number of greens hit in regulation by 10 percent, a golfer may also set a goal to go through the same routine before every shot. It is thought that the more one focuses on process goals, the less that person will worry about how she performs and hopefully will then perform better. Thus, the athlete, through learning to set process and performance goals rather than outcome goals, is setting goals that she has control over.

Sport psychologists have found that athletes often set goals that are not specific and not measurable (Rabasca, 1999). Also, athletes often set goals that cannot be controlled. Athletes often set goals that focus on winning, but they may have little control over whether they win. Their team may have an off night, a key team member

outcome goals—Goals that are related to winning and losing or to specific results of a competition.

process goals—Goals that specify what the athlete should focus on while performing a sport skill.

performance goals—Goals that are related to various statistics that can help a person become better at what he or she is trying to do.

> *How much success do you want? Many athletes achieve some success without using formal goal setting, but virtually every great athlete who consistently wins uses some form of goal setting. Based on our experiences, the USOC sport psychology program believes that using goal setting is as necessary as having a coach.*
>
> **Sport Psychology Staff**, United States Olympic Committee (2008, p. 7)

might become ill or get injured, or the other team may get some lucky breaks, and none of this is under that athlete's control. Kirschenbaum (1997) has presented the SMART acronym to help athletes set effective goals: Goals are specific, measurable, attainable, and realistic and they have a specific time frame.

Imagery

Mental imagery involves using the mind to re-create a picture of a sport skill that an athlete is working on perfecting. It also involves visualizing the on-field or on-court strategy from a tactical perspective. Athletes practice the skill by imagining themselves moving to various positions and seeing themselves play offensive and defensive strategies. But imagery is not only the ability to see oneself in the mind's eye executing a skill. It is also the ability to use all the senses—tactical, olfactory, auditory, and kinesthetic—to re-create and vividly control the pictures in the mind (Weinberg & Gould, 2007). Athletes use imagery to control emotions and reactions to certain events that might not go the way they want them to. Thus, they can practice responding in a positive way and allow themselves to get back to focusing on the process, not the outcome.

> *I have used visualization techniques for as long as I can remember. I always visualized my success. It wasn't until later in my career that I realized the technique is something most people have to learn. I had been practicing the principles naturally my entire life. I visualized how many points I was going to score, how I was going to score them, how I was going to play and break down my opponent.*
>
> **Michael Jordan** (1998, p. 64)

Imagery is a skill that helps athletes pursue their goals, but it is not always practiced in a systematic manner. A sport psychologist or mental training consultant can teach athletes how to use the skill of mental imagery in a systematic way.

Visualizing success can help an athlete stay motivated and confident (Paivio, 1985). Also, when an athlete is faced with a distraction, having visualized that distraction can help the athlete prepare more optimally. Imagery also can help athletes visualize specific strategies (Weinberg & Gould, 2007). Athletes are taught to use imagery to mentally prepare for competition (Suinn, 1972); they also use it during time-outs and breaks during competitions (Hall, Rodgers, & Barr, 1990). Athletes use imagery when rehabilitating from injuries (Driediger, Hall, & Callow, 2006) and in down times, such as right before going to bed at night (Hall, Rodgers, & Barr, 1990). Many athletes use the imagery process while studying videotape or film.

Cross country coaches have used guided imagery to mentally prepare their athletes before competition. A team might have a meeting to discuss the next day's race. Then all the athletes lie on their backs in the meeting room and begin to use relaxation and breathing techniques to get into a calm state. Then the athletes are guided mentally through visualizing and thinking in detail about everything that will happen on the day of the competition. The next day when they compete, they may feel nervous, but having the feeling that they have been there before may help them get into a more relaxed state (Doss-Antoun, 2006).

Jason Hirsh, a player for the Colorado Rockies, describes his use of visualization as preparation for practice and competition. Hirsh says that he has always learned visually and can remember learning to ride a bike as a child just by watching somebody else do it. He uses visualization to focus on the technical aspects of pitching and to work on the control of his pitches. Harding (2007, para. 13-16) says, "Hirsh visualizes himself at first from the outside, first from behind the mound, then from a close-up view of his upper body." Hirsh says this about his visualization: "I am seeing the path I want it to follow…Say I'm throwing the slider, I am seeing the arc of the slider." Using the visualization methods in practice appears to help Hirsh develop the correct mind-set for competition. He says, "Then I can go out to the mound on game day, and I can focus on the catcher's glove."

NBA Hall of Fame player Isiah Thomas provides an excellent example of how he used imagery to work on mentally preparing for NBA Championship games:

> I used a lot of visualization in terms of who I would be guarding and who would be guarding me. When I was walking down the street for, say, lunch I would imagine those individuals in front of me. I'd imagine going around them. Most of the time I was guarded by Byron Scott and Magic Johnson. But whenever I got on a roll, Michael Cooper would guard me. Preparing for him, I'd visualize myself as George Gervin, because Gervin was a player who gave Cooper problems. So I'd try to imitate some of the things that Gervin did when he came off a screen—how he got his feet square and set and shot the ball. ("Handling the Pressure," 2007, section 5, para. 7-8)

When athletes are taught imagery, they are educated about the skill, then they acquire the skill. They then use the skill both in practice and in competition. Mental training consultants and sport psychologists may provide an assessment instrument so that athletes can evaluate their level of use and skill in imagery techniques. For example, the sport psychology staff of the United States Olympic Committee provides an imagery assessment instrument that helps the athlete identify the areas of imagery in which they currently have strengths and areas of the skill in which they can improve (Sport Psychology Staff: United States Olympic Committee, 2008). Then they provide specific exercises for athletes to practice in order to help them improve their ability to imagine situations more vividly and to control their images. Mental training consultants might also help athletes create audiotapes or MP3 files that provide guided imagery for the athletes to listen to before practicing or competing.

Related to the imagery process is the use of motivational highlight DVDs or videotapes. Consultants might develop highlight videos of the athlete practicing and competing; athletes can watch these to aid them in their ability to visualize successful performances and to build their confidence.

Not only can athletes benefit from the skill of learning mental imagery, but coaches also can benefit from the use of mental imagery in preparing themselves for practices and competition (Thelwell, Weston, Greenless, & Hutchings, 2008). One coach who discussed his use of visualization was Phil Jackson (Jackson and Delehanty, 1995, p. 121): "Before each game I usually do forty-five minutes of visualization at home to prepare my mind and come up with last-minute adjustments. This is an outgrowth of the pre-game sessions I did when I played with the Knicks."

Relaxation

The ability to control **anxiety** and relax under pressure has been of interest to psychologists, physical educators, and physicians for a long time. Drs. Dan Czech and Jonathan Metzler use anxiety-reducing techniques in helping football players train for the NFL Combine, which involves four days of testing the physical and mental abilities of players who are thought to have a chance of being drafted by an NFL team. Dr. Czech said, "We teach the players how to regulate themselves, through breathing techniques, progressive relaxation, and meditation. In addition, we take the time to just listen and work through some of the debilitating thoughts they may be thinking. Once they master these concepts and work through some of their worries and anxieties, the players can put themselves in position to perform at optimal levels when they really need it" (Floeckher, 2007, para. 19-21).

anxiety—Feelings of nervousness, worry, and apprehension.

Martens (2004) suggests that uncertainty and how they view success are the main reasons that athletes have anxiety. Martens suggests that to lower athletes' levels of anxiety, coaches should have athletes focus on achieving their potential and making their best effort; they should not focus on the final score or the outcome.

In his book *The Essential Wooden: A Lifetime of Lessons on Leaders and Leadership* (Wooden & Jamison, 2007), John Wooden explains that he wanted his athletes to be able to deal with pressure in competition. So he tried to simulate pressure during daily practices. Coach Wooden did this by creating very intense and focused practices that were similar to the actual atmosphere that the athletes would face in the game. Coach Wooden trained his athletes to be mentally ready for pressure by simulating the pressure in his practices. He also lessened the stress and pressure by not having his team focus on fear of losing or excessive concern about winning a competition.

Psychology Insight

Lawson (1928) recognized the importance of keeping Olympic athletes relaxed and ready for competition. Lawson believed that helping athletes stay relaxed was one of the most important jobs of the medical staff that was working with United States Olympic athletes.

Sport psychology and mental training consultants teach various relaxation and anxiety-reducing techniques to athletes to help them stay in the right frame of mind. These are progressive relaxation, biofeedback, meditation, and breathing techniques (Weinberg & Gould, 2007). Gould and Udry (1994) reviewed the research literature on the use of techniques to manage stress and found that these techniques can be helpful to athletes.

Progressive Relaxation Edmund Jacobson developed the technique of progressive relaxation, which involves tensing certain muscle groups and letting go of the tension in those muscle groups throughout the body to achieve a relaxed and calm state. In an interview with sportswriter Grantland Rice (Rice, 1935, p. 32), Jacobson said the following:

> It is possible to be at high tension and then relax completely, to relax every muscle in the body. Those able to do this will be much better athletes and will last much longer than those that don't. It is one of the most important factors connected with sport—every branch of sport.

Jacobson also supported the concept of relaxation training for golfers and athletes by saying, "But if he could learn in advance just how to relax every muscle, which is not too difficult, it would be a great help. It would make golf much easier and much simpler, just as it would make any other sport much easier and simpler" (Rice, 1935, p. 32).

Biofeedback Biofeedback is a technique in which an athlete is hooked up to a computer via electrodes attached to the fingers or the torso. The athlete learns to control physical tension as demonstrated on the computer screen by relaxing the mind and body. As Peterson (2005) suggests, this technique provides the athlete with information from the physiological component of the body, which then can be controlled by the mind through the use of various techniques to help relax the body. Peterson notes that the quick feedback provided by the technological devices allows athletes to know if what they are doing is helpful in managing the arousal.

Meditation Phil Jackson is a coach who believes in helping athletes stay relaxed and calm through the use of meditation. Jackson, winner of nine NBA Championships with the Chicago Bulls and the Los Angeles Lakers, brought in a consultant, George Mumford, to teach players how to relax under pressure and learn the skill of meditation, in which athletes use their minds to help relax their bodies. In one method of meditation, athletes will repeat a word to themselves that they will focus on. As they repeat the word they try to let all thoughts pass through them and not consciously think about anything while meditating. By allowing the words to pass through and not focusing on their thoughts the athletes allow themselves to become more relaxed (Vargas-Tonsing, 2006).

Breathing Techniques Breathing techniques are also taught to athletes to help them reduce anxiety and become more relaxed. One breathing technique is diaphragmatic breathing. In this technique, the athlete takes long deep breaths, allowing the lungs to fill while the diaphragm expands. The exhalation phase is also long. This slow, rhythmic breathing helps the athlete to relax.

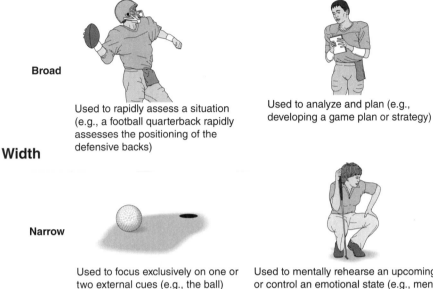

Broad

Used to rapidly assess a situation (e.g., a football quarterback rapidly assesses the positioning of the defensive backs)

Used to analyze and plan (e.g., developing a game plan or strategy)

Width

Narrow

Used to focus exclusively on one or two external cues (e.g., the ball)

Used to mentally rehearse an upcoming performance or control an emotional state (e.g., mentally rehearsing a golf putt or taking a breath to relax)

External   **Internal**

Direction

FIGURE 3.2 Nideffer's model describes the focus of concentration as broad or narrow and as external or internal.

Reprinted, by permission, from Weinberg and Gould 2007.

Concentration

Harvey Dorfman and Karl Kuehl, in their book *The Mental Game of Baseball: A Guide to Peak Performance* (1995), say that almost all the professional athletes they talk to want to learn how they can improve their concentration for sport performance. However, this technique is not easy to learn (Dorfman & Kuehl, 1995). A mental skills consultant or a sport psychologist can help an athlete learn the skill and practice the skill more often.

Nideffer (1976) developed a model of concentration that has two dimensions: width and direction. Nideffer suggests that the width of concentration can be broad or narrow, and the direction of concentration is external or internal (figure 3.2). The key to successful sport performance is the ability to focus on the proper aspects of the task so that an athlete is in the moment while performing the task.

> *I am firmly convinced that to be great at anything it takes the ability to focus correctly for the required period of time to complete the task at hand.*
>
> **Dr. Richard Gordin** ("Special Feature: Dr. Rich Gordin's Golf Tips," 2007, section 5, para. 1)

Athletes need to be aware of what is going on in the external environment and also be aware of their internal thoughts. Athletes can be taught to focus on the important cues at the correct time during competition. They can be taught various ways to assess their concentration levels and then learn skills to improve their ability to focus during practice and competition. One of Martens' (1987) suggestions for assessing and practicing concentration is the use of a concentration grid exercise, in which an athlete has a certain amount of time to cross out as many numbers as possible, in order, on a sheet of 100 randomly placed numbers.

Harvey Dorfman, author of *Coaching the Mental Game* (2003), describes a conversation with professional baseball player Jamie Moyer regarding why Moyer had recently been in a slump. Through their conversations, Moyer realized that he had not been using the concentration grid exercise that had helped a great deal. Moyer began to use the training exercise again and then began to improve.

Another exercise that Martens (1987) describes is the stork stand. The athlete practices standing on one foot (stork position) and maintaining that position for as long as possible with the arms outstretched and the eyes closed.

In addition to these exercises, routines are taught extensively by mental skills consultants and sport psychologists. Preperformance and precompetition routines help athletes focus on the task at hand and be in the moment in order to perform successfully. Athletes may be given worksheets to fill out, which involve creating a detailed precompetition focusing plan and also a competition focusing plan. If something were to go wrong in competition, the athletes have a written plan that they can refer to in order to refocus and get back into concentrating on the task at hand (Leith, 2003). A preperformance routine would be used in individual sports or parts of a team sport that have self-paced components. Mental skills consultants may teach a pre-event or preshot routine to athletes in golf, track and field, and gymnastics and also athletes in team sports who are performing self-paced activities. In American football, linemen can be taught pre-play routines (Ravizza & Osborne, 1991).

Like many basketball players, Gilbert Arenas uses a preshot routine before his free throws. Arenas says, "Everything is mental, but if you remember to stay with your same technique you will be fine. If you stay confident, make sure you are doing the same thing over and over, the free throws will fall" ("The Art of the Free Throw," 2007, para. 4).

Self-Talk

Similar to the psychological skills of imagery and relaxation, self-talk has long been used as a performance-enhancement tool. This skill was actually discussed at the first Olympic congress to discuss sport psychology in 1913 in Lausanne, Switzerland. Self-talk in the early 1900s was referred to as autosuggestion. As mentioned in chapter 1, in the 1940s Dorothy Yates (1943) taught boxers to use positive affirmations, and in the 1950s David F. Tracy worked with the St. Louis Browns on the use of positive affirmations and other psychological skills (Tracy, 1951).

You can see the effects that self-talk can have on performance by looking at the example in figure 3.3. Self-talk is a skill in which athletes practice repeating posi-

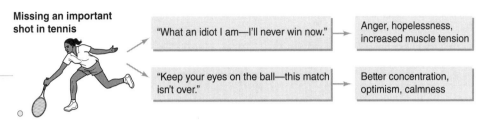

Missing an important shot in tennis

"What an idiot I am—I'll never win now." → Anger, hopelessness, increased muscle tension

"Keep your eyes on the ball—this match isn't over." → Better concentration, optimism, calmness

FIGURE 3.3 **An example of the effects of negative and positive self-talk.**

Reprinted, by permission, from Weinberg and Gould 2007.

tive thoughts to themselves to build confidence. Self-talk also can be used as an instructional component (Anderson, Vogel, & Albrecht, 1999) or to motivate an athlete to push through a competition when he is fatigued (Weinberg, Smith, Jackson, & Gould, 1984). Often athletes say disparaging things to themselves that will lessen their confidence and put them in a bad mood. But by working with mental training consultants or sport psychologists, athletes or coaches can learn how to become aware of what they are saying to themselves and then make their self-talk much more positive. Also, sport psychologists or mental training consultants can help athletes learn to use cue words so that they can be more focused on the task at hand or can refocus to get back to the necessary level of concentration to execute a skill (Rushall, Hall, Roux, Sasseville, & Rushall, 1988).

Just as in physical training, it is important for athletes to train their minds to think positively and to use their thoughts to focus on the task at hand. Athletes sometimes think about the past when they are supposed to be focused on the present, or athletes may think about their lack of specific skills during a competition. Athletes may say things to themselves that are not controllable, such as "I have to win this game" or "We should be beating this team." Also, athletes may have thoughts that are overly perfectionist (Vallance, Dunn, & Causgrove Dunn, 2006).

Fortunately, many techniques can help athletes improve their self-talk. One is the thought-stopping technique (Ziegler, 1987). When an athlete has a negative thought, she says, "Stop," and then replaces the thought with a more positive thought. Another technique is the development of a plan for focusing during competition that incorporates the use of self-talk (Orlick & Partington, 1988). For example, an athlete can create a plan for what he will say to himself at critical points of the competition so that he can focus on thoughts that will be process oriented and focused on what the athlete can control.

Research Support for Teaching Mental Skills to Athletes

The mental skills that are taught to athletes have been studied to determine their efficacy in improving performance. It appears that more successful athletes use mental skills more often than less successful athletes (Gould, Guinan, Greenleaf, Medbery, & Peterson, 1999). Also, reviews of the literature conducted by Greenspan and Feltz (1989), Vealey (1994), and Weinberg and Comar (1994) support the use of psychological interventions for enhancing athletes' performances. Although much of the research has been positive, much more research on psychological interventions needs to be conducted. Gardner and Moore (2006, p. 73) have suggested that to improve research in the study of performance-enhancement interventions, "empirically supported treatment criteria" should be used, meaning the findings would be verifiable and not merely anecdotal.

Who Provides Performance-Enhancement Services to Athletes?

As noted previously, the teaching of mental skills to athletes occurs in various settings by various people. Sport psychologists and mental training consultants assist high school students, university student-athletes, Olympic and national team athletes, and professional athletes. In all of these settings, coaches are also involved in providing mental skills training to their athletes.

Consultants at the High School Level

Athletes at the high school level may have access to full-time mental skills consultants if they are training at an elite-level sport academy. Also, high school student-athletes may obtain mental training consulting from professionals in private practice or from sport psychology consultants at local universities. As noted in chapter 2, some universities provide sport psychology services to the community for a fee. The Boston University Athletic Enhancement Center and the University of Pittsburgh Medical Center's Mental Training program provide mental training services to the local community and high school athletes. Also, hospitals are beginning to offer sport psychology services to high school and adult competitive recreational athletes. The Massachusetts General Hospital Sport Psychology Paces Institute provides services to high school athletes.

Graduate students who are gaining applied experience in the field of sport psychology also provide services to high school athletes. An article in *APA Monitor Online* (Munsey, 2007) explains how Dan Leidl and Joe Frontiera, doctoral students in the West Virginia University sport psychology program, began providing mental training to a high school basketball team that was overcoming a difficult season.

Consultants at the University Level

At the university level, some athletes have access to full-time sport psychology consultants. However, many more might have access to part-time mental training coaches or consultants who provide sport psychology services to a specific team (Kornspan & Duve, 2006; Kornspan, Shimokawa, Duve, & Pinheiro, 2007). Athletes training at a sport academy that is part of a university also may have access to mental training consultants. Of course, as at the high school level, athletes without access to sport psychology consultants at their school may access services from consultants in private facilities or in private practice.

Consultants at the Olympic and National Team Levels

Stotlar and Wonders (2006) studied 28 national governing bodies affiliated with the U.S. Olympic teams and found that 54 percent of the governing bodies had sport psychologists as part of their performance-enhancement staff. Many nations have full-time sport psychologists who provide mental training services to national-level athletes. The Australian Institute of Sport (AIS) has a staff of sport psychology professionals who focus on providing mental training services to athletes. Canada has sport psychology and mental training professionals who work for their various Canadian Sport Centres. The Hong Kong Society of Sport and Exercise Psychology employs mental training consultants. The English Institute of Sport has a national lead sport psychologist, who directs the provision of sport psychology for England. Sean McCann's chapter in *Doing Sport Psychology* (McCann, 2000), titled "Doing Sport Psychology at the Really Big Show," explores the ways in which mental training is used with Olympic athletes.

Consultants at the Professional Level

At the professional level, athletes may have access to mental skills consultants or sport psychologists through their team or a professional sport league or organization. Many professional sport organizations list sport psychologists in their staff directories. Some agents also provide these services for their athletes. Professional athletes in individual sports such as golf and tennis have hired mental training consultants and sport psychology consultants to enhance performance.

The Boston Red Sox baseball organization provides mental training and performance-enhancement services to their athletes. There are approximately 150 athletes in the Red Sox minor league system; Bob Tewksbury works with about 20 to 25 of those athletes. Tewksbury believes the number of athletes using the services he provides will continue to increase to possibly almost half of the athletes in the minor league system (Mullen, 2007).

Coaches at All Levels

As stated earlier in the chapter, coaches are instrumental in providing mental skills training to athletes in all settings. An example is a cross country coach who encourages her athletes to mentally prepare for a race the day before competition by thinking about the course. The coach may then assist the athlete in generating an imagery script related to the course (Brewer, 2000). Damon Burton and Thomas Raedeke (2008), in their book *Sport Psychology for Coaches*, provide coaches with the knowledge to implement a mental skills training program with their athletes. A coach also might decide to bring in a sport psychologist or a consultant in mental skills training to provide group lectures on a sport psychology topic. After listening to the lectures in a group format, some athletes might decide they would like to begin working with a consultant on an individual basis.

The Short of It

- The importance of teaching mental skills to athletes is becoming much better understood by both athletes and those who support athletes, including coaches and sport administrators. Mental skills training is now considered an important part of the training process along with training physically, tactically, and technically.

- Athletes are taught the psychological skills of goal setting, imagery, relaxation, concentration, and self-talk to enhance their performance.

- Mental skills training is provided in many settings: youth sport academies, high schools, universities, Olympic and national training centers, and professional sport settings.

Enhancing the Performance of Teams

In this chapter, you will learn the following:

✓ What team cohesion is and the benefits of developing cohesion

✓ The main theories of how sport teams form

✓ What strategies coaches and sport psychologists provide to teams to enhance cohesion

✓ Research support for the types of interventions that are provided by sport psychologists to enhance team chemistry and cohesion

"Every season there are numerous examples of teams that have all the right talent to compete for the championship but end up losing and falling painfully short of their goals. Occasionally, it is bad luck or an off day, but more often than not it is due to a lack of teamwork."

Jeff Janssen
(2002, p. 6).

The members of the U.S. soccer team were racing up the steps of a building on the campus of the University of Georgia, singing the theme from the movie *Rocky*. This was a drill devised by their mental training consultant, Dr. Colleen Hacker. In another team-building drill, they hiked down a cliff; half the team was blindfolded while the other half was led down the cliff by a partner. The athletes and coach of the team, Tony DiCicco, felt that Dr. Colleen Hacker was instrumental in helping the team become successful. Mia Hamm said, "Colleen's meant so much to this team. She's like a final piece to a puzzle. . . . Our team chemistry has always been one of our strengths, but she's made it 10 times better" (Shipley, 1999, para. 5).

Hacker (2001b, p. 17) described the importance of team building in providing mental training to athletes:

Team building is an invaluable part of any team's success. But team building isn't just playing games or having fun, or having a break from training. We take team building very seriously, even though we're laughing often times during the team building session. We can work on problem solving, communication, developing leadership, handling adversity, dealing with frustration, cooperating with one another, increasing interpersonal understanding and risk taking. It's amazing when we're doing trust dives or trust falls, you see elite athletes suddenly get tense and worried. Without question there is a lot of growth that occurs.

The topic of how teams form was discussed as early as 1913 at the first Olympic Congress on the psychology and physiology of sport in Lausanne, Switzerland. Dedet presented a lecture on how teams follow a life-cycle approach throughout the season (Kornspan, 2007b). Today, it is clear that coaches and sport psychologists believe it is important to build teams that are able to work together effectively. This chapter explores the aspects of an effective team and how consultants and coaches create programs to improve the cohesion of athletic teams and organizations.

Overview of Team Building

Team cohesion describes how a team comes together socially and in their athletic tasks. In general, teams with higher team cohesion are thought to perform better (Carron, Colman, Wheeler, & Stevens, 2002). This section explores the benefits of team building and gives examples of what successful coaches have to say about team building.

> **team cohesion**—How a team comes together both socially and in their athletic tasks.

Benefits of Team Building

Team building develops cohesion among the athletes on the team. The two types of cohesion are social cohesion and task cohesion (Carron, Widmeyer, & Brawley, 1985). **Social cohesion** is about getting athletes to enjoy the process of working together and helping individuals on the team develop camaraderie. **Task cohesion** is an analysis of how individuals on the team work together to achieve a common goal. From a standpoint of team victories, it appears that task cohesion is more important (Williams & Widmeyer, 1991). But to help athletes have a truly satisfying and enjoyable experience, mental training consultants and sport psychologists believe that social cohesion is important.

> **social cohesion**—A measure of how much athletes enjoy the process of working together and the extent to which individuals on the team develop a camaraderie.
>
> **task cohesion**—A measure of how well individuals on the team work together to achieve a common goal.

Individuals need to work together in the process of becoming a team. The linear theory of group development suggests that individual athletes go through four stages when becoming a team: forming, storming, norming, and performing (Tuckman, 1965). The forming stage is the beginning of the season, when individuals on the team are just starting to get to know each other. In the storming stage, conflict within the team occurs. Competition for positions might occur, and individuals who are competing against each other might not get along (Leith, 2003).

During the storming stage, it is helpful to let athletes know their roles and responsibilities so that the team can transition smoothly into the norming phase (Leith, 2003). Dean Smith, retired head coach of men's basketball at the University of North Carolina, provides an excellent example of this: Smith had one-on-one meetings with his athletes and let them know where they stood after about the first three weeks. He did not tell his athletes that they needed to improve to beat someone out of a position. He tried to encourage an athlete who would not be a starter to continue to work hard because things could change if that player continued to improve. Coach Smith thought that if he encouraged competition for starting positions among the players, he would have created athletes who were focused on their own interests and not those of the team. This would have gone against one of his main missions of having athletes play together as a team (Smith & Bell, 2004).

The third phase of forming a team is the norming phase. This occurs when the team begins working together and performing with more task cohesion. The final stage, performing, occurs when the team has become a well-oiled machine and there are few problems. The team is focused on the process, and individuals on the team know their roles well.

Janssen (2002) proposes that team building can facilitate both on-the-field success and athletes' satisfaction with the sport experience. In terms of success, building a cohesive team can be helpful since it might stop personal conflicts from occurring. Team building can help a team commit to a goal by staying focused on performance improvement. Janssen also suggests that very successful teams are usually focused on **task goals** 90 percent of the time. Teams that have moderate success are usually focused on the task goals 50 percent of the time, while the other 50 percent of the time they are dealing with external issues that are affecting the team. Teams that are not effective are focused on task goals 10 percent of the time and are focused on external issues the other 90 percent of the time.

> **task goals**—Goals focused on achieving successful physical performance.

Regarding athletes' satisfaction with the sport experience and the process of being part of a team, Janssen (2002, p. 9) says, "While the majority of coaches and athletes get involved in sport for the challenge and joy of winning, a sense of satisfaction from the close relationships which you and your players develop is often an unmentioned, yet important reward of the team building process."

Successful Coaches on Team Building

Many coaches go to great lengths to create an atmosphere in which athletes on the team get to know each other and get along well with each other. Coach Dean Smith believes in helping his players develop a team-first attitude: "We constantly thought about ways to make the team concept stronger. We called it chemistry; the better chemistry among the players, the stronger the team" (Smith & Bell, 2004, p. 125). Smith had players on the team change roommates on road trips, and for the first semester on campus athletes were assigned roommates. Coach Smith believed that an attitude of unselfishness was instrumental to team success.

> *Good teams become great ones when the members trust each other enough to surrender the "me" for "we." This is the lesson Michael [Jordan] and his teammates learned en route to winning three consecutive NBA championships.*
>
> **Coach Phil Jackson** (Jackson & Delehanty, 1995, p. 21)

Coach John Wooden also believed in getting his teams to play with great unity. One of the blocks on Wooden's pyramid of success is cooperation. He thought that if individuals and teams were to reach their potential, they would have to be able to get along well and cooperate with each other. When recruiting players, Coach Wooden looked for character traits that indicated the athletes were team players (Wooden & Jamison, 2007). He wanted UCLA teams to develop cooperation so that they could achieve their competitive potential. He also wanted individuals on the team to put the needs of the team before individuals' needs. Coach Wooden wrote, "UCLA team members were taught that teammates were responsible for their success: 'It takes ten hands to make a basket.' They were instructed that whenever a Bruin scored, that player was to give a nod or a wink to the assisting teammate. One player asked, 'Coach Wooden, what if he isn't looking at me?' I said don't worry, I'll be looking" (Wooden & Jamison, 2004, p. 112).

Moran (2004) discusses how the captain for the England Ryder Cup team wanted to find out what he could do to increase the cohesion of his team members. Sam Torrance, the captain, consulted with well-known soccer coaches Sven Goran Eriksson and Alex Ferguson (Moran, 2004). According to Moran, the message Torrance received was to treat all of the athletes in a similar way. In preparing his Ryder Cup team, Torrance used slogans to inspire his team. One slogan was "Out of the shadows come heroes" (Moran, 2004, p. 216).

Another consultant helping an athletic team with team-building exercises was Dr. Jack Stark at the University of Nebraska. It was the end of the 1990 football season and the Nebraska team had just lost three of their last four football games. As Dr. Stark said, "We wanted to have a way for the players to become more unified" (Shulte, 2002, para. 5). So early in 1991, Dr. Stark helped the team start a unity council, a group of team members who met weekly to discuss issues that the team was dealing with. The council members were elected by their teammates, and the meetings were conducted without any coaches present (Shulte, 2002). The unity council provided the team with a comfortable environment in which they could discuss concerns and then bring those concerns to the coaching staff. Interestingly, Nebraska has brought back the unity council under new coach Bo Pelini (Hudgens, 2008).

During the 2003 football season, Bobby Bowden, national championship coach for Florida State University, created a unity council similar to the type of council Jack Stark created with the Nebraska football team. According to Bowden, the purpose of the unity council was to provide the athletes with a way of meeting with him to express concerns they might have about anything (Thomas, 2003).

Pat Riley, coach of the 2006 NBA championship team the Miami Heat, focused on creating a cohesive team atmosphere throughout the 2006-2007 NBA season and playoffs. Riley continually repeated the phrase "15 strong" during the playoffs (Shipley, 2006). He had a

Psychology Insight

Coaches and sport psychology consultants look for innovative ways of developing cohesive teams. Every season during training camp, Ken Hitchcock, coach of the Philadelphia Flyers, includes activities to help his hockey team work on bonding. For three seasons the Flyers went to West Point and the Naval Academy to work on building team chemistry with consultant Dr. Nate Zinsser, the director of the Center for Performance Enhancement at the United States Military Academy at West Point. One exercise that the team participated in was a ropes course, which can help individuals overcome fear and put trust in the teammates who are guiding them through the course. Coach Hitchcock said, "The physical and mental experiences there, that is what we are looking for. We are looking for chemistry" (Pannaccio, 2006, F3).

bowl of thousands of cards; one side of each card said "15 strong" and the other sides had pictures of trophies, family, and the team (Sheridan, 2006). Coach Riley placed the bowl of cards in the locker room and used them as a reminder of team cohesion. Riley said, "We just kept piling them in. I had a little wheelbarrow and I would dump a bunch in and Shaq [O'Neal] would dump some in and we just kept building it up" (Hu, 2006, para. 16).

Mike Krzyzewski (Coach K), the national championship coach of the men's basketball team at Duke University, uses the analogy of the fist as a symbol he teaches his team in order for them to focus on teamwork and togetherness. Each finger represents a word:

> Each separate finger that makes up The Fist symbolizes a fundamental quality that renders a team great. For my teams we emphasize five words . . . communication, trust, collective responsibility, care, and pride. I believe that any of these traits alone is important. But all five together are tough to beat. (Krzyzewski & Spatola, 2006, p. 170)

Coach K explains that a fist is much more powerful than five fingers held alone and not touching each other. This is similar to basketball, where five players must work together rather than as individuals in order to achieve success. Coach K's goal in using the fist as a symbol is to remind his athletes to work together in order to achieve their purpose.

Obviously many of the greatest coaches believe in the importance of developing a cohesive team from a social as well as a task perspective. The sport psychology staff of the United States Olympic Committee has found that most of the national governing bodies believe team building is important to success in international competition (McCann, 2007).

Where Does Team Building Occur?

Leith (2003) describes team building as when a coach provides a way of helping athletes develop a high level of togetherness. The hope is that team-building activities foster trust, open lines of communication, and improve social support among teammates. Two types of team-building procedures discussed in the literature are an indirect approach and a direct approach (Bloom & Stevens, 2002).

Indirect Approach

An indirect approach occurs when a mental training consultant or sport psychologist meets with the coaches to explain the various activities to be conducted with the team, and then the coach implements these activities with the team. This approach usually has four stages (Carron, Spink, & Prappevessis, 1997; Carron & Dennis, 1998).

In the first stage (the introduction stage) of the indirect approach to team building, the consultant and the coach meet; the consultant or sport psychologist explains the benefits of helping a team become more cohesive (Carron, Spink, & Prappevessis, 1997). The consultant and coach then create various strategies and interventions in order for the team to develop more cohesiveness. In the second stage, the consultant presents a model to the coach about the ideal outcomes of the intervention. The consultant and coach discuss how the intervention can enhance various elements of a successful team and the main principles behind developing these successful elements. The third stage of the indirect method of a team-building intervention is a practical component in which the consultant and the coach use a brainstorming procedure to determine as many specific ways as possible to build cohesion within the athletic group. In the final stage, the coach presents the strategies to the team (Carron, Spink, & Prappevessis, 1997; Weinberg & Gould, 2007).

Direct Approach

In the direct approach to team building, the mental skills consultant or the sport psychologist provides the team-building services directly to the athletes (Cox, 2007). An example is Dr. Hacker's work with the U.S. World Cup soccer team: She met directly with the athletes and taught them various team-building exercises.

In describing her work with the U.S. World Cup soccer team, Hacker (2001a) said that team building was an important activity that she provided to the team in addition to teaching imagery, concentration, relaxation, goal setting, self-talk, and other mental training tools. Hacker (2001a, p. 363) wrote, "Team building activities serve a critical role assimilating strong personalities and unique individuals into a unified and collective whole (i.e., 'the team before me')." She explained that individuals cannot hope that team chemistry will just happen by chance, but that action-oriented efforts are needed in order for team chemistry to build among the coaches and athletes.

Dr. Hacker says, "Adventure programming and team building activities embrace and encourage adaptation, creativity, risk taking, and the development of problem solving skills, and they help individuals of all ages to trust, cooperate, risk, achieve and grow" (Hacker, 2000a, para. 1). She describes in detail how to go about planning team-building sessions with athletes: The consultant would start with a planning phase, which involves thinking through what is being taught to the athletes. Then the team-building session begins with an icebreaker, which is similar to a warm-up that athletes might use for a physical practice session. After the icebreaker, the consultant provides the rules of the sessions to the athletes so that they know what is expected of them. Then the athletes go through various team-building exercises to help them learn a specific concept that the coach, mental skills training consultant, or sport psychologist may be teaching. After the athletes complete the team-building exercises, the consultant should help the team through a debriefing stage in which the athletes and the consultant discuss various lessons that may have been learned from the exercises. Hacker emphasizes that the debriefing component may be just as important as, or even more important than, the actual team-building exercises. Finally, consultants follow up with the team throughout the year to ensure that the coach and athletes continue to discuss the lessons learned in the team-building sessions (Hacker, 2000b).

Janssen (2002) discusses four steps in a direct team-building process: assessment, strategy, implementation, and evaluation. As with the other approaches to team building, one of the objectives is to understand as much about the team as possible. Janssen provides a survey instrument that can be given to the team as an assessment of the present level of team building. This instrument asks players to respond to statements in seven categories: goals, roles, commitment, dealing with conflict, communication, team cohesion, and positive leadership. Examples of items on the inventory include: "Players on the team generally respect and trust each other" and "The team's success is a high priority for most players" (Janssen, 2002, p. 26). After the assessment phase, the consultant develops a strategy to implement team building to improve the areas of team cohesion that need to be improved. One of the best ways to educate people in these areas is to have a game or activity in which the student-athletes can experience the mental skill being taught or discussed. The third stage is implementing the plan and teaching the skills. The final stage is an evaluation of the effectiveness of the team-building activity. Ways to evaluate the effectiveness of team building include asking the athletes directly what they thought of the activities or having the athletes fill out a survey asking them about the effectiveness of the team-building assessment and activities (Janssen, 2002).

What Team-Building Activities Are Taught to Athletes?

Athletes can use many activities to enhance team cohesion and to focus on an area that the team needs to enhance in order to improve their performance. Some excellent resources provide many types of activities that can teach various concepts to athletes. Janssen (2002); Dale (2003); Dale and Conant (2005); and DiCicco, Hacker, and Salzberg (2002) describe many activities that can build team cohesion. The human knot, team transport, the trust walk, the tire sing-along, strung together, and blindfolded shapes are some of the activities that Janssen (2002) describes.

A variety of activities can be conducted with a team to help build chemistry (Lasser, Borden, & Edwards, 2006). These include practice drills, team meetings, team-bonding sessions, and team activities.

Practice Drills

A 7-10 spare-shooting drill in bowling, in which the bowlers practice shooting both 7- and 10-pin spares from the full rack of 10 shots, helps team members initiate conversation in practice drills. Through this drill, the team can discover who is strong in spare shooting and who needs to improve in this area. This drill encourages the athletes to talk to each other about what techniques they can use to improve their scores. After athletes begin to discuss how to help each other, they often spend even more time practicing while encouraging each other to improve (Lasser, Borden, & Edwards, 2006).

Team Meetings

Team meetings are an opportunity for athletes to build cohesion by making positive comments to each other and working on problem solving. Meetings allow the athletes to share information with each other and develop a bond. Cohesion can be enhanced in team meetings when athletes discuss their thoughts on how the team communicates, the goals of the team, and various conflicts that involve the whole team.

Team-Bonding Sessions

Team-bonding sessions can help an athletic team become more cohesive through self-disclosure and conversations about personal feelings related to practicing and competition as well as life in general. At the annual team-bonding session for the U.S. bowling team, team members end their session by forming a circle and saying, "I'm your teammate and I'm here for you no matter what" (Lasser, Borden, & Edwards, 2006, p. 310). Consultants or sport psychologists may facilitate these types of meetings; as Lasser and colleagues (2006, p. 310) say, "For a meeting of this type to be successful, there needs to be an experienced leader who is comfortable facilitating group process. The leader sets the tone and provides guidance during any moments of distraction or conflict." Holt and Dunn (2006) found that a bonding session in which athletes disclose personal stories and information about their lives provides an increased understanding of individuals in the group, improved confidence, and more cohesion among the group.

Team Activities

These activities are not related to the sport that the athletes are training for. An example of a team activity is taking a professional football team bowling. For two straight years Mike Shanahan, coach of the Denver Broncos, cancelled the last practice of his team's minicamp and instead took his team bowling (Mason, 2006).

Research Support for Teaching Team Building

Team building is one of the newer techniques introduced into the literature on mental skills training for athletes. Therefore, not much research has been conducted on the effects of team building as a mental training tool to help teams perform more optimally (Bloom & Stevens, 2002).

Various studies in the sport psychology literature have found team building to be effective. Voight and Callaghan (2001) found that athletes in their study believed the team-building intervention increased team unity. Senecal, Loughead, and Bloom (2008), in a study analyzing the effects of team-building interventions on the perceptions of team cohesion in basketball players, found that team cohesion was higher for the goal-setting intervention group than for the control group (a group that did not participate in a season-long team-building intervention). Newin, Bloom, and Loughead (2008), in an analysis of the perceptions of coaches who implemented a team-building intervention throughout the season, found that coaches who implemented the intervention believed that the athletes enjoyed the intervention, and that it helped them acquire life skills. The coaches also believed the intervention helped the athletes with teamwork.

Who Provides Team-Building Services to Athletes?

Team-building activities are provided by mental skills training consultants and sport psychologists. Often a consultant is brought in to meet with an athletic team to provide team-building sessions or a day of team building. As covered in chapter 3, at the high school level consultants from local universities, sport academies, or private practice might be contracted by local high schools to provide team-building sessions. This may also be the case at the university level; however, some universities or athletic teams may have their own full-time or part-time consultants who facilitate team-building sessions for the athletic teams. At the professional and Olympic level, teams may have mental training consultants or sport psychologists on staff who provide these services, or they may hire consultants to provide these services. Some individuals have developed their own companies related to helping athletic teams and businesses enhance cohesion through team-building activities and leadership skills training.

⭐ SUCCESS STORY

Jeff Janssen, Janssen Sports Leadership Center

Courtesy of Jeff Janssen.

Jeff Janssen began his consulting career as a peak performance consultant and assistant life skills director at the University of Arizona athletic department, where he worked with national championship and Pac-10 championship teams ("Janssen Peak Performance," 2007). Janssen's success at the University of Arizona is well documented. After eight years at Arizona, Janssen left and started his own company, Janssen Peak Performance. The company provided team-building services and various seminars, including a championship team-building workshop, to athletes and businesses. Recently, Janssen renamed his business the Janssen Sports Leadership Center and shifted his focus to working with college athletic departments to develop leadership skills in both student-athletes and coaches.

The Short of It

- Team cohesion includes both social cohesion and task cohesion and describes how a team comes together both in social situations and on the field of play.

- According to the linear theory of group development, teams go through four stages when becoming a team: forming, storming, norming, and performing.

- Many of the greatest coaches believe that team-building interventions that increase team cohesion are important to success.

- Sport psychologists and mental training consultants provide team-building consulting to athletes and coaches using both direct and indirect approaches.

- Team-building activities include practice drills, team meetings, team-bonding sessions, and team activities.

- Sport psychologists and mental training consultants provide services to athletes either as consultants for coaches or as part of an organization's staff.

Creating a Positive Sport Environment

Leadership, Motivation, and Communication

In this chapter, you will learn the following:

✓ Why creating a positive coaching environment is important

✓ What sport and exercise psychologists teach coaches to help them create positive environments

✓ Where and how sport and exercise psychologists educate and consult with coaches on providing a positive developmental sport environment

"A good parent, teacher, coach, or leader— and really they're all the same—must understand human nature."

John Wooden
(Wooden & Jamison, 2004, p. 127).

One of the most exciting stories of the 2006 NCAA Men's Basketball Tournament was the team from George Mason University. Most would not have believed that a "mid-major" team, one of 65 chosen to participate, would make the Final Four. But in 2006, George Mason University did make the Final Four. Throughout the season, Coach Jim Larranaga often spoke to his good friend Dr. Bob Rotella, a top consultant and former director of the sport psychology program at the University of Virginia. During George Mason's Final Four run, Larranaga said, "Through the last 20 years as a head coach, Bob has helped me relax and enjoy the process." (O'Connor & Kapsidelis, 2006, p. C14). Rotella also met with the coaching staff and athletes before the season started. During these meetings Rotella told the team, "Are you willing to believe that you and Duke are the best teams in the country? You can believe that or you can believe another team is the best. We are what we think about ourselves. Believe in your talent" (Robbins, 2006, p. 97). Rotella said of Larranaga, "Jimmy really understands that every word he says in practice is going to have some impact on the players' minds, the way they're thinking, the way they're feeling" (Steinberg, 2006, p. E1).

During the 2004 baseball season, Coach Horton of the Cal State Fullerton baseball team brought mental training consultant Ken Ravizza in to consult with the athletes and coaching staff. Ravizza began working with the coaching staff first. Coach Horton believed that many of the problems that were occurring with the team were related to the mental approach that the coaches were taking. Horton said, "We were chipping on umpires, yelling at players, and getting wrapped up in negative thinking. Ken gave us tools to use as coaches that allowed us to take blows and keep going" (Smith, 2005, para. 48). The Cal State baseball team went on to win the national championship in 2004. Coach Horton believed Ravizza's work was helpful:

> When I look back on it now, I can see that we started the season without our mental game in order. . . . As soon as we began to work the mental game, we started to win. There is no doubt in my mind that Ken's help was what turned a 15-16 season start into a national championship season, and I am more convinced than ever that mental skills training is an essential piece of the puzzle. (Smith, 2005, para. 6)

One of the main roles of a sport psychology consultant is to help athletes, coaches, exercisers, and various sport personnel enjoy the experience of being involved in sport and physical activity. Since the mid-1960s sport psychologists have been researching and studying how leadership and group dynamics can affect the sporting experience. Sport psychology practitioners have been using this research in teaching coaches how to create positive sport environments. In fact, the importance that the sport psychology profession places on educating coaches is shown through an entire issue of the journal *The Sport Psychologist* being devoted to coaching education. Also, the Association for Applied Sport Psychology (AASP) listed educating coaches and parents as a service provided by consultants ("About Applied Sport and Exercise Psychology," 2008). But many coaches and administrators still consider the main role of sport psychology consultants to be providing mental training services to help only *athletes* improve performance. This chapter focuses on the role that sport psychologists play in consulting with and educating coaches in order to create positive sport environments.

Importance of Creating a Positive Sport Environment

One of the main lines of research conducted by sport and exercise psychologists has analyzed why youth are motivated to participate in sport and also why they stop participating. A main reason youth participate in sport is that it is fun (Ewing & Seefeldt, 1989). Likewise, one of the main reasons that children stop participating in organized sport is that it is *not* fun. Thus, coaches, parents, and administrators who understand how to provide a positive and supportive atmosphere can help youth continue to participate in sport. Continually keeping children participating in sport has health benefits and allows them an opportunity to learn skills that can be transferred to other areas of their lives.

Articles have been written about problems occurring at sporting events because of inappropriate behavior by fans, coaches, and parents. Also, some coaches are being forced to leave their jobs or to change their behavior because of their style of coaching. Some coaches who have used an authoritarian style of coaching have been asked to resign from their positions. Here is a hypothetical situation: A coach of a top-level elite club soccer team is described as having a dictatorial approach to motivating the team. As personal and performance problems mount for the team, the coach is fired. The assistant coaches take over and provide a much more positive environment and the team goes on to a very successful season.

Here is a similar scenario: A high school baseball coach is asked to change his coaching style and apologize to his team after many of the athletes approach the athletic director about the coach's negative coaching behavior. Could situations like these be prevented if a sport psychology consultant had provided consulting to the coach? Although it can't be determined for sure, it may be possible that a sport psychology consultant can help coaches interact more positively with athletes.

Why Consultants Are Needed

Not enough coaches are being trained to coach. Coaches at the highest levels of university and professional sports are often seen being visibly angry with the referees. Occasionally coaches shout at or humiliate athletes for making mistakes. Because many youth sport and high school coaches see elite coaches exhibiting these behaviors, they often believe that this is the best way to coach. Sport psychologists have spent years researching and understanding more positive ways to coach that have been shown to be effective in improving athletes' performance. And sport psychology consultants can actively play a role in helping coaches learn to lead in a positive way.

Sport psychologists have learned that a win-at-all-costs philosophy is a major factor in creating a negative sporting environment (Martens, 2004). This philosophy often fosters an authoritarian or command style of leadership and does not provide an enjoyable environment for the athletes.

In light of the research findings on the benefits of a positive coaching environment, clearly there is a need to have more sport psychology consultants working with coaches at all levels. As Smoll and Smith (2006) point out, interventions for elite athletes get the most attention in sport psychology. They explain the importance of sport psychology professionals' helping to create a more positive sport environment at the youth level:

> Most coaches are fairly well versed in the technical aspects of the sport, but they have rarely had any formal training in creating a healthy psychological environment. It is here that sport psychologists are capable of making significant contributions, by developing and conducting educational programs that positively affect coaching behaviors and thereby increase the likelihood that youngsters will have positive sport experiences. (Smoll & Smith, 2006, p. 459)

To help create positive sporting environments, coaches and administrators can bring in sport psychology consultants to assess the type of **leadership style** that athletes prefer and that coaches believe they are providing. See the sidebar for descriptions of leadership styles in coaching (Martens, 2004). A sport psychology consultant can administer the Leadership Scale for Sports (LSS) (Chelladurai & Saleh, 1980) to both the coaches and the athletes. The consultant then compares the coaches' and athletes' perceptions on how the team is being led. If the perceptions are not consistent, the consultant can then work to create more positive communication between the coaches and athletes so that tension between them is lessened and the environment is more conducive to athletes' training (Leffingwell, Durand-Bush, Wurzberger, & Cada, 2005).

leadership style—The way in which a coach trains and interacts with athletes.

Successful Coaches and Positive Sport Environments

Creating a positive sporting environment through a developmental leadership style is an effective way of achieving two main objectives in sport: good performance and fun. The field of sport psychology analyzes the behavior of expert coaches. Jim Tressel (football coach at Ohio State) and Phil Jackson (coach of the Los Angeles Lakers) are renowned for being positive communicators who incorporate sport psychology concepts into their work with their teams.

STYLES OF COACHING

command style—A negative approach to communicating, which involves using fear and intimidation to control athletes' behavior.

submissive style—An approach in which the coach functions more as a babysitter and lets athletes do what they want.

cooperative style—A focus on developing a positive relationship with athletes. The coach listens and communicates in a positive way and allows athletes to participate in the decision-making process.

After the 2007 National Championship football game in which Ohio State lost, Tressel still viewed his athletes as champions:

> Starting with these four guys up here, who have been great leaders, and 14 other seniors and a bunch of great kids, we've been awfully proud of the way they represented college football and Ohio State and they have achieved a lot on the field. Fell short this evening, but you know they're champions in my book. (Rice, 2007, para. 5)

Similarly, Phil Jackson continues to be seen as a positive coach day in and day out in practices. According to Tex Winter, Phil Jackson communicates with his athletes in a positive manner: "The important thing is that he doesn't destroy their confidence. So many coaches do that. It's his demeanor, the way he handles people, the way he communicates what he wants done. He does this in a very positive manner, even in very stressful situations" (Abbott, 2006, para. 13).

> *People never care how much you know until they know how much you care.*
>
> **John C. Maxell**

Harvey Dorfman, a well-known mental training consultant in baseball, is an excellent example of how and why sport psychology concepts that stress a positive approach can and should be implemented with coaches. Dorfman (2003) was brought in to consult with a university baseball team. On the first night, Dorfman and the coaching staff went out to dinner, where the head coach explained to Dorfman that the team was quitting and not putting forth enough effort during games. One of the assistant coaches asked the head coach if he had told Dorfman how he acts when the team starts to lose. The assistant explained that when the team started to lose, the head coach would start to exhibit anger and display negative nonverbal communication. The head coach would shut down and not talk to anyone when the team was not performing well. After Dorfman heard about this issue, he explained to the head coach what the problem was. Dorfman spent much time working with the coach to help him understand how his behavior was affecting the team.

Where Do Coaches Learn to Create a Positive Environment?

The example of Dorfman's work with the coaching staff at the university level, which involved individual consulting, may be the most optimal. However, there are other ways that coaches, parents, and administrators can learn about psychological principles in order to create a positive environment for their athletes. University courses in sport psychology that cover concepts and tactics involved in creating a positive athletic environment are excellent learning opportunities. The International Council for Coach Education (ICCE) created the Magglingen Declaration, which summarizes 10 main challenges that should be addressed by the coaching profession ("The Magglingen Declaration," 2008). One of the challenges is to create more athlete-centered sport environments. Also, this declaration suggests that competencies of coaches should be developed.

In the United States, students obtaining a coaching major or coaching minor are often required to take courses in sport psychology, especially if the coaching education program is accredited by the National Council for Accreditation of Coaching Education (NCACE), a division of the National Association for Sport and Physical Education (NASPE) ("NCACE Domain Specific Review," 2008). In Australia, the National Coaching Accreditation Scheme offers a sport psychology component as part of their intermediate course on the general principles of coaching ("Intermediate Coaching General Principles," 2008).

An additional benefit of sport psychology coursework is that the skills learned are often transferable to other areas of life. According to Gould (2002, p. 247), "Many AAASP members are transferring what they have learned about facilitating human performance in sport to other domains such as music, the arts, business, and the military." There are excellent opportunities to apply the principles of a positive approach to behavior in business settings (Jones, 2002). Although applying sport psychology to business settings may be a way for sport psychology consultants to earn additional income, if a student's main interest is in practicing psychology in business settings full-time, training in industrial-organizational psychology is suggested.

Additional settings in which coaches can learn how to create a more positive environment include clinics, conferences, and workshops. National organizations have begun to promote the importance of coaching education. These programs often offer licenses or certifications. As part of these certification or licensing programs, coaches learn how to use the principles of sport psychology in creating a positive developmental coaching environment. Many national governing bodies (NGBs) offer training and workshops that include information about coaching the psychological elements of those specific sports. Examples of such NGBs are the Amateur Swimming Association (UK), United States Soccer Federation, and USA Cycling. The Coaches Association of British Columbia has partnered with the Canadian Sport Psychology Association in offering a Sport Psychology Conference for Coaches ("Sport Psychology Conference for Coaches," 2007). The Australian

CENTERS THAT PROVIDE SPORT PSYCHOLOGY AND MENTAL TRAINING SERVICES

Boston University Athletic Enhancement Center
www.bu.edu/aec

Harvard University Athletic, Academic, and Personal Excellence (AAPEX)
http://aapex.harvard.edu

University of Pittsburgh Medical Center
http://sportsmedicine.upmc.com/mentaltrainingprogram.htm

University of Vermont Center for Health and Well-Being
www.uvm.edu/~chwb/counseling

West Point Center for Enhanced Performance
www.dean.usma.edu/centers/cep/default.htm

Western Washington University Center for Performance Excellence
www.wwu.edu/cpe/cpe_staff.htm

University of North Texas Center for Sport Psychology and Performance Excellence
www.sportpsych.unt.edu

Football Coaches Association offers accreditation for coaches; a component of this accreditation is a focus on the welfare of the athletes ("AFL Coach Accreditation Courses," 2008).

What Methods Do Consultants Teach to Coaches?

As students learn more about the field of sport and exercise psychology, they spend more time studying topics such as leadership, motivation, communication, and reinforcement. These topics are the building blocks of what sport psychology consultants teach to coaches to help them learn to create a positive environment.

Coaching Philosophies

As discussed in chapter 3, two main leadership philosophies involve having athletes focus on the process, not the outcome, and having athletes focus on what they can control and not worry about what they cannot control. Sport psychology professionals often help coaches overcome these problems as well.

Sean McCann (2006), head of the United States Olympic Committee's sport psychology department, describes an experience in which he was consulting with a high-level Division I football team. The team was not performing up to expectations and was having difficulty beating their archrival. McCann knew

Psychology Insight

Dean Smith, former men's basketball coach at the University of North Carolina at Chapel Hill, says, "Making winning the ultimate goal is usually not good teaching. Tom Osborne, the great former football coach of the University of Nebraska, said that making winning the ultimate goal can get in the way of winning. I agree. So many things happened in games that were beyond our control: the talent and experience of teams, bad calls by officials, injuries, bad luck" (Smith & Bell, 2004, p. 29).

what the problem was when he went into the meeting with the coaches. One of the signs displayed a rule that stated that a team that wins most often is the one that makes the fewest mistakes. McCann explained that this philosophy focuses the athletes and staff on what not to do rather than on what they should do, which is to address the task at hand. McCann recommends that coaches choose various specific positive goals that they can help athletes focus on and that help athletes to be less worried and distracted about the outcome of competition. Through the help of a sport psychology consultant, a coach can learn this important leadership concept so that athletes can play better under the pressure of competition.

Leadership, Motivation, and Communication

In addition to teaching coaches a philosophy of creating a positive environment, sport psychologists and mental training consultants provide coaches with information about leadership. One issue of debate is whether coaches are born or made. Some people believe successful coaches are born. Alternatively, some believe that coaches can learn how to be successful through experience and training (Weinberg & Gould, 2007). Most sport psychologists would support the belief that people can learn how to use a positive leadership style by allowing athletes to be a part of the decision-making process and using positive reinforcement to lead athletes toward success.

extrinsic motivation—External and sometimes tangible rewards or recognition (such as trophies, money, or praise from a coach) that drive an athlete to achieve.

intrinsic motivation—Internal factors that drive an athlete to achieve, such as satisfaction and enjoyment of an activity or the attainment of a personal-best time in a race.

Sport psychologists believe that intrinsic motivation is more optimal than **extrinsic motivation,** such as the use of trophies, money, or other rewards that are dependent on winning (Metzler, 2002). However, it should be noted that extrinsic rewards, when used properly, can be motivating to athletes. For example, a coach who acknowledges and provides positive feedback to an athlete who is learning a new skill can be a very powerful motivator. It is important for coaches to use extrinsic rewards correctly so that they do not undermine an athlete's intrinsic motivation (Martens, 2004).

Intrinsic motivation comes from athletes' wanting to participate in a sport because of the enjoyment and satisfaction they feel and the achievement of personal goals. A coach's cooperative leadership style usually leads to creating a more intrinsically motivating atmosphere where athletes strive for success and focus on improvement rather than take on a win-at-all-costs philosophy. Through scientific research and applied practice, sport psychologists have developed views similar to those of great coaches about the importance of intrinsic motivation. Christian Klemash, in his book *How to Succeed in the Game of Life* (2006), presents the philosophies of prominent coaches, such as Red Auerbach, Joe Torre, Bill Walsh, and John Wooden. These coaches believe that ultimate success occurs when an individual gives his best effort and is able to reach his potential through attempting to improve his abilities each day. This can be summed up by John Wooden's definition of success: "Success to me is a peace of mind, which is the direct result of self-satisfaction in knowing you made the effort to become the best of which you were capable. Success is coming as close as possible to reaching your maximum potential at whatever task you're involved in" (Klemash, 2006, p. 23).

A common technique that is taught to coaches to help create a positive atmosphere is communicating positively. During a practice situation, a coach usually uses the IDEA approach: *i*ntroduce and *d*emonstrate a skill, *e*xplain the skill, and then *a*ttend to that behavior (Martens, 2004). While attending to the athletes' performance of various skills and drills, the coach is observing and analyzing and then deciding if and when she should provide feedback. When the coach decides to provide corrective feedback, it is believed that the best way to do so is through a positive approach. One approach is the compliment sandwich approach, described in figure 5.1.

The compliment sandwich approach involves helping the athlete focus on future-oriented instruction. First the athlete is provided with a positive statement indicating what she did well. Then the coach provides that athlete information about what she needs to do to improve her performance the next time she does the skill. Finally, the coach provides a positive statement to continue to motivate the athlete (Smoll & Smith, 2006). Sport psychology consultants also teach coaches to be aware of their nonverbal communication, since much communication occurs in nonverbal ways.

FIGURE 5.1 **By using a compliment sandwich, the coach helps develop a positive atmosphere on the team.**

Reprinted, by permission, from Weinberg and Gould 2007.

Research Support for Providing a Positive Sport Environment

Frank Smoll and Ron Smith (2006) have conducted research analyzing coaching behaviors. One of the main findings was that regardless of how well a team did, athletes still seemed to enjoy the experience more if they had a positive coach. Athletes who played for a positive coach were more likely to report feelings of greater confidence and enjoyment than those who played for a coach who displayed more negative behavior. Based on their findings, Smoll and Smith created a behavioral training program to determine whether training could help coaches behave more positively and whether or not it was more enjoyable to play for coaches who were taught these leadership behaviors. Smoll and Smith (2006) concluded that training programs can be effective in teaching coaches how to relate to athletes in a positive way.

Psychology Insight

Research that has analyzed John Wooden's and Jerry Tarkanian's coaching behavior showed that they focused on providing positive instructional feedback to their athletes (Weinberg & Gould, 2007).

Who Provides Consulting on Positive Sport Environments?

Those trained in sport psychology have various career options in educating coaches on sport psychology concepts. The *Graduate Training and Career Possibilities* brochure includes coaching educator as a career option for those with graduate training in sport psychology (Van Raalte & Williams, 1994). People trained in sport psychology also may choose to work for sport organizations or as consultants to coaches.

Coaching Education Programs

Those trained in sport psychology may work for national coaching education programs that train coaches in creating a positive developmental atmosphere and educate coaches on the psychological aspects of coaching. Nonprofit sport organizations who provide coaching education hire directors to fulfill this capacity. Many sport psychology and peak performance consultants provide coaching workshops and clinics to coaches, parents, and administrators.

Three well-known programs providing coaching education to coaches in the United States are the American Sport Education Program, the Program for Athletic Coaches Education (PACE), and the Positive Coaching Alliance. Coaching education programs in the UK are based on the United Kingdom Coaching Certification (UKCC). The Coaching Association of Canada has a national certification program for training coaches. In Australia, coaching education is provided through a National Coaching Accreditation Scheme.

The Positive Coaching Alliance was started in 1998 by Jim Thompson. The organization has created partnerships with over 1,000 youth sport organizations and has provided thousands of workshops that teach coaches how to create a positive sport environment ("About PCA," 2008).

The Coaching Effectiveness Training (CET) program was created by Ron Smith and Frank Smoll. This is a two-and-a-half-hour workshop that trains coaches in providing positive reinforcement and helping children focus on the enjoyment and improvement aspects of competition rather than focus only on winning (Smoll & Smith, 2006).

University athletic departments also provide consultation to coaches. At Ohio State University, Buckeye Psychological Services provides coaches the opportunity to consult with a psychologist. The University of North Texas Center for Sport Psychology

⭐ SUCCESS STORY

Rainer Martens, Founder of the American Sport Education Program

One of the most influential people in the field of sport and exercise psychology is Rainer Martens. Martens received his undergraduate degree in physical education at Emporia State University in Kansas and his master's degree in exercise science at the University of Montana. He then received his doctorate in physical education, specializing in sport psychology, at the University of Illinois. From 1968 to 1984, Martens was a professor at the University of Illinois, where he focused his research on competitive anxiety in sport. He was also the sport psychologist for the U.S. Nordic ski teams from 1978 through 1984. In 1976, he began conducting research on children's sports and especially the influence of coaches' and parents' behavior on young athletes. This led him to launch the American Sport Education Program (originally known as the American Coaching Effectiveness Program) as a division of Human Kinetics, which Martens founded in 1974 ("About ASEP," 2008). In 1978, Martens published *Joy and Sadness in Children's Sports,* and that book along with ASEP helped lead the movement to improve youth sports through educational programs. ASEP became the largest program to train coaches in the United States (Martens, 2004). A coaches' training course, called Coaching Principles, is provided by ASEP. It is based on Martens' book *Successful Coaching* (2004), one of the best-selling coaching books of all time. This course has been instrumental in providing interscholastic state high school associations with certified instructors to educate coaches about the philosophical and psychological elements in creating a positive sport environment ("About ASEP," 2008). Sport and exercise psychologists interested in educating coaches about the philosophy and psychology of coaching can become certified instructors through ASEP. Information about becoming a certified instructor is available at the ASEP Web site at www.asep.com.

provides many workshops that teach coaches specific skills to improve their coaching ability. One workshop they offer is Positive Coaching for Youth Sports.

Consultants Providing Direct Services to Coaches

It is important for sport psychology consultants who work with individual athletes to also know how to help coaches create a positive sporting environment. A coach might call a sport psychology consultant to help athletes enhance performance, but the consultant might have to spend just as much time with the coaches to educate them on helping athletes from a psychological perspective (Dorfman, 2003).

Many sport psychology consultants offer workshops and clinics to educate coaches on creating optimal psychological environments for athletes. Jeff Janssen operates a consulting company, the Sports Leadership Center (formerly Janssen Peak Performance), which provides leadership workshops for coaches. These workshops are titled Coaching: The Seven Secrets of Successful Coaches. Janssen provides information to coaches about developing a positive **coaching philosophy,** developing athletes' confidence, and creating trust between themselves and the athletes they work with ("Janssen Peak Performance," 2005). Other consultants meet individually with coaches. As more sport psychology consultants are hired full-time and part-time by athletic departments, there most likely will be more opportunities for sport psychology professionals to continue consulting with coaches.

coaching philosophy—A coach's views on the best way of leading a team.

> *Coaches are performers just like athletes and they face the same mental skills challenges. . . . They have to make instant decisions under pressure and they are susceptible to the same emotion and focus issues as athletes. I work with coaches at Tennessee on controlling their level of emotion, staying focused on what is important, and understanding when they are being most effective in getting their message across.*
>
> **Joe Whitney**, director of mental training at the University of Tennessee
> (Smith, 2005, section 6, para. 1)

There are more applied opportunities for those trained in sport psychology to work with coaches and athletes at the youth sport level. Five full-time mental conditioning professionals are employed at the IMG Academies ("Mental Conditioning: Coaches," 2008). The International Junior Golf Association school has hired an individual to work with athletes and golf instructors on developing athletes' mental game and applying sport psychology concepts ("Mental and Physical Training," 2008).

The Short of It

- Sport and exercise psychologists can teach coaches to create a positive psychological environment so that athletes enjoy the process of participating in sport.

- Sport psychology consultants teach coaches about various philosophies of coaching and about leadership, motivation, and communication styles that can improve the sport environment.

- Coaches can learn about creating a positive sport environment through coaching organizations, workshops, clinics, and individual consulting.

Assessing Athletes' Mental Skills

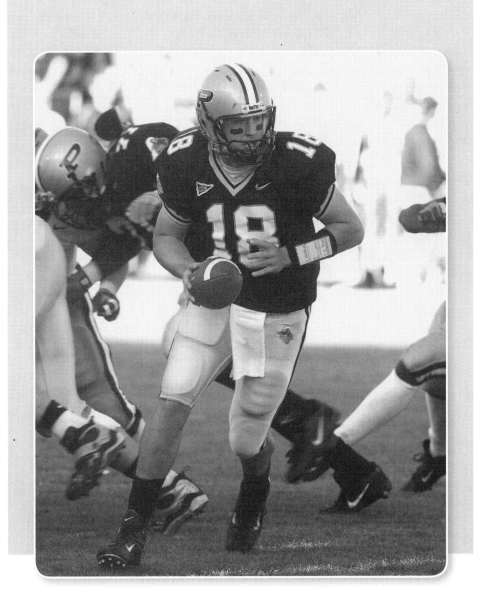

In this chapter, you will learn the following:

✓ The history and purposes of psychological assessment for athletes and coaches

✓ The types of psychological assessment services that are provided to athletes and how assessment is provided

✓ The types of instrumentation that professional sport organizations use when selecting players

✓ How organizations use assessments to help athletes improve their mental skills after they have been selected for teams

---

"I strongly believe that psychological assessments are very useful and that not enough focus is given to them in my sport."

Petra Cada, Canadian table tennis player (Leffingwell, Durand-Bush, Wurzberger, & Cada, 2005, p. 89)

At the National Football League (NFL) Combine held every spring, university football players perform physical and mental tests in order to be evaluated for the upcoming NFL Draft. Potential NFL draftees take an intelligence test, known as the Wonderlic Personnel Test, and various other psychological tests. Athletes often take additional psychological tests provided by individual teams that they meet with. Some athletes take the Troutwine Athletic Profile (TAP) (Chappell, 2006).

Bill Polian, president of the Indianapolis Colts, said regarding psychological testing, "You want to look at the whole person, not just the football player" (Chappell, 2006, para. 5). Rich McKay, current president and former general manager for the Atlanta Falcons, believes that testing can be helpful but should not be used as an end-all: "I view the (tests) like you would a workout at the combine or the 40-yard dash. It's a cross check, is all it is. It's another way of looking to see if there is an issue that you didn't otherwise know was there" (Chappell, 2006, para. 21).

Overview of Assessment for Sport Organizations and Teams

Assessment was one of the first areas of emphasis in applied sport psychology. Some of the first studies of athletes involved assessments of reaction time, which at the time was considered a part of psychology and physical education. Studies of reaction time later became part of the field of motor learning in the United States. In the 1890s E.W. Scripture investigated athletes' reaction times, and in the early 1900s sport personnel and psychologists studied it (Kornspan, 2007a). In 1913, after testing three football players at his psychology laboratory at the Univer-

assessment—A testing process that can be based on inventories, observations, or oral interviews.

sity of Nebraska, Harry Kirke Wolfe believed that psychological testing could help football coaches select athletes for their teams (Brannon, 1913).

Hugo Munsterberg, one of the most well-known psychologists in the history of psychology, wrote in his 1916 book *Psychology, General and Applied*, "The football players may be psychologically examined; their reaction time may be measured in thousandths of a second in order to determine the individual differences and to study changes in their rapidity of response under different conditions" (p. 455).

In 1920, psychologists Albert Johanson and Joseph Holmes at the Columbia University psychology laboratory evaluated Babe Ruth to determine what made him such a great home-run hitter. They tested Ruth's quickness, strength, attention, vision, breathing, steadiness, and reaction time (Fuchs, 1998). They found that in relation to the average person, Ruth seemed to have faster reaction times, higher levels of coordination, and more quickness (Fullerton, 1921). In the 1920s, Coleman Griffith and Walter R. Miles, who were studying the psychology of athletics, were interested in the assessment of reaction time. As mentioned in chapter 1, one of Griffith's first tasks when he joined the faculty advisory staff of Bob Zuppke's University of Illinois football team was aiding the coaches in team selection ("Psychologist to Aid Selection of Illini Athletes," 1922). Griffith also conducted assessments of the Chicago Cubs baseball team in 1938 and 1939 (Green, 2003).

Intelligence of athletes has long been a topic of interest for physical educators and psychologists. Psychologists began aiding coaches in assessing athletes' intelligence during the 1920s. In the 1930s Paul Brown used various psychological instruments in selecting athletes for the Massillon High School, in Massillon, Ohio, football team (Kornspan, 2006).

What Types of Characteristics Do Sport Psychologists Assess?

Today, assessment is an important part of sport psychology and mental training. Questions relate to whether athletes have psychological characteristics that make them more successful. Just as the field of strength and conditioning focuses on enhancing athletes' physical skills, mental conditioning focuses on enhancing athletes' mental skills. Both in strength and conditioning for physical skills and mental conditioning for mental skills, assessment is usually the first step in creating an intervention to help the athlete.

Beckmann and Kellmann (2003) note that although assessment in sport psychology has been a controversial topic, many consultants use assessment instruments. These authors believe that psychological assessment should be used in guiding interventions with athletes.

What Types of Assessments Are Used?

Assessment consists of the use of psychological inventories and tests, interviews, and observations of coaches and athletes. O'Connor (2004) analyzed the types of assessments that consultants use with athletes. O'Connor was specifically interested in finding out how consultants were using surveys in assessing various mental skills and psychological issues. Most of the respondents (66 percent) used surveys or questionnaires in their consultations with athletes, and the instruments most used were the Test of Attention and Interpersonal Style (TAIS) (Nideffer, 1976) and the Profile of Mood States (POMS) (McNair, Lorr, & Droppelman, 1971). Assessments also exist for analyzing such areas as competitive stress and anxiety, overall mental skills, and specific mental skills such as imagery and confidence. The NFL uses the Wonderlic Personnel Test in assessing athletes entering the NFL Draft. The Troutwine Athletic Profile is also used by NFL teams (Chappell, 2006).

Another assessment often used at the individual level of sport psychology is an initial interview in which athletes are asked to describe their thoughts, feelings, and emotions during their best performances. Then the consultant asks the athletes to describe their thoughts, feelings, and emotions during their worst competitions (Orlick, 2000). This exercise shows athletes how being aware of their thoughts and feelings during their best performances can influence performance. Through this assessment, consultants can show athletes that during their best performances they may be displaying the types of psychological characteristics that successful athletes display. In mental skills training, athletes can assess each of their mental skills and then practice trying to improve various mental skills.

Where Do Assessments Occur?

Assessment is part of most mental training and sport psychology work and is used in mental skills training, team-building services, clinical sport psychology, monitoring of burnout and overtraining, and in exercise psychology for the general population beginning or maintaining fitness programs (McCann, Jowdy, & Van Raalte, 2002). Assessment occurs at the high school, university, Olympic, and professional levels of sport. Usually assessments take place in an office setting in which an athlete is asked to complete a survey or questionnaire. Assessment of mental skills can also take place online. Athletes may be asked to respond to various interview questions if they are meeting a sport psychologist for draft assessment. Also, a sport psychologist may observe an athlete during a game or practice and analyze the athlete's behaviors.

How Is Assessment Used in Sport Psychology?

Although there is not complete consensus in the field about how psychological assessment should be used, there appear to be general ways in which it is being used in sport. General managers of professional sport teams ask sport psychologists and consultants to provide psychological testing and interview athletes in the selection process, assess players' mental strengths and weaknesses once on the team, and provide neuropsychological and clinical testing for athletes.

Assessing an Athlete's Mental Skills: Preselection

Cox (2007) suggests that there has long been an interest in whether one's personality traits can predict successful athletic performance. There used to be much interest in the relationship of psychological testing to athletic performance, but many studies did not find a relationship between personality and how one performed athletically. Thus the amount of research related to psychological testing and athletes has decreased considerably. Despite this trend, Cox suggests that since psychological testing is prevalent in professional sport, it is important for students of sport psychology to understand this specific area.

Sport psychology consultants often conduct assessments of athletes on professional sport teams and provide team managers with information that they can use as part of the athlete-selection process (McCann, 2005). Sport psychologists assess athletes through observation of their performance in practice, through interviews, or through scores on various intelligence and personality tests. In 2001 the Dallas Cowboys brought their own psychologist to the NFL Combine in Indianapolis (Hill, 2001). Some athletic teams also hire human resource companies to conduct psychological profiling of athletes before the draft begins ("Transcript, Giants General Manager Jerry Reese," 2007).

Personality Tests A personality test administered at the NFL Combine is the Troutwine Athletic Profile, a 75-question assessment that takes about 20 minutes to complete. The test reveals athletes' mental and emotional weaknesses (Jones, 2007). The Cleveland Indians baseball team uses a general personality test, the 16PF, to assess their potential draft picks (Vinella, 2003).

Intelligence Tests At the NFL Combine each February, athletes who are trying out for a position in the NFL go through a variety of physical tests. Athletes also take the Wonderlic Personnel Test, a 50-question intelligence test that takes 12 minutes to complete.

The Australian Rules Football League also has begun to focus on using psychological testing for draft purposes (Kelly & Hickey, 2004). Marc Portus, the sport science manager for Cricket Australia's Centre of Excellence, has discussed how psychological testing is being used in identifying talent in cricket: "The purpose of the testing is to provide a service to the athletes and the states so they can get to understand these guys a bit better, the way they think, the way they cope with pressure, the way they regard themselves" (Smith, 2007, p. 85).

Interviews With Athletes Psychologists may also be involved in interviewing athletes when teams are making decisions on whom to select. Roarke (2006) reported that because the process of interviewing athletes at the National Hockey League Central Scouting Service Combine has become so important, many teams have sport psychologists taking

> ### *Psychology Insight*
>
> Psychological testing can wear out athletes at the NFL Combine. On one day, Joe Thomas, a rookie offensive lineman for the Cleveland Browns, took six consecutive psychological tests for various teams for over five hours. Also, an athlete heading out to the Combine can be nervous about psychological testing. Thomas said, "The stuff you're nervous about is all the psychological testing. You get nervous about that stuff, meeting coaches for the first time. You're trying to make a good impression on those guys" (Thomas & Fox, 2007, para. 4).

> *There's one team—I know this for a fact—that interviews the players, and the team will ask their psychologist what he thinks [after sitting in on the interview]. If he says I wouldn't take this guy, they don't take him.*
>
> **Frank Bonello**, director of central scouting with the
> National Hockey League (Molinari, 2004, para. 15)

part in the interview process. The interview process for potential draft choices also has become an important part of the NFL Combine and thus more team psychologists have become involved in the interview process. Rich McKay, the former general manager and now the president of the Atlanta Falcons, in discussing the importance of the interview, said, "It seems like the individual interview has become a bigger and more important piece of the puzzle. This kind of stuff has been part of the corporate hiring process for years, so why not us?" (Pasquarelli, 2007, para. 11).

Sport Managers' Opinions on Psychological Assessment   Dan O'Dowd, general manager of the Colorado Rockies, explained the use of psychological testing by his organization in preparation for the Major League Baseball Draft. Major League teams can use psychological testing if an athlete authorizes it. The Major League Baseball scouting bureau has a standard test, or an organization can use its own specific test. The Rockies use their own test on potential draftees. O'Dowd said, "It's just one tool we use to evaluate the player, but certainly not the only tool" (Harding, 2006, para. 20).

Tony DiLeo, assistant general manager and now interim head coach of the Philadelphia 76ers, when asked about the importance of the psychological characteristics of athletes that they consider drafting, said, "We can see what is on the outside, we can see how fast they are, how well they shoot the ball or dribble, or whatever. But it's harder to find out what's inside. We try to do that with psychological testing. We try to do that with our background checks and just talking to other coaches or players who played against this player" ("Tony DiLeo Speaks," 2007, para. 57).

Billy King, former general manager of the 76ers, further commented on the role of psychological assessment of athletes: "I think it's important not just playing on the court [but] spending time talking to them. They spend time with [team psychologist] Dr. [Joel] Fish. I'm sure they enjoyed that time. It really gives us a chance to get to know them as people. We'll ask them questions and find out some more about them, get to know them as people, not just basketball players" ("2007 Post Draft Press Conference," n.d., para. 1).

Assessing an Athlete's Mental Skills: Postselection

Player evaluation and development are important considerations at the professional level. Some organizations make it a priority to develop the mental skills of athletes by assessing their mental skills when they are first brought to the organization. Organizations can then learn where an athlete needs to improve mentally and try

⭐ **SUCCESS STORY**

Joel Fish, PhD, Center for Sport Psychology

Joel Fish is a professional sport psychologist who provides psychological testing for the Philadelphia 76ers basketball team. Fish, captain of his high school baseball team, graduated from Lower Merion High School in Pennsylvania in 1971 (Adams, 2002) and went on to complete his bachelor's degree from Clark University, his master's degree from Temple University, and his PhD from the University of Wisconsin at Madison ("Joel Fish, PhD, Director," n.d.). In 1989, Dr. Fish opened the Center for Sport Psychology (Adams, 2002) which is located in Philadelphia, Pennsylvania. Additionally, Dr. Fish serves as the sport psychologist for the University of Pennsylvania athletic department.

Dr. Fish provides each potential draftee with a psychological test of 120 questions and then asks the potential draftee 25 questions regarding how the athlete would respond in certain situations. Fish compares the results to those of previous athletes. Moore (2007, para. 13) said, "It's Fish's job to help the Sixers determine how coachable a draft pick is. Is he a guy who needs to be encouraged, or does he respond to a tongue lashing? How much support does he need off the court?" Fish said, "It's trying to understand what they feel and when and how they handle that feeling" (para. 15). He continues, "The most important thing, to me, is there are situations you can't prepare for, that you can't script answers for. You're really seeing the patterns of how they react and how they make decisions. I can compare the answers to 200 players I've asked these questions to. I think it gives a real indicator of certain personality traits" (para. 18).

Fish believes that an emphasis placed on psychological assessment of potential draftees provides the 76ers with an advantage over teams that do not use this service. Fish explained his role in conducting the psychological assessment: "I don't have a crystal ball. My role is to pass the information [along to management]. They take that and plug it in with a lot of other factors. The decisions are theirs" (Moore, 2007, para. 22).

Fish is also asked to observe the athletes at their individual workouts: "Being part of the workout gives me insight into how a player can deal with pressure." Fish continued, "When you have NBA executives watching your every move, that is pressure" (Narducci, 2007, p. E12).

to help the athlete improve his or her mental game. Coach Dean Wurzberger said the following:

> Most coaches place a high value on determining the psychological strengths and weaknesses of the athletes they are coaching. In my experience, motivation and confidence are especially big areas of interest for soccer coaches. From a practical standpoint many coaches would find psychological testing to be very similar to physical fitness testing. It can help us identify each individual's psychological strengths and weaknesses and then act on that knowledge by implementing an appropriate training program. (Leffingwell, Durand-Bush, Wurzberger, & Cada, 2005, p. 87)

The Cleveland Indians baseball team assesses the technical aspects as well as the physical and mental aspects of athletes' development. When athletes enter the Cleveland organization, their mental skills are evaluated and their strengths and weaknesses in these skills are determined. After the assessments, the athletes meet with their coaches to discuss plans for the three areas. The athletes can meet with the mental skills training consultant to help them improve the mental aspects of their game. Each season at spring training, the Cleveland organization also provides the athletes with mental skills training manuals and lectures and discussions (Vinella, 2003).

Neuropsychological Assessment

One problem in sport that is gaining more attention is the incidence of concussion. Professional athletes sometimes play with concussions or return too early from a concussion to participate in practices and competitions. Neuropsychologists can use the Impact computer program, which was created at the University of Pittsburgh Medical Center to assess athletes' readiness to return to practice and competition (Mihoces, 2007). An athlete is assessed with the computerized system when he is free of any head injury (i.e., when he has *not* been hit on the head). Then if he does get hit on the head, he can be tested to determine whether his profile is different from his normal state. If it is different, the athlete can be told that he is not ready to return. When the normal and postinjury evaluations line up, the athlete can be cleared for competition (Mihoces, 2007). The NFL is taking the testing of athletes for concussions very seriously. All NFL athletes will have to take a baseline test using the Impact system to see where they are during normal functioning (Mihoces, 2007).

Clinical Assessment Screenings

Another area of assessment that is starting to be used by university athletic departments relates to clinical issues (McCann, Jowdy, & Van Raalte, 2002). Team Enhance, developed at the University of Tennessee, uses clinical assessments to help athletes with off-the-field problems (Moshak, 2003). The assessments involve lifestyle surveys and observations of behaviors. The lifestyle questionnaire screens student-athletes for eating disorders and abuse of alcohol or other substances.

Issues in Psychological Testing

Over the years, the question of whether psychological tests should be used for team selection has been discussed in the sport psychology literature. Weinberg and Gould (2007) believe that teams should not use psychological tests alone when deciding whether to select an athlete. They suggest that if a psychological test is used with a battery of other tests that are reliable and valid, then psychological tests can be of some use:

> Using personality inventories alone to select athletes or cut them from a team is an abuse of testing that should not be tolerated. When psychological tests are used as part of a battery of measures to help in the athlete selection process, three conditions should always be kept in mind (Singer, 1988). First the particular test must be a valid and reliable measure. Second, the user must know what personality characteristics are key for success in the sport of interest and the ideal levels of those characteristics needed. Third, the user must know how much an athlete can compensate in some characteristics for the lack of others. (Weinberg & Gould, 2007, p. 38)

Research Support for Using Assessments With Athletes

Although assessment instruments are used by professional teams to aid in making decisions about athlete selection, it appears more research is needed in order to understand how these tests can be best used. The use of psychological testing is becoming more widespread, and the field of sport psychology should continue to work to understand psychological assessment issues in more detail.

One important area for the field of sport and exercise psychology to continue to focus on is creating assessment instruments that are sport specific and also valid and reliable. The field of sport psychology has begun to create sport-specific inventories that are psychometrically sound (i.e., the researcher can test the instruments for reliability and valid-ity). **Reliability** is the repeatability of a score on a test. For example, if an athlete takes a mental skills test and then retakes the same test a week later, the scores from both tests should be similar. **Validity** relates to whether a test measures what it is supposed to measure. For example, if an assessment is supposed to measure levels of anxiety, is anxiety, in fact, what the test actually measures? Generally, once the test has been found to be valid and reliable, then it can then be marketed for widespread use. However, Leffingwell and colleagues (2005) point out that determining if an instrument is valid is a continuing process and thus consultants should understand the current literature in order to determine whether a specific test should be used. Many sport psychology assessments have been found to be psychometrically sound over the long term, but there is some debate as to whether assessments tested for reliability and validity with the general population should be used with athlete populations. Sport psychologists should use such tests with caution.

reliability—The repeatability of a score on a test. A measure of reliability is whether athletes with the same skill levels repeatedly score the same way on a test.

validity—Whether a test measures what it is supposed to measure.

Nideffer and Sagal (2001), in their book *Assessment in Sport Psychology,* support the need for the field of sport psychology to continue to use psychological tests. They believe that tests, in addition to other information, should be used as part of the process of making decisions: "While tests alone should not be used to make selection and screening decisions, they should be a part of the decision-making process" (p. 5). It is also important to try to validate the information gained from tests through other methods, such as observing the individual and conducting interviews. Based on the information gained from observations in other settings, the tester can determine whether the scores on the test appear to be accurate (Nideffer & Sagal, 2001).

Who Provides Psychological Testing Services?

Most of the services that are discussed in this chapter are provided by individual sport psychologists at the elite level of sport, such as for professional sport teams. Certainly at the high school, university, and professional levels, the use of assessment instruments to aid in mental skills training can be helpful. Companies also provide assessment services to professional sport teams. A provider of psychological tests for the Major League Baseball Association is the Winslow Research Institute. Another organization that provides testing services for NFL and NBA teams is Human Resource Tactics. Professional sport teams, such as in baseball, football, basketball, and hockey, may employ their own consultants who complete the psychological testing and interview professional draft picks.

The following are companies that develop and sell instruments related to assessment in sport psychology:

- Enhanced Performance Systems: The Attentional and Interpersonal Style (TAIS) Inventory
- Psymetrics: Winning Profile Athlete Inventory (WPAI)
- Troutwine and Associates: Troutwine Athletic Profile (TAP)
- The Winning Mind: The Athlete's Mental Edge
- GolfPsych: Mental skills assessment for golfers online
- Fitness Information Technology: Group Environment Questionnaire, Sport Imagery Questionnaire, and Flow Scales
- Mind Plus Muscle from the Institute for Applied Sports Psychology: OMSAT
- Ohio Center for Sport Psychology: Nine Mental Skills Measurement Kit CD
- ProCoach Systems: Sport Psychology Quotient Assessment

Most sport and exercise psychologists use assessments on the job. Careers in sport psychology assessment are scarce but are available with companies such as those previously listed or as consultants with professional sport teams.

The Short of It

- Sport psychology assessment focuses on measuring various psychological traits and mental skills of athletes.
- Psychologists have been interested in the psychological assessment of athletes since the beginnings of the field of sport psychology.
- University and professional organizations use the services of consultants to provide psychological testing for athletes.
- Psychological testing is used in evaluating players' mental skills and clinical issues, and it is used in athlete selection and concussion assessment.
- Companies also provide mental skills assessment for athletes.

CHAPTER 7

Caring for Athletes

General Well-Being and Recovery From Injury

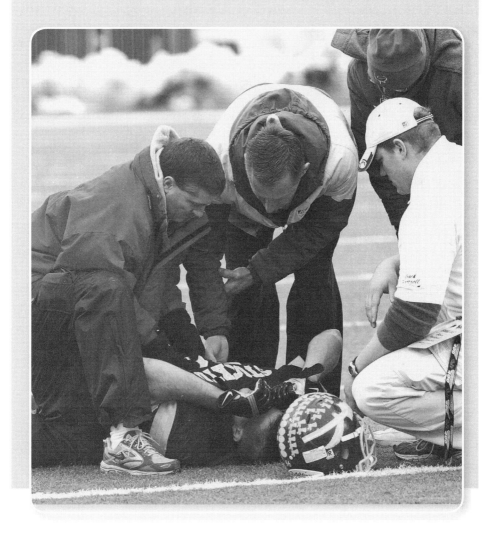

"Excellence in every part of your life is a decision—decide to excel."

Terry Orlick
(2007, p. 3)

When Dwayne Jarrett, now a National Football League player with the Carolina Panthers, was a student-athlete at New Brunswick High School in New Jersey, he said he did enough academically to get by and stay eligible. But Jarrett realized that he was not on track to be eligible to play at the NCAA level. The Play It Smart program began at Jarrett's school, and Jarrett began to improve his academic performance. Jarrett said, "Because of the Play It Smart Program, I took school more seriously and developed my study habits" (Esfarjani, 2006, para. 4). To develop study habits, Jarrett and other athletes on the team met three times a week with their academic coach and then studied in groups. Jarrett said, "Going into my first year of college it would have been much tougher without the organization and management skills I learned" (Esfarjani, 2006, para. 11).

Sport psychologists and related professionals are increasingly called on to help athletes with general life skills and personal development. The care of athletes relates not only to personal development but also to recovery from injury. This chapter addresses these two topics separately under the broad category of caring for athletes.

What Is Psychology of Rehabilitation From Athletic Injury?

Athletic injuries are very common in sport. One of the most important aspects of training for athletes is to try to stay injury-free so that they can continue to practice. However, because injuries are common in competitive sport it is important for sport psychologists and mental training consultants to understand how they can provide support services to injured athletes. See figure 7.1 for an example of the prevalence of athletic injuries in competitive sport.

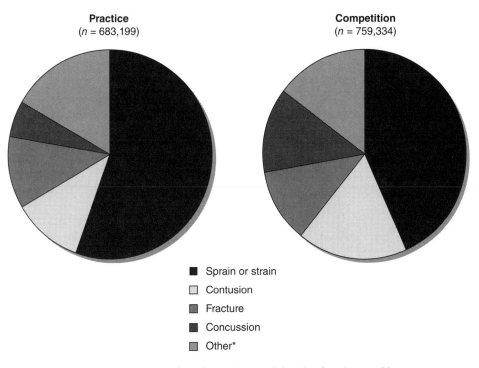

Practice
(n = 683,199)

Competition
(n = 759,334)

- ■ Sprain or strain
- ☐ Contusion
- ▨ Fracture
- ■ Concussion
- ▨ Other*

* Includes other injuries (e.g., lacerations or dislocations) and reportable
health-related events (e.g., heat illness, skin infections, or asthma attacks).

FIGURE 7.1 High school sport-related injuries suffered in practice and competition in the 2005-2006 school year, by diagnosis.

From Comstock et al. 2006.

Some believe that the psychology of rehabilitation from athletic injury actually starts before an injury occurs. Some athletes believe they may have been more susceptible to an injury because of the amount of stress they were under. Iona McKenzie, a triathlete, said, "I'd been rowing for about seven or eight years completely injury-free. But during that year I fractured a rib and soon after that healed, I injured my lower back. Both are fairly common injuries for female rowers, but I don't feel like either would have happened if my body hadn't been so weakened by how much stress I was under" (Wadyka, 2007, para. 6).

The American College of Sports Medicine (ACSM) released a consensus statement that suggests that a relationship exists between life stress and athletic injury. Athletes who experience more stress either in or away from the competitive arena are at greater risk for becoming injured while participating in sport activities: "Certain subpopulations of athletes, such as those experiencing high life stress and low personal coping skills, may be even at a greater risk of sustaining athletic injury" (ACSM, 2006, p. 2031). Andersen and Williams created a model to show some of the ways stress contributes to injury (figure 7.2).

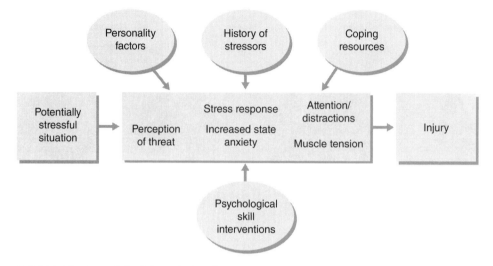

FIGURE 7.2 A model of the relationships between life stress and athletic injury.

Reprinted, by permission, from Weinberg and Gould 2007. Adapted, by permission, from Andersen and Williams 1988.

It appears that athletes who are less stressed are less prone to becoming injured. Thus, a mental training consultant can play a role in reducing the chance of athletic injury by helping athletes manage their stress.

Athletes often sustain injuries that make it difficult if not impossible to continue to play their sports. These injuries can last a few days, weeks, months, or even a whole athletic season. Sometimes these injuries can even be career ending. Athletes are often provided with services from an athletic trainer or physical therapist to help them recover from injury. But some athletes may become depressed or withdrawn and have difficulty dealing with their injuries. Sometimes an injured athlete needs assistance in dealing with personal or clinical psychological issues that may occur because of an athletic injury.

How Do Athletes Respond to Injury?

Often athletes have emotional responses to injuries that force them out of their sport. Sometimes athletes experience an injury in the same way people experience grief. Loss experienced by athletes sometimes is similar to a model of loss described by Elisabeth Kübler-Ross, which includes five stages: denial, anger, bargaining, depression, and acceptance. For example, an athlete may deny that the injury is as severe as what she has been told and may see herself quickly recovering and returning to action. When the athlete does not return to action quickly, she may become angry at teammates, coaches, friends, and family. In the bargaining stage, the athlete may make promises to coaches, herself, or God with the hope of recovering quickly from injury. The fourth stage is depression. In this stage the athlete may become sad and doubt her ability to come back from the injury. The final stage of the grief model related to an athletic injury is acceptance. In this stage, an athlete begins to recover from injury through treatment and begins to accept the injury. This grief model has been helpful in understanding how athletes respond to athletic injuries, but other models seem more realistic in terms of how athletes respond (Cornelius, 2002; Weinberg & Gould, 2007).

Udry, Gould, Bridges, and Beck (1997) explain that athletes may experience most of these emotions but not all. Athletes first go through an information-processing stage that involves inquiries about recovery time and the pain. Inconvenience and how the injury will affect the athlete's life are concerns in this stage. The athlete then goes through an emotional phase that may fatigue the athlete and cause isolation or denial. The third stage is the positive outlook and coping stage, in which the athlete begins to accept the injury and adopts a positive style of coping with the injury.

A more recent model of how athletes respond to athletic injury is called the cognitive appraisal model (Brown, 2005). This model is focused on the meaning an athlete places on the athletic injury. If an athlete has been competitive and has gone through many minor injuries before, he might be able to cope well with the injury. However, if an athlete who has not competed at a high level incurs the same injury, he may not be able to cope with the injury in a positive way as easily.

Regardless of the theoretical model that is used to show how athletes deal with injury, it seems clear that athletes who experience injury often have emotional reactions and that the counseling process or mental skills training can aid them in the recovery process (Cornelius, 2002). Of course, not all athletes will need counseling, but support groups and sport psychologists can assist athletes in coping more positively. And through the teaching of mental skills, consultants may even be able to help athletes return from injury more quickly.

Referrals to Sport Psychologists

An injured athlete is often referred to a sport psychology consultant by an athletic trainer or a medical professional in a **sports medicine clinic.** However, sports medicine physicians seem to believe that not enough sport psychologists or mental health counselors are available to treat the number of athletes they provide services for, so only 24.8 percent refer their patients to a sport psychologist for an injury-related issue ("2006 Sports Medicine Sport Psychology Survey," 2006).

sports medicine clinic—A medical center that specializes in treating athletic injuries.

Weinberg and Gould (2007, p. 454) offer warning signs an athletic trainer might see that would lead him or her to refer an athlete to a mental health professional:

- Feelings of anger or confusion
- Obsession with the question of when the athlete can return to play
- Denial
- Repeatedly coming back too soon and experiencing reinjury
- Exaggerated bragging about accomplishments

- Dwelling on minor physical complaints
- Guilt about letting the team down
- Withdrawal from significant other
- Rapid mood swings
- Statements indicating that no matter what is done, recovery will not occur

The ACSM consensus statement (2006, p. 2031) suggests that "Problematic emotional reactions occur when symptoms do not resolve or worsen over time, or the severity of the symptoms seems excessive relative to other injured athletes."

The issue of helping athletes work with a sport psychology consultant is an important one in the field. Based on the research, not enough injured athletes are using the services of sport psychologists or mental skills training consultants (Heaney, 2006). Many athletes and athletic trainers may not understand how sport psychology can aid in the recovery from an athletic injury. Also, there may be little access to sport psychology services and a stigma related to seeking help from sport psychologists.

There are a few ways to improve this situation. Heaney (2006) suggests that sport psychology consultants educate sports medicine professionals involved in injury rehabilitation about the benefits that sport psychology can provide to injured athletes. Also, athletic trainers should be direct service providers. That is, they should have counseling skills so that they can aid injured athletes. Helping athletic trainers understand when to refer injured athletes to sport psychology consultants could ensure that more athletes receive the needed services.

What Interventions Are Provided to Injured Athletes?

Counseling may help injured athletes learn how to comply with the suggested physical rehabilitation, overcome pain, and cope with stress. Experiencing an athletic injury can be very difficult to deal with. Dr. Aimee Kimball, University of Pittsburgh mental training consultant, said, "It's definitely an emotional hurdle. A lot of times the sport is so important to the athletes, it is like they are losing a significant part of themselves" (Ross, 2006, para. 2).

> *Any injury can certainly cause feelings of depression and even anger in an individual about losing their athletic outlet. I help patients to focus on the future and realize that an injury doesn't mean a loss of ability. It is a minor setback—a challenge to overcome.*
>
> **Dr. Thomas Ferraro** ("Winthrop's Sports Medicine Program," 2004, para. 7)

Brewer and Petitpas (2005) discuss a four-phase process of providing psychological assistance to athletes who have sustained athletic injuries. The first phase is rapport building, in which the sport psychologist listens to the athlete and the psychologist explains the injury and the meaning of the injury. The second phase focuses on educating the athlete about the injury. In this phase, the sport psychologist may ask the athlete what she knows about the injury and determines whether she has a realistic understanding of what she has experienced. The third phase, skill development, is when the sport psychologist and the athlete select various psychological interventions. The helping professional begins to teach psychological skills to the athlete and helps the athlete use these skills. In the fourth phase, the injured athlete begins to practice and apply the various skills she has learned. Also, during this phase the helping professional evaluates the injured athlete's progress toward meeting the goals of the treatment.

Williams and Scherzer (2006) note that the same mental skills that are used for performance enhancement—such as self-talk, imagery, goal setting, and relaxation—are helpful in the rehabilitation of an injured athlete. Education is an important component when working with an injured athlete. The consultant may have to teach the athlete that it is all right to feel upset about the injury and to show emotions, but the consultant should also help the athlete avoid feeling hopeless. Mental training consultant Dr. Aimee Kimball said, "The first thing to do is to help them deal with stress. A lot of times athletes are supposed to control their emotions and they're supposed to be seen as tough. I let them know that other people have experienced this and it's OK to be upset" (Ross, 2006, para. 3).

Goal Setting

An important step in the recovery process is helping athletes set short-term and long-term goals for daily rehabilitation and return to practice and competition. Goal setting can also be used to help athletes focus on the number of physical exercises that should be done in rehabilitating the injury. Highly motivated athletes may want to do too much; therefore they need to stick to their goals so they do not risk reinjury (Weinberg & Gould, 2007). Brown (2005, p. 232) also suggests that goal setting is very helpful: "Effective goal setting is the cornerstone of rehabilitation."

Mental Imagery

Cornelius (2002) describes four types of imagery training that can help athletes involved in the injury rehabilitation process: mastery imagery, emotive imagery, body rehearsal, and coping imagery. Mastery imagery involves seeing oneself successfully completing the physical exercises necessary for the recovery from injury. Emotive imagery is seeing oneself with positive energy for specific anticipated events. Coping imagery involves mentally rehearsing a difficult event and seeing oneself handling the event and dealing with it. For example, the athlete can practice visualizing the pain involved in the rehabilitation process and see herself coping with it. Body rehearsal involves visualizing an injury, such as a fracture, actually healing itself and getting stronger.

Wrisberg and Fisher (2005) present an excellent example of how imagery and mental rehearsal can help athletes recover from injury by practicing the sport mentally when they may be unable to practice their sport physically: A heptathlete had to undergo surgery to repair her shoulder. Her rehabilitation lasted for five months, and twice every day she spent 10 to 15 minutes mentally practicing. During each mental rehearsal, she saw herself throwing the javelin. At the conference championship two weeks after she had been cleared to resume practicing, she broke her personal record in the javelin. Wrisberg and Fisher (2005, p. 58) wrote, "Considering the absence of physical rehearsal she experienced in the months before this meet, it is amazing that she was able to achieve such a feat. At the very least, mental rehearsal kept her in touch with the demands of her sport and made her feel she was doing something to enhance her return to participation."

Positive Self-Talk

Injured athletes can be taught how to become aware of what they are thinking and learn to talk to themselves more positively during the rehabilitation process. The importance of self-talk during rehabilitation is illustrated in figure 7.3, which shows the possible consequences of negative and positive self-talk. Williams and Scherzer (2006, p. 584) provide an example of an athlete who is going through a difficult rehabilitation session in a training room. She says to herself, "This is awful. This hurts too much to be beneficial. These exercises will probably cause me more harm. Besides, I've been doing this for three days now, and I can't see any progress. It would be a lot easier to just let the injury heal on its own." This is an example of negative self-talk and inner dialogue. By learning the skill of positive self-talk, the athlete will learn more beneficial ways of dealing with the injury. Williams and Scherzer (2006, p. 584) suggest that the athlete should say, "Stop. These exercises hurt, but it's okay. They'll pay off. I'm lucky to have knowledgeable people helping me. I'll be competing soon because I'm doing these exercises."

Relaxation

Relaxation training can help athletes alleviate the stress that occurs when they are trying to overcome pain. Cornelius (2002) suggests that techniques such as progressive relaxation developed by Edmund Jacobson, the relaxation response developed by Benson, and meditation can help athletes deal with pain and stress when recovering from an athletic injury.

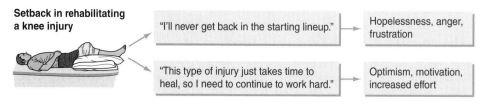

FIGURE 7.3 An example of the effects of negative and positive self-talk on an injured athlete.

Reprinted, by permission, from Weinberg and Gould 2007.

Group Counseling: Support Groups for Injured Athletes

Support groups are often coordinated by sport psychologists or other helping professionals. At the University of Tennessee, student-athletes who suffer an injury that ends their competitive season are required to attend the Team Enhance injury support group. The group meets weekly for 90-minute sessions. They begin each session by discussing their feelings and how they are progressing in the rehabilitation process. Then the group facilitator leads group discussion in various areas. Kristin Martin, who facilitated the support groups, said, "They'll talk about stuff like specific coping skills, grief work, or dealing with the loss of their sport" (Anderson, 2004, para. 24). To evaluate progress and success, some support group facilitators use written feedback: Athletes anonymously fill out an evaluation form in which they state whether they enjoyed the group and whether the group was helpful.

> *It's therapeutic to hear that there are other people going through similar types of situations. The idea is to empower the athletes with skills and help normalize their situation by helping them realize there are other people going through similar things.*
>
> **Dr. Dave Yukelson**, coordinator of sport psychology services for the Penn State University athletic department (Anderson, 2004, para. 7).

Research Support for Injury Counseling

Studies have shown that athletes who have been taught psychological skills may be positively affected in their recovery from athletic injury. A study by Hamson-Utley, Martin, and Walters (2008) found that athletic trainers and physical therapists believed the use of psychological skills was instrumental in the process of recovery from athletic injury.

Who Provides Sport Psychology and Counseling Services to Injured Athletes?

Providing services to injured athletes is a common practice of many sport psychologists regardless of their setting. Some individuals working full-time, part-time, or on a consulting basis provide psychological services to injured athletes at sports medicine clinics because that is where injured athletes often go to work on their physical rehabilitation. Most of these clinics are university- and hospital-based. However, Brewer (1998) cited research suggesting that only 2 percent of sports medicine clinics had psychologists on staff. Based on the 2006 Sports Medicine Sport Psychology Survey, this may be a problem since sports medicine professionals may not know of sport psychologists in their area to refer their athletes to ("2006 Sports Medicine Sport Psychology Survey," 2006). Thus, more collaboration between professional sport psychology and sports medicine organizations is necessary in order to set up referral networks for injured athletes with psychological problems.

What Are the Unique Developmental Concerns of Athletes?

In addition to caring for athletes' sport injuries, sport psychologists are beginning to focus on caring for athletes' general well-being. Traditionally, the field of sport psychology has focused on helping athletic teams to enhance performance and aiding athletes in enjoying the sport experience. However, a trend in sport psychology is to also focus on helping athletes deal with issues outside of their sports. Sport psychology can also be viewed as a field that can use sport to teach athletes how to enhance development of life skills.

Understanding the unique development of student-athletes can aid those working with athletes in providing more effective programming. As Miller and Wooten (1995, p. 172) note, "The academic, social, and personal well-being of the student-athlete is a growing concern for coaches, athletic support staff, and counselors." As sports become a major focus of an athlete's life, other areas of life may receive less attention. Thus, student-athletes may have unique concerns that students not involved in sports may not have. Specialized programming has been created for student-athletes in areas related to academic, career, and personal concerns.

In response to the unique needs of athletes, athletic counseling has emerged as a specialty area within counselor education, and its future seems bright (Petitpas & Buntrock, 1995). Athletic counseling has become established as an important part of academic support services for student-athletes and is a developing area in the field of sport psychology (Sachs, Burke, & Salitsky, 1992).

Career Concerns

One important area in which athletic counselors, life skills coordinators, and sport psychologists can help athletes is career development. Many career issues are unique to an athlete population. For example, athletes may have a delayed level of career maturity. Their often unrealistic development of purpose may delay athletes from thinking about career plans. Additionally, an athlete may have a high level of **external locus of control,** which means that he has not been held accountable for the outcomes of his experiences either on or off the field of play (Kornspan & Etzel, 2003). He may feel as if he is being told what to study rather than truly making a career choice on his own. With an understanding of these unique needs, athletic counselors and sport psychologists can more optimally aid the athletes they work with.

external locus of control—A belief that things happen to a person based on luck or chance.

Academic Concerns

In addition to the unique career concerns of athletes, sport psychology professionals have focused on assisting athletes with academic concerns. Athletes devote a great deal of time to their sports and may have difficulty managing their time in order to balance academics and athletics. Thus, time management is an important skill that professionals can teach athletes.

Greenspan and Andersen (1995) discuss the role conflict that can occur for student-athletes. Student-athletes may view academics as challenging, unrewarding, and time consuming, whereas they view sport as fun, exciting, and instantly rewarding. When an athlete is referred to counseling for academic issues, it is important to determine if role conflict may be causing the academic problems.

Student-athletes also face many academic pressures. They may feel pressure to keep up their grade-point average for eligibility purposes, or they may lack confidence in their ability to succeed academically. In helping student-athletes, sport psychologists, academic counselors, and life skills coordinators can teach study skills to improve academic performance (M.B. Andersen, 2002).

Personal Development

Sport psychologists can help athletes with personal development, including managing the various life transitions that athletes experience. Athletes often need help in adjusting to new levels of competition both on and off the playing field. In addition, athletes are provided support services for dealing with retirement from athletics at various levels of competition (Van Raalte & Andersen, 2007).

Athletes can also have trouble developing relationships with others (Lanning, 1982). Athletes tend to spend the majority of their time with teammates and thus have the opportunity to form friendships only with other athletes. This can lead to isolation and makes it difficult for athletes to form friendships when they retire from competition or when they are in environments outside of sport settings.

Emotional issues related to an athlete's self-worth may also be a unique concern. Athletes may have a difficult time when they realize they may not be the best on the team (Lanning, 1982). Also, high levels of stress that student-athletes face may affect their level of psychosocial development (Ferrante, Etzel, & Lantz, 1996), which in turn may affect the athletes' academic, career, and personal concerns.

Where Are Personal Development Services Provided and Who Provides Them?

Programs have been developed to provide assistance in the unique experiences that athletes face at the youth sport, high school, university, and professional levels. These programs help athletes with academic issues, career development, and personal concerns.

Youth Sport Development Organizations

Organizations, many of which are nonprofit, are being developed that teach life skills through sport. Most of these organizations have an executive director and a board of directors who oversee the organization. A curriculum is developed, and program coordinators or coaches and instructors teach both the sport and life lessons through the sport experience. The sidebar lists organizations that provide youth development programs through sport.

YOUTH DEVELOPMENT PROGRAMS THROUGH SPORT

The following are organizations that teach life skills through sport participation.

America Scores (soccer)
www.americascores.org

First Tee (golf)
www.thefirsttee.org

Girls in the Game (general sports)
www.girlsinthegame.org

Harlem RBI (baseball)
www.harlemrbi.org

Hoops 4 Hope (basketball)
www.hoopsafrica.org

LEAP (Life Enhancement through Athletic and Academic Participation)
www.jfku.edu/leap

MetroLacrosse (lacrosse)
www.metrolacrosse.com

PowerPlay NYC (general sports)
www.powerplaynyc.org

SOS Outreach Society (snow sports)
www.sosoutreach.org

SquashBusters (squash)
www.squashbusters.org

Squash Smarts (squash)
www.squashsmarts.org

Team-Up for Youth (general sports)
www.teamupforyouth.org

Tenacity (tennis)
www.tenacity.org

Athletic Departments: High School Level

The National Football Foundation has started a program, Play It Smart, that focuses on the development of life skills for high school student-athletes. Part-time coaches provide academic support services to student-athletes (Petitpas, Van Raalte, Cornelius, & Presbrey, 2004).

A focus of the Play It Smart program is to teach athletes how they can apply skills learned in sport to other areas of life, such as academic performance. In the academic coach pilot program, student-athletes raised their grade-point average from 2.16 to 2.54. Also, 98 percent of the seniors in the Play It Smart program graduated from high school, and 83 percent entered a university program (Petitpas, Van Raalte, Cornelius, & Presbrey, 2004).

Student-athletes appear to support these programs. Ray McElrathbey believed that he would not have received a scholarship to Clemson University without the academic support services and the academic coach he had in high school through the Play It Smart program. McElrathbey said, "When I got to Mays I had a GPA of 1.8. Nobody was holding me accountable. The people paid a lot of attention to me and held me accountable. It was huge for me" (Barnhart, 2007, p. 14E).

Ken Wafer, an academic coach in the Kansas City area, explained that before the program was initiated, it was difficult to keep students interested in class after the football season was over. Student-athletes would lose eligibility, but now the Play It Smart program keeps students focused on doing well academically. As an academic coach, Wafer monitors study halls, provides tutoring help, educates student-athletes on the course work necessary for college, and provides assistance preparing for standardized college placement tests (Kerkhoff, 2007). Additionally, Wafer helps the student-athletes learn career-development skills such as interviewing effectively.

Athletic Departments: Community Colleges and Universities

Historically, providing support to student-athletes has been discussed since the 1930s ("Aided Freshman Athletes," 1930). By the late 1950s universities began to consider hiring individuals to provide academic support services to student-athletes. University of Texas football coach Darrell Royal saw the need for these services. He hired Lan Hewlett to be an academic counselor for the University of Texas football team. Hewlett became known in media reports as the "Brain Coach."

Athletic departments at the university level have also begun to focus on student-athletes' academic, career, and personal concerns. However, some athletic departments may be focusing more on student-athletes' eligibility and graduation rates than on their deeper career and personal concerns. A way to assist athletes is to divide services into four areas: academic advising, life skills, counseling for clinical issues, and provision of mental skills training. Academic advising is a traditional way for most athletic departments to provide support, but some larger institutions are providing a life skills development approach to helping student-athletes, which focuses on helping athletes with personal concerns through educational seminars and workshops or academic courses. Broughton and Neyer (2001, p. 51) stress the importance of meeting the various needs of student-athletes: "A model program would include appropriately trained personnel who can access and treat student-athletes' academic, athletic, and personal needs. Without this kind of support, student-athletes will continue to have needs unmet, to the detriment of their growth and potential as students, athletes, and young adults." The NCAA's CHAMPS/Life Skills (Challenging Athletes' Minds for Personal Success) program, discussed later in this chapter, attempts to meet many of these needs.

One way in which athletic departments at the university level have begun to focus on the personal development of student-athletes is by providing access to academic support service personnel, who provide orientation programming, career development programming, academic support, and life skills programming (Carodine, Almond, & Gratto, 2001). Academic support for student-athletes includes specific services such as a freshman orientation, monitoring eligibility, helping arrange class schedules, and providing career assistance. Athletes making the transition from high school to university often have difficulty and may need an orientation course. During this transition course they may be taught coping skills to help them deal with stress.

Student-athletes may have difficulty choosing a major or they may have a foreclosed identity, which means that they do not explore the various academic majors that are available because they feel already committed to a career path (Miller & Kerr, 2003). According to Miller and Kerr (2003, p. 198), "Identity foreclosure exists when an individual prematurely commits to a career or lifestyle without adequate exploration of available opportunities and ideologies." Also, student-athletes may face difficulty in dealing with retirement from athletics at the end of their academic years. Academic support service staff can help student-athletes ease into retirement from athletics.

In the United States, the National Association of Academic Advisors for Athletics (N4A) supports the academic and personal success of college student-athletes. The N4A defines their members' work as follows:

> N4A members are academic support and student services personnel who are committed to enhancing the opportunities for academic, athletic, and personal success for collegiate student-athletes. These objectives are achieved primarily by providing informed, competent advising and by serving as a liaison between the academic and athletic communities on college campuses across the country. ("What Is the N4A?" 2007, para. 1)

Individuals who participate in this organization are life skills coordinators, psychologists, academic advisors for student-athletes, and various other professionals who help promote life skill development and academic excellence of student-athletes.

Athletic Counselor   Academic athletic counseling is a career track for students who have studied sport and exercise psychology:

> Academic athletic counselors often organize academic tutoring services, monitor academic progress, assist in academic scheduling, and provide other support services for college student-athletes. In larger universities, academic athletic counselors may be assigned to work with a specific team on academic, personal, or sport performance issues, and/or may provide specialized services, such as career development, new student orientation, substance abuse prevention, learning disabilities assessment, or life skills development. (Van Raalte & Williams, 1994, section 6, para. 4)

Advisors commonly are told that they are viewed as a person who helps keep student-athletes eligible. In reality, the academic advisor obviously does not keep the student-athletes eligible; that is the student-athletes' responsibility. The academic advisor helps student-athletes learn strategies for becoming successful students. Academic advisors monitor the eligibility of student-athletes to ensure that they are meeting the requirements set forth by the NCAA or the athletic conference in which the university is competing. Additionally, academic advisors and other academic support service personnel for student-athletes provide encouragement and information about the various resources on campus that can help the student-athletes have a successful university experience (Meyer, 2005).

NCAA CHAMPS/Life Skills Coordinator   In the United States, CHAMPS/Life Skills coordinators provide services to NCAA student-athletes. This program began in 1994 with 46 institutions and has added approximately 40 colleges and universities each year. The CHAMPS program focuses on helping student-athletes in five main areas: academic excellence, athletic success, career development, personal development, and community service ("Welcome to the NCAA CHAMPS/Life Skills Program," 2007).

The academic part of the CHAMPS/Life Skills program includes teaching student-athletes various life skills for success in the classroom, such as time management and goal setting. Tutoring and advising are also part of the academic component. The athletic component focuses on providing student-athletes with the necessary equipment, facilities, administrative support, and travel arrangements to allow the athlete to achieve athletic success (Carodine, Almond, & Gratto, 2001). Career development involves guiding athletes in exploring career options and selecting courses of study. It also prepares student-athletes for retirement from competitive sport. Personal development focuses on educating student-athletes about issues such as eating disorders, substance abuse and prevention, depression, personal concerns, and communicating with others. The fifth component of the NCAA CHAMPS/Life Skills program involves providing student-athletes with information about and access to community service opportunities (Carodine, Almond, & Gratto, 2001).

As of June 2008, 627 NCAA colleges and universities were participating in the NCAA CHAMPS/Life Skills program; 330 of the schools were NCAA Division I institutions, which are required to participate. Division II and Division III programs are not required to participate ("CHAMPS/Life Skills: Frequently Asked Questions," n.d.). Currently, 16 percent of these programs have individuals whose full-time job is to be the CHAMPS/Life Skills coordinator ("CHAMPS/Life Skills: Frequently Asked Questions," n.d.). Some universities also have assistant coordinators. Most full-time coordinators are providing services at the NCAA Division I schools, but over time it is hoped that more participating universities will create full-time CHAMPS/Life Skills coordinator positions within their athletic departments.

Professional Sport Leagues and Teams

Professional sport leagues provide services through their league offices and specific club teams. As discussed in chapter 2, the National Football League (NFL) has a player development program whose purpose is "To challenge NFL players to be lifelong learners while pursuing continuous improvement in family relations, social interactions, personal growth, and career development during and beyond their careers as NFL football players" ("Player Development," 2007, para. 1).

The NFL player development program has four main areas: player assistance services, continuing education, internships for career development, and education on financial aspects. Each team in the NFL has a player development director whose job focuses on providing these services to athletes. Some teams are even developing their own player development departments ("Player Development at the Clubs," 2007).

The National Basketball Players Association (NBPA) has player programs as well as career development programs. The career development program has a director and four career counselors ("Career Development Program," 2008). The NBA and NBPA work together to help athletes with their educational and career goals in order to prepare them for life after basketball. The philosophy of the Player Program Department of the National Basketball Players Association is as follows:

> Based on the experiences of its membership—NBA players—the NBPA has learned that numerous unique and extraordinary situations challenge professional basketball players. Apart from the pressure of having to perform on court, the NBPA has come to understand and appreciate the multitude of off-court situations that players regularly have to confront. How a player handles these off-court challenges can have as much of an impact on his career in the NBA and his future as his on-court performance. ("Player Programs," 2008, para. 1)

The NFL player development program has a variety of services that aid athletes with various personal issues and life concerns. Player assistance services help players gain a sense of life satisfaction and are aimed at helping athletes with off-the-field issues. Life skills seminars and educational workshops are provided to NFL players ("Player Development at the Clubs," 2007).

A focus on transition has also become an important part of the player development services that are provided to professional athletes. Major League Baseball (MLB) offers the rookie career development program, the NFL offers rookie orientation, and the NBA has an orientation week. Professional sport leagues also provide services to help athletes with the transition out of sport. One example is a symposium for retired NFL athletes.

Performance lifestyle advisors help athletes involved in professional leagues and organizations, such as the English Cricket Board, the Welsh Rugby Union, and the Rugby Football Union ("Performance Lifestyle," 2008). The Welsh Rugby Union provides services in three areas: career development, educational advising and guidance, and lifestyle advice and support ("About Performance Lifestyle," 2008). Professional sport organizations also have player welfare managers, who provide athletes resources to deal with off-the-field issues and help to make sure the athlete is treated well.

Programs for Elite Athletes

Programs have been developed worldwide to help elite athletes. The British Olympic Committee has performance lifestyle advisors on staff to help their athletes in training; they provide guidance on issues related to time management, financial advising,

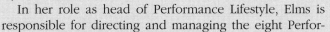

⭐ SUCCESS STORY

Susie Elms, Scottish Institute of Sport

Susie Elms is the head of Performance Lifestyle® for the Scottish Institute of Sport. Elms received her undergraduate degree in physical education from Dunfermline College of Physical Education, Edinburgh. She received a postgraduate certificate in Athlete Career and Education Management from the Australian Institute of Sport. Before beginning her work as head of the Performance Lifestyle program for the Scottish Institute of Sport in 1999, Elms was a lecturer in sport coaching and development at Telford College in Edinburgh ("Meet Our Experts," 2008; "Performance Lifestyle," 2008).

In her role as head of Performance Lifestyle, Elms is responsible for directing and managing the eight Performance Lifestyle managers affiliated with the Scottish Institute of Sport and works directly with the athletes and coaches to integrate, manage, and create a lifestyle that is conducive to performance ("Performance Lifestyle," 2008). She explains the responsibilities of her job: "You need to manage distractions to focus on performance. . . . I deal with integrating a sport with everything else that goes on with an athlete's life. It's about minimizing the distraction to allow them to focus on their performance. So I work with coaches to identify what their plans are over a year or four years. And based on that, I work with athletes to work out where to fit everything in" (Howden, 2006, section 4, para. 1). Elms comments on the importance of helping athletes prepare for life after sport: "With athletes it can be a real trauma when they're no longer in their sport. One day they're a medalist, one day they've retired and they don't know who they are. I call it transition, so working with athletes in this way you can help take the stress out so they can focus on their performance now" (Howden, 2006, section 4, para. 5).

Courtesy of Susie Elms.

career advising, and media education ("Performance Lifestyle," 2008). The Canadian Sport Centres have lifestyle managers and coordinators who provide athletes with retirement and transition services, educational services, financial services, career services, and counseling for personal issues ("Life Services," 2008). The Scottish Institute of Sport has a performance lifestyle coordinator and eight performance lifestyle advisors working at their various locations ("Meet Our Experts," 2008). The Irish Sports Council employs a director of athlete lifestyle services. The Australian Institute of Sport has career and education advisors and coordinators who work with national-level athletes ("Position Description," 2008; "Careers and Education," 2008). Victoria University in Australia has created a graduate certification program in providing career counseling to elite performers ("Career Counseling for Elite Performers," 2008).

The U.S. Olympic Committee athlete career program helps athletes who are still competing as well as those who have retired from sport ("USOC Athlete Career Program," 2008). Additionally, businesses and organizations have been developed to help athletes with the acquisition of life skills, such as the National Consortium for Academics and Sports, Crites and Associates, and the Athletes for Life Foundation.

Research Support for Personal Development Services

Much more research is needed in order to show that assisting athletes with life skills can be helpful. One promising area of research is the evaluation conducted by Petitpas and colleagues (2004) on the Play It Smart program for high school student-athletes. Other studies support the need for life skills and transition programs for professional athletes. The NFL Players Association survey in 2002 found that of 500 recently retired athletes, almost two-thirds had some emotional issues (Skolnick, 2007).

Studies have also evaluated NCAA CHAMPS/Life Skills programming. Samuelson (2003) surveyed students on the academic component of the CHAMPS/Life Skills program and found that they had a positive attitude about and belief in the effectiveness of the program. Goddard (2004) found through a survey of 163 Division I student-athletes that they perceived all components of the CHAMPS/Life Skills program as positive.

The Short of It

- The field of sport psychology focuses not only on performance enhancement but also on helping athletes with various off-the-field concerns, including career decisions, education, personal issues, and injuries.
- When dealing with athletic injuries, athletes often go through various stages of emotions. Sport psychology professionals can aid athletes in dealing with injuries.
- Sport psychology has begun to focus on helping athletes at all levels learn life skills that can enhance their psychosocial development.
- Professionals are coordinating programs that teach life skills to youth through sport, providing academic and athletic counseling to student-athletes, and helping elite athletes deal with various issues off the field.

CHAPTER

Helping Athletes With Mental Health Issues

A Clinical Approach

In this chapter, you will learn the following:

✓ What clinical sport psychology is
✓ Where clinical sport psychology takes place
✓ The types of services that clinical sport psychologists provide to athletes

"It has increased to the point where 15% to 20% of our student athletes are dealing with major depression."

Dr. Jennifer Carter
(Gardiner, 2006,
section 2, para. 8)

Hack (2005) relates a story of an athlete who benefited from the services of a sport psychologist in dealing with off-the-field problems: The athlete was an excellent basketball player coming out of high school, and she was labeled as having incredible potential. But, as a college athlete, she felt that she was not performing up to her potential, and she started exhibiting signs of withdrawal and irritability. One day the player became emotionally distraught, and the coach realized that she needed assistance. The coach sent her to a mental skills consultant, who found that the personal issues the athlete was dealing with were beyond his area of expertise. The athlete then began working with a sport psychologist. After some sessions with the sport psychologist, she began to understand how her off-the-field issues were affecting her on-court performance. Over the next two years of counseling, she was able to develop skills in order to regain her happiness and continue her success as a professional athlete.

Although life skills and educational support services are provided to help athletes with career, academic, and personal concerns, sometimes athletes, just like the general population, need assistance for more serious mental health problems, such as depression, eating disorders, anxiety disorders, addictions, and attention-deficit disorders (Bennett, 2007). As mental health issues receive more attention in the media, athletic directors and general managers of professional sport teams have begun to see the importance of staff who can provide clinical services to their athletes. The National Collegiate Athletic Association (NCAA) organized a conference of psychologists who provide psychological services to university athletic departments (Hosick, 2005b).

Other organizations throughout the world are focusing on the mental health issues of their athletes. The Australian Sports Commission has developed a network of specialists who can provide clinical and personal counseling for athletes in Australia. Also, clinical counseling professionals affiliated with the Canadian Sport Centres provide counseling services for athletes. The English Institute of Sport has a clinical psychologist on their sports science team.

Although consultants with training in educational sport psychology can provide performance-enhancement services to athletes, the services discussed in this chapter are usually provided by licensed mental health professionals. Even if sport psychology students do not plan to practice clinical sport psychology, it is important that all consultants understand mental health issues since they may be working with athletes who need referrals to clinical sport psychologists.

What Is Clinical Sport Psychology?

Clinical sport psychologists work with people who have mental health problems. They are usually trained in clinical or counseling psychology and often have received additional training in sport psychology and the sport and exercise sciences (Weinberg & Gould, 2007). Clinical and counseling sport psychologists are trained to help athletes with issues outside of the sport environment (McCann, 2005).

> *The athletic experience can be very stressful to some athletes, and negatively affect their performance or their ability to function as healthy human beings. In these cases, sport psychologists trained in counseling psychology or clinical psychology are needed.*
>
> **Richard H. Cox**, 2007, p. 10

Moore (Winerman, 2005) reports that her work as a university counseling and sport psychologist is about 20 percent focused on traditional sport psychology, about 60 percent on counseling-related issues, and about 20 percent a combination of performance-enhancement and clinical issues. Gary Bennett (2007), a licensed psychologist hired by Virginia Tech University to help student-athletes with mental health concerns and other psychosocial developmental issues, reports that only 20 percent of the athletes he sees seek assistance for performance-only issues.

Dr. Sam Maniar, a leader in working with the NCAA on mental health issues of athletes, reports the following:

> The NCAA has really been pushing for mental health care of student-athletes. I think that all of us have made some false assumptions about student-athletes because they are so successful. We think they are less susceptible to emotional difficulties, but the research now coming out is that they are suffering from depression, anxiety, relationship difficulties, at least the same amount as the general student population, and we know that 10% of that population suffers from clinical depression. (Porentas, 2006, section 4, para. 13)

Psychology Insight

Psychologists providing services to student-athletes report that approximately 15 to 20 percent of athletes are clinically depressed. In addition, sport psychology practitioners who work in athletic departments report seeing clinical issues such as eating disorders and anxiety (Harris, 2006a). One university sport psychology department reported that from 2000 to 2003 approximately 25 percent of the visits with the sport psychologists were related to performance concerns (Harris, 2006b). That means the other 75 percent of the visits were for non-performance-related, counseling, or clinical concerns.

Responsibilities of a Clinical or Counseling Sport Psychologist

Sport psychologists in university settings are now providing clinical services to athletes. Visits to sport psychologists are for issues such as eating disorders, depression, anxiety, self-mutilation, and thoughts of suicide (Harris, 2006b). Figure 8.1 lists the typical duties of a counseling or clinical psychologist providing services for a university athletic department (Carter, 2005).

One of the questions that often arises when dealing with clinical or counseling issues of athletes is why there is a special need for a clinical *sport* psychologist to work with athletes. Dr. Nicki Moore, a sport psychologist for the University of Oklahoma, notes, "Someone who's not familiar with the intense level of significance that sport plays in the life of a student-athlete—particularly at a Division I school—can be well intentioned but have a disconnect with the student" (Winerman, 2005, section 4, para. 2).

The NCAA's interest in mental health issues of student-athletes is shown in the manual *Managing Student-Athletes' Mental Health Issues* (Thompson & Sherman, 2007), which is divided into five chapters covering mood disorders, anxiety disorders, eating disorders, substance abuse, and managing and treating mental health issues. The manual aids coaches in understanding mental health issues and recognizing signs and symptoms, and it provides guidance on referring athletes to mental health professionals.

Where Does Clinical Sport Psychology Take Place?

University athletic departments hire sport psychologists with backgrounds in working with student-athletes on mental health issues and also individuals with sport psychology training to provide performance-enhancement services to student-athletes (Gardner, 2007). Clinical sport psychology also takes place at the professional and Olympic levels of sport. At the Olympic level, the United States has five sport psychologists who provide comprehensive sport psychology services. The U.S. Olympic Committee's sport psychology staff reports that half of their work with athletes is related to personal or clinical issues ("USOC Sport Psychology Services," 2008). The Canadian Olympic Committee employs sport psychologists to work with their athletes, as do New Zealand and Australia.

Many sport psychologists in private practice provide clinical psychology services. O'Connor (2007) suggests that clinical sport psychologists are gaining more acceptance as part of the sports medicine services.

What Occurs in Clinical Sport Psychology?

In counseling, the first phase is determining where an athlete is and where she wants to go. This usually involves the athlete's completing paperwork and various assessments for an evaluation of the concerns and symptoms. Then a plan is created and

FIGURE 8.1

Common Work Duties for Counseling or Clinical Psychologists in University Athletic Departments

CLINICAL AND COUNSELING DUTIES

- ☐ Individual therapy with varsity college student-athletes
- ☐ Group therapy with teams for clinical issues (trauma, eating disorders, etc.)
- ☐ Crisis management
- ☐ Creating and delivering wellness programs
- ☐ Consulting with medical staff (physicians, athletic trainers, dietitians)
- ☐ Assessment
- ☐ Individual therapy with high school, professional, and recreational athletes
- ☐ Supervising the clinical work of graduate students and postdoctoral fellows
- ☐ Participating on athletic department alcohol and drug committee
- ☐ Consulting with athletic department administrators
- ☐ Participating in case conference (colleague supervision)
- ☐ Applying research findings to clinical work

PERFORMANCE-ENHANCEMENT DUTIES

- ☐ Meeting with sport teams to enhance mental skills
- ☐ Facilitating team-building exercises
- ☐ Attending practices and competitions
- ☐ Meeting with individual athletes or small groups for mental skills training
- ☐ Consulting with coaches
- ☐ Delivering educational workshops to coaches
- ☐ Delivering presentations to college, high school, and professional teams or camps

RESEARCH AND TEACHING DUTIES

- ☐ Preparing grant proposals
- ☐ Collaborating with athletic and academic departments on research projects
- ☐ Reviewing the research literature in areas of interest
- ☐ Collecting and analyzing data
- ☐ Writing manuscripts and presentations
- ☐ Presenting at professional conferences
- ☐ Teaching sport psychology and/or counseling classes

SERVICE DUTIES

- ☐ Participating on university wellness task forces
- ☐ Mentoring students
- ☐ Responding to e-mail, phone calls

Reprinted, by permission, from Morgan et al. 2005.

intervention begins. The counselor will continue to evaluate the athlete to determine if she is improving (Bennett, 2007).

Assessment is an important component of providing clinical sport psychology services. Gardner and Moore (2006) have developed a multilevel classification system for assessing an athlete in a clinical sport psychology framework. That system classifies issues and concern into four areas: performance development, performance dysfunction, performance impairment, and performance termination (Hack, 2007). The performance development classification describes an athlete who is doing well and seeks to learn skills to improve performance. This assessment usually leads to an intervention focused on mental skills training. Performance dysfunction occurs when an athlete sees the sport psychologist for a performance problem, but off-the-field psychological issues appear to be the main cause of the problem. Interventions for athletes in this classification include counseling and mental skills training. Performance impairment occurs when an athlete presents with clear clinical issues. Often these issues affect performance, but the main focus of intervention is helping the athlete with the clinical issue. Performance termination usually focuses on an athlete's departure from sport. Usually the main intervention in these cases is counseling to help the athlete's transition.

Mental Health Issues Treated by Clinical Sport Psychologists

As the previous sections discussed, athletes often meet with sport psychologists to get help for issues such as depression, eating disorders, substance abuse, and anxiety. This section describes these psychological issues in more detail.

Depression

Depression is a feeling of extreme sadness that lasts for a long time. Also, this sadness usually is seen interfering with a person's normal daily functioning. Thompson and Sherman (2007) outline various signs and symptoms of depression: feeling sad with episodes of crying, anger, or irritability, feelings of worthlessness, extreme fatigue and low energy, negative thoughts, possible suicidal thoughts, and sleeping and eating problems.

depression—A condition of extreme sadness that lasts for a long time.

Approximately 10 percent of the population is depressed (Thompson & Sherman, 2007). Three common causes of depression are an extremely negative life event, biological reasons, and negative thinking. Reasons for depression can also be related directly to an athlete's participation in sport. An example is athletic injury. When a student suffers an athletic injury in practice or competition, it can lead to depression. Also, it is possible to become depressed because of overtraining. Coaches and mental training professionals need to understand and assist athletes with depression because athletes who are depressed may be at risk of developing injuries. Depression appears to be common among student-athletes. It is important to seek early intervention for athletes who are depressed;

to assess depression, a mental health instrument should be used. The Center for Epidemiological Studies (CES-D) Depression Scale is an effective assessment instrument (NCAA, 2007). Etzel, Watson, Visek, and Maniar (2006) provide suggestions for athletic departments in helping student-athletes with depression. First the staff should be trained to recognize and refer athletes to mental health professionals if the athletes exhibit signs of depression. Also, the athletic department should have in place a network of mental health professionals whom student-athletes can be referred to.

Eating Disorders

Two of the most common **eating disorders** are anorexia nervosa (commonly referred to as anorexia) and bulimia. Characteristics of anorexia include refusal to maintain body weight within 15 percent of the minimum normal weight for that person. A person with anorexia nervosa is extremely fearful of gaining weight and experiences a disturbance in body image, such as feeling fat even when obviously thin. For females, there is the absence of three menstrual cycles in a row. Bulimia is an eating disorder in which a person tries to maintain normal weight by bingeing and purging at least twice a week for over three months (Weinberg & Gould, 2007).

The sport environment may sometimes increase the risk of occurrence of an eating disorder. Approximately 2 to 3 percent of female university student-athletes have eating disorders. Many of these student-athletes are in sports that require a low percentage of body fat (Hellmich, 2006), such

eating disorder—A condition characterized by abnormal eating behaviors.

as gymnastics, diving, cross country, and figure skating. A study by Carter found that 15 percent of university athletes had symptoms of disordered eating, but these were at a subclinical level, which means they did not technically have eating disorders (Grabmeier, 2002). Carter (Grabmeier, 2002, para. 5) says, "In general, eating disorders among college athletes are no more prevalent—and may be slightly less prevalent—than among college students at large." Carter goes on to say, "We're trying to prevent eating disorders by identifying those at risk early enough to help them. We're also educating coaches, trainers, and others about how to identify athletes who may have symptoms of eating disorders" (para. 15).

The diagnosis of eating disorders is similar to that for depression: Athletes can complete an assessment instrument for eating disorders. Team Enhance, developed by the University of Tennessee's women's athletic department, created a program to identify and prevent eating disorders in athletes. Loucks and Nattiv (2005) recommend that athletes be screened for eating disorders before the start of each season. Also, regular time periods for testing should be developed.

Intervention strategies can be provided for athletes with eating disorders; education is one such intervention that can be used as a prevention tool. The focus of educational interventions should not be on discussion of eating disorders, but on teaching healthy eating in order to improve sport performance. Cogan (2005) recommends that coaches be educated and apply various strategies. For example, coaches can stop weighing athletes and stop having athletes weigh in in a group setting.

The main intervention for an athlete with an eating disorder is individual therapy. Group therapy can also be effective. Athletes can benefit from having a multidisciplinary treatment team to aid them in overcoming the eating disorder. These treatment teams usually consist of a sport psychologist, dietitian, physician, and athletic trainer (Cogan, 2005).

Clinical sport psychologists in university athletic departments may also be part of committees that address eating disorders. Bennett (2007), a clinical sport psychologist with the Virginia Tech athletic department, is part of a nutrition and performance committee, which observes athletes who may be at risk for developing eating disorders. This committee meets once a month.

Substance Abuse

Substance abuse issues are a major concern when counseling athletes on mental heath issues. University student-athletes are considered a population at risk for alcohol abuse (Etzel et al., 2006). Athletes sometimes use **performance-enhancing substances,** such as steroids and human growth hormone, which can increase muscle mass and speed but can cause physiological and psychological problems.

Some athletes use substances such as marijuana and alcohol for recreational purposes. One of the best ways to help prevent substance abuse is through education.

performance-enhancing substances—Substances, usually illegal, that provide athletes with an unfair physical advantage over their competitors.

Drug workshops during the preseason can be an effective preventive strategy (Bacon, Lerner, Trembley, & Seestedt, 2005). Assessment for substance abuse is also important. Coaches and sports medicine professionals can observe athletes they think might be at risk. Drug testing is another way of preventing athletes from using illegal and dangerous drugs (Brewer & Petrie, 2002). Sport psychologists can inform athletes about drug testing and the consequences of testing positive for banned substances. Similarly, sport psychologists can inform athletes about case studies in which athletes had problems with certain substances.

Sport psychologists may also be part of the process of drug testing of student-athletes. Bennett (2007), in his role as a clinical sport psychologist for the Virginia Tech athletic department, serves on the substance abuse committee, which creates substance abuse policy and also meets to discuss the cases of any student-athletes who have positive drug tests. In the Rutgers University sport psychology program, student-athletes and coaches attend yearly educational sessions on substance abuse. Student-athletes who test positive for a substance must receive individual counseling from the staff ("Rutgers University Sport Psychology Program," 2007).

Anxiety Disorders

Anxiety disorders are the most common type of mental illness in the United States. Approximately 40 million people have an anxiety disorder (NCAA, 2007). The most common type of anxiety disorder is a generalized anxiety disorder. According to the National Institute of Mental Health, a **generalized anxiety disorder** can be described as extreme tension and worry that lasts for a long time, even when there is nothing going on that should lead one to feeling anxious ("Generalized Anxiety Disorder," 2008). Other anxiety disorders are panic attacks and obsessive-compulsive disorder. According to *2007-2008 NCAA Sports Medicine Handbook*, student-athletes with an anxiety disorder often welcome referrals to mental health professionals.

> **generalized anxiety disorder—** Extreme tension and worry that lasts for a long time, even when there is nothing going on that should lead one to feeling anxious.

A few professional athletes have discussed their difficulties with anxiety disorders. Earl Campbell, in his book *The Earl Campbell Story: A Football Great's Battle With Panic Disorder* (Campbell & Ruane, 1999), describes how he overcame issues related to a panic disorder.

> **phobia—**Extreme irrational fear that is debilitating to the individual.

One of the most interesting sport-specific types of **phobias** involves an athlete who suddenly has difficulty making a routine sport move that he has been able to make for years (Silva, 1994). For example, a baseball player cannot make the throw from second to first base or cannot make the throw back to the pitcher. In treating these types of sport phobias, clinical sport psychology services are usually recommended.

According to Durand and Barlow (2006), what phobic athletes face is a heightened level of performance anxiety, which becomes a performance phobia. Although these athletes may not fear being in social situations, they fear having to perform a skill and are worried about embarrassing themselves in public and being judged by others.

Research Support for Clinical Sport Psychology Services

Unfortunately, there has been little literature on issues related to clinical sport psychology. However, that appears to be changing: A periodical that addresses this very necessary area of research, the *Journal of Clinical Sport Psychology*, began publication in January 2007. Based on current literature, Brewer and Petrie (2002, p. 316) note the following:

> For sport and exercise participants with diagnosable psychopathology, appropriate treatment can improve their quality of life and enhance their sport or exercise. In the absence of empirical data suggesting otherwise, diagnosis and treatment of psychopathology in sport and exercise participants should be the same as with nonparticipants.

Although treating athletes for mental health concerns is similar to treating the general population, it is important that the psychologist be knowledgeable in working with athletes (Winerman, 2005, para. 6 and 18). Thus, knowledge of sport psychology and the exercise sciences would seem to be helpful for a psychologist treating an athlete with a mental health concern. Sport psychologists are likely to understand the significance and context of sport in the athlete's life and make connections that general psychologists might not be able to make.

⭐ **SUCCESS STORY**

Kirsten Peterson, Senior Sport Psychologist, United States Olympic Committee

Courtesy of Kirsten Peterson.

Kirsten Peterson has been a sport psychologist with the United States Olympic Committee (USOC) since 1996. Peterson received her master's degree in sport psychology from the University of Illinois. She completed a predoctoral internship in sport psychology at the United States Olympic Training Center (USOTC) and then obtained her doctoral degree in counseling psychology from the University of Illinois ("USOC Performance Enhancement Team," 2008). As a student, Peterson was actively involved as a student representative in the Association for the Advancement of Applied Sport Psychology (AAASP) ("Where Are They Now?" 2008). Peterson is both a licensed psychologist and an AASP-certified consultant.

In addition to being a senior sport psychologist at the USOTC, Peterson has been the manager of the United States Olympic Committee's sport psychology registry and has served as the president of Division 47, the Exercise and Sport Psychology Division of the American Psychological Association.

Dr. Peterson offers this advice to students: "Make sure that the life of an applied sport psychologist is what you want to do. Talk to people doing that sort of work. Find out how things work and decide if that kind of lifestyle fits who you are. Then I would strongly encourage you to think about (a) getting your doctorate and (b) getting it in psychology. By being licensable as a psychologist, many more applied work doors are open to you, and you get to use the word psychology as part of who you are" ("Where Are They Now?" 2008, para. 9).

Who Provides Clinical Sport Psychology Services?

The services discussed in this chapter are provided by mental health professionals who have received proper training and authorization through an evaluation or test of their knowledge to provide mental health services in their state or country. In the United States and Canada, mental health professionals obtain licensure status in order to provide services as a psychologist. In Australia, a similar evaluation procedure is referred to as registration ("Working as a Psychologist," 2008). The hope is that individuals providing clinical sport psychology services to athletes would also have training in sport psychology and the sport and exercise sciences.

Professional counselors, licensed psychologists, sport psychologists, sport psychiatrists, and licensed social workers may provide mental health services to athletes. A licensed psychologist has received a doctorate in psychology and has met the requirements for licensure or registration in the state or country in which he or she plans to practice. Individuals trained in professional counseling also work with athletes on various issues. Bacon and colleagues (2005) describe a licensed counselor as someone who has at least a master's degree in counseling and is licensed in the state in which he or she is practicing. A licensed social worker typically has a master's degree in social work and is licensed to practice independently.

Many athletes have clinical as well as performance issues; therefore, some students of sport psychology are seeking graduate training in order to help athletes enhance their performance on the field as well as to help them with clinical or counseling issues. Dr. Maniar explains his counseling role for college student-athletes: "I provide counseling for student-athletes, the same kind of things you and I would go to psychologists for, relationship problems, academic problems, depression, anxiety, bereavement, grief. Some more serious things sometimes, things like substance abuse or dependence, very rarely, but sometimes we see suicidal ideations, things like that" (Porentas, 2006, para. 22).

Because many students and professionals are interested in providing holistic services to athletes, and there is a need for these services, some graduate programs in sport psychology are being created to provide multidisciplinary training in which students are trained to provide mental skills training as well as clinical and counseling services to athletes (Kornspan & Lerner, 2005). Examples of these types of graduate programs are West Virginia University, University of Missouri, University of North Texas, JFK University, and Boston University (Burke, Sachs, Fry, & Schweighardt, 2008). Dr. Leonard Zaichkowsky, director of the sport psychology program at Boston University, noticed a change in the type of presenting concerns that athletes have. In response, Zaichkowsky (2006) saw the need to change the graduate program to allow students to become eligible to pursue licensing as mental health counselors after completing all the requirements of the graduate program.

The Short of It

- Clinical sport psychology services help athletes with issues outside of the sport environment.
- Sport organizations and leagues throughout the world have an increased interest in meeting the needs of athletes in the area of clinical services.
- Sport psychologists provide assistance for athletes' clinical issues, including depression, eating disorders, anxiety disorders, and substance abuse.
- Those who have training in psychology or counseling and have met their state's or country's requirements to practice can provide clinical sport psychology services to athletes.
- Graduate programs are being developed that prepare students to work with athletes both on mental skills training and on clinical sport psychology issues.

Using Psychology to Encourage Involvement in Exercise and Fitness

In this chapter, you will learn the following:

✓ The importance and main functions of exercise psychology

✓ Where exercise psychology services take place

✓ The types of exercise services and interventions that clients are provided

✓ Research that has been conducted to support interventions

✓ Who provides exercise psychology services to the general population

> "'Exercise maintainers' of all levels stick with fitness because they have fun doing it."
>
> **Dr. Jay Kimiecik**, associate professor of health promotion at Miami University (Harr, 2003, para. 2)

Kelly Belkeir joined a fitness center a few years ago. Like many people, she went to work out once and then did not return for another workout. A main reason she did not return was that she felt uncomfortable and did not believe she was obtaining the necessary help from the staff ("YMCAs Offer Customized Workout Programs," 2005). But she was still interested in beginning an exercise program, so Kelly decided to join the local YMCA. Kelly's experience the second time was much better. The YMCA had started a new program called the Coach Approach. Kelly received fitness coaching during her weekly exercise process. She met with a wellness coach, who helped her stick to her exercise routine. The coaches helped Kelly determine the best time to exercise in order to manage her time.

Similarly, Carla Brooks was 52. She had worked out and exercised before, but often had trouble maintaining a physically active lifestyle (Sarnataro, 2005). Carla said, "I'd get started and do pretty well for a while, but I'd get busy and drop off" (section 1, para. 2).

To stay motivated, Carla worked with a wellness coach, who focused on helping her stay active. Carla said, "Each time I met with the coach, she had a topic to talk about. She gave you tools to deal with when you didn't feel like exercising or got off track" (Sarnataro, 2005, section 2, para. 15). While working with a wellness coach for a one-year period, Carla was very successful in meeting her physical activity and weight loss goals.

The American Heart Association (AHA) published a statement recommending that medical professionals provide exercise and physical activity counseling:

> We know many doctors have less time to visit with each patient. Still most patients say that if their doctors told them to be physically active, they would listen. Doctors need to ask questions at every visit about what kinds of activity and how much activity each patient is getting. If doctors don't have time to counsel, they can refer patients to other healthcare team members. These may include nurse case managers, certified exercise professionals trained in behavior-change programs, and sports nutritionists. ("Exercise [Physical Activity] Counseling," 2007, para. 2)

The Move for Health program was established by the World Health Organization (WHO) in 2002. This organization has referred to the problem of physical inactivity as a global public health problem: "Effective public health measures are urgently needed to improve physical activity behaviours in all populations" ("Physical Inactivity: A Global Public Health Problem," 2008, para. 3). Many nations have begun to address this problem by creating programs to increase the physical activity of their citizens. Healthy Active Australia is one such program developed by the Australian government. The Sport England organization's mission is to help the population of England become more active through sport.

In response to the need to address physical inactivity, many nations' government agencies have created jobs that focus on strategies to increase the physical activity behavior of the citizens in the community. These types of positions are also developing in the private sector. The following are types of jobs that focus on changing the physical activity behavior of the general population:

- Health and physical activity manager
- Manager of physical activity promotion
- Physical activity coordinator
- Physical activity development officer

What Is Exercise Psychology?

Exercise psychology is the study of psychological factors that determine continued participation in regular physical activity (Anshel, 2006). Exercise psychology focuses on helping people learn to enjoy exercise and change their behavior in order to make exercise a regular part of their daily lives. Table 9.1 provides some comparisons between sport psychology and exercise psychology. Mental skills training consultants certified through the Association for Applied Sport Psychology (AASP), health and wellness coaches, and physical activity advisors and counselors can work with exercisers to help them adhere to their exercise routines. This is important because obesity rates are continuing to increase, which puts people at increased risk for developing various diseases. This public health problem has led the Centers for Disease Control and Prevention (CDC) to focus on helping the U.S. population become more physically active. The CDC reports that 60 percent of adults are not engaging in enough physical activity ("Report of the Surgeon General: Adults," 2007).

Psychology Insight

The U.S. surgeon general's report (2007) indicates that 25 percent of Americans do not exercise at all, which puts them at increased risk of becoming obese and therefore at much higher risk of developing various diseases, such as heart disease and diabetes. According to the CDC, becoming more physically active and engaging in regular exercise routines help people reduce the risk of developing various diseases; maintain muscle, bone, and joint health; and reduce symptoms of anxiety and depression.

TABLE 9.1 Sport Psychology vs. Exercise Psychology

Characteristic	Sport psychology	Exercise psychology
Clients	Athletes and coaches	The general population
Services provided	Mental training: teaching athletes skills such as goal setting, imagery, relaxation, and concentration	Focus is on providing support for individuals who are in the process of making physical activity a daily part of their lives
Goals	To help athletes learn skills to enhance their mental game and perform more optimally	To help exercisers overcome barriers that stop them from making physical activity a daily part of their lives, and help individuals adhere to a physically active lifestyle

Many people do not exercise enough, and some do not exercise at all. The role of professionals in this area is to help people begin exercising and support them in continuing their physical activity throughout their lifetime. There is a need for more sport and exercise psychology professionals to provide consulting and exercise coaching services to public and private facilities. There is also a need to place sport psychology students in jobs involving wellness coaching, behavioral change, and physical activity consulting.

> *Doctors, insurance companies, and legislators are beginning to understand that prevention is the best way to keep medical costs down. In the not-too-distant future, physicians may refer patients to wellness coaches along with prescribing medications to treat medical conditions that can be prevented, improved, or cured by exercise, nutrition, weight control, and stress management.*
>
> **Randy Littlejohn (2005, p. 71)**

Where Does Exercise Psychology Take Place?

Ideally, exercise psychology services would be provided in a variety of facilities, such as fitness centers ("Stansbury Fitness and Wellness Center," 2007), community recreation centers, nonprofit fitness facilities, university recreation centers, physicians' offices, and community programs. Because applied exercise psychology is a very new field, it is just beginning to be applied in these types of settings. Professionals are providing support in fitness centers and nonprofit fitness centers ("Meet the Coaches," 2007). Clients may meet with exercise psychology professionals in hospital-based weight-management programs or at medical centers that provide surgical weight-loss programs.

Another area where exercise psychology can occur is in cardiac rehabilitation. Cardiac patients can benefit from the exercise support process, and it can help them adhere to exercise over a long period. Programs also have been created that study physical activity counseling to determine whether it can help people adhere to exercise (Tulloch, Fortier, & Hogg, 2006).

What Services Are Provided in Exercise Psychology?

The YMCA approach is a model that helps people have successful fitness experiences. People trained in sport and exercise psychology can use this type of intervention model at YMCAs, fitness facilities, or in other settings. The Coach Approach is for YMCA members who are interested in seeking help in the process of exercise. The program helps people set short-term and long-term goals for fitness. Participants can continue to meet with wellness coaches in order to continue making progress toward their fitness goals. Dr. Jim Annesi developed the program at Atlanta-area YMCAs. The focus of the program is to make exercise a habit for people and to address the problem of new members' dropping out. About 55 to 65 percent of people drop out of exercise programs within the first few months. According to Annesi, the Coach Approach has decreased that percentage (Sarnataro, 2005).

In the Coach Approach program, a coach conducts assessments of clients' physical and mental states and then helps them ease into exercise, making sure they do not do too much too soon. The wellness coach meets at least once a month with members to help them stay focused on their programs and overcome challenges in order to maintain regular physical activity. Jennifer Unruh summarizes the purpose of the program: "It's a **behavioral change** tool for people who have a hard time sticking with exercise and [let] everything else in life come first" (Sarnataro, 2005, para. 4). This is a practical approach for implementing the concepts of exercise psychology into the physical activity environment.

behavioral change—A change made in a person's life that becomes a part of their everyday routine.

stages of change—A theory that involves five phases that a person goes through to reach a permanent behavioral change.

As with many programs aimed at helping exercisers maintain their exercise habits, the YMCA program is based on the **stages of change** theory, or the transtheoretical model (Dishman & Buckworth, 2006). This model involves six stages of behavioral change, shown in figure 9.1. The first stage is precontemplation. People in this stage are not exercising and are not thinking about

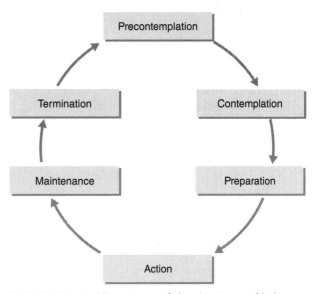

FIGURE 9.1 Cyclic pattern of the six stages of behavioral change.

Reprinted, by permission, from Weinberg and Gould 2007.

starting an exercise program. The second stage is contemplation. People in this stage are thinking about starting an exercise program. The third stage is the preparation stage, in which people begin planning to exercise. The fourth stage is action, in which people have begun to exercise on a regular basis but have done so for less than six months. The fifth stage is maintenance, in which people have exercised consistently for over six months, though it is possible that they will still relapse and stop exercising, at which point they might begin the cycle again. Once people have been exercising for five years and are unlikely to stop, they have ended the cycle and are in the termination stage. An intervention can be chosen based on the stage that an exerciser is in.

What Interventions Are Used in the Exercise Process?

Once people who have not exercised in a long time begin exercising, they have the challenge of continuing to exercise, which is very difficult. In fact, on average, without any successful interventions to help them, about 50 percent of people who start exercising drop out within the first 6 to 12 months (figure 9.2). One goal of exercise psychologists is to find successful strategies to help people continue with their exercise programs. One promising strategy involves providing a person with an exercise coach who teaches mental skills that can help the person stick with the process of daily exercise (Annesi, 2003).

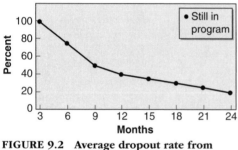

FIGURE 9.2 Average dropout rate from exercise programs.

Reprinted, by permission, from Dishman, Washburn, and Heath 2004.

Goal setting and social support are two of the strategies that performance-enhancement consultants and wellness coaches use in helping people adhere to exercise routines. The literature suggests that social support can help people remain physically active (Orsega-Smith, Payne, Mowen, Ho, & Godbey, 2007).

The strategies that performance-enhancement consultants and wellness coaches teach to exercisers are similar to the skills that mental training consultants teach athletes in order to help them improve performance. **Cognitive-behavioral skills** are among the strategies taught to exercisers to help them adhere to programs. These skills include goal setting, decision balance, self-monitoring, enhancement of self-efficacy, and relapse prevention (Buckworth & Dishman, 2002).

In goal setting, exercisers learn to set both short-term and long-term goals. The research literature suggests that goal setting can help exercisers stay physically active (Shilts, Horowitz, & Townsend, 2004).

cognitive-behavioral skills— Skills for addressing the thoughts that influence a person's feelings and behaviors.

Decision balance occurs when exercisers write down what they believe their short-term and long-term benefits will be when participating in a regular exercise program. Also, this strategy allows exercisers to determine what barriers might arise in the process and thus provides them with strategies

⭐ SUCCESS STORY

Jim Annesi, Director of Wellness Advancement for the YMCA of Metropolitan Atlanta

Jim Annesi, PhD, has been on the faculties of Rutgers University and the United States Sports Academy and has held appointments with the Veterans Affairs Health Care Systems, Elizabeth General Medical Center, and Enhanced Performance Technologies. Throughout his career, he has been interested in developing evidence-based methods that empower individuals to maintain their health behaviors. In fact, he has written numerous articles and three books on the subject.

Courtesy of Jim Annesi.

Annesi became the director of wellness advancement at the Metro Atlanta YMCA in 2000 ("Research and Development," 2007), where he created an exercise behavioral change program for YMCA members that became known as the Coach Approach. This program focuses on helping exercisers learn the skills to help them adhere to exercise. Each exerciser consults with a wellness coach who provides support in the exercise process. The program is now in 19 cities in the United States and Canada and also in Italy and England ("YMCA Helps All Family Members to Adopt Healthy Behaviors," 2007). Annesi maintains an active research program focused on exercise adherence, weight loss and maintenance, and the effects of physical activity on depression, anxiety, self-image, and other mental health and quality-of-life factors.

In addition to the Coach Approach, Annesi's protocols of Youth Fit For Life and the Health and Fitness Experience are applied in a variety of health promotion and preventive medicine settings in the United States, United Kingdom, Italy, Japan, and Canada.

---

for overcoming those barriers (Buckworth & Dishman, 2002). Recent research has found this technique to be helpful in changing physical activity behavior (Wankel & Thompson, 2006).

The technique of self-monitoring can be taught by performance-enhancement consultants, physical activity counselors, or wellness coaches to keep people motivated to exercise (Gleeson-Kreig, 2006; Buckworth & Dishman, 2002). Self-monitoring involves keeping track of exercise behavior patterns and staying aware of thoughts and feelings while monitoring exercise behavior. Through self-monitoring, people can determine various barriers and cues that can cause them to stop exercising and learn how to plan ahead to overcome those barriers.

Positive self-talk can help people adhere to exercise programs. One method involves going through an inventory of excuses to avoid exercise and then learning to recognize the excuses. People can then learn to talk to themselves positively about exercising (Kirschenbaum, 1997).

West Virginia University's Mission Possible program provides support to obese people while they are participating in exercise programs. The program involves six group counseling sessions, individual counseling sessions, and a support group, and provides a safe and nonintimidating environment in which to learn about making the necessary lifestyle, physical, and emotional changes for lifelong healthy living ("Stansbury Fitness and Wellness Center," 2007).

Research Support for Exercise Psychology Services

In the implementation of the Coach Approach intervention with exercisers, Annesi and Unruh (2004) found that, over a six-month period, a control group (which did not receive coaching) dropped out at a rate of 62 percent, whereas the experimental group (the group that did receive the coaching) had a dropout rate of 38 percent. Proper, Hildenbrant, Van der Beek, Twisk, and Van Mechelen (2003) found that physical activity counseling of people involved in workplace exercise programs increased adherence to exercise. Batik and colleagues (2008) found support for the effectiveness of the Physical Activity for a Lifetime of Success (PALS) program in increasing the amount of physical activity that adults over the age of 65 participate in.

Evidence indicates that counseling people to be more physically active is helpful (Breckon, Johnston, & Hutchinson, 2008). A study analyzing the active lifestyles approach found that the roles and responsibilities of physical activity advisors are very important to the success of a program aimed at increasing physical activity (Wormald, Waters, Sleap, & Ingle, 2006).

Dr. Steven Blair from the Cooper Institute for Aerobics Research and colleagues were instrumental in analyzing the effects of counseling on physical activity behavior change. Blair and colleagues (1998) explained the activity counseling trial (ACT), which was a study aimed at understanding the effectiveness of physical activity counseling. Results from the activity counseling trial (Writing Group for the Activity Counseling Trial Research Group, 2001) showed that counseling and education can help individuals enhance physical fitness by increasing their adherence to physical activity guidelines.

Who Provides Exercise Psychology Services?

Providing applied exercise psychology services to the general population is a very new area of service provision in sport psychology. In fact, the literature on AASP-certified physical activity consulting is virtually nonexistent. There has been a change in recent years to emphasize coaching and physical activity counseling in the fitness industry. Physical activity counselors, physical activity consultants, and exercise interventionists are now providing support to exercisers using techniques that have been studied in exercise psychology.

Wellness Coaches

As discussed previously, one program that focuses on providing support to people involved in physical activity is the YMCA Coach Approach program, which provides many opportunities for students trained in sport and exercise psychology. YMCA wellness coaches provide support to members to help them remain physically active. These coaches use a variety of strategies, including goal setting, self-monitoring of physical activity, and time management. Similar types of jobs are available at companies in the health and fitness industry. Wellness coaches and health coaches working in these settings provide a variety of services, including coaching employees to help them become more physically active and maintain their activity programs.

An organization that has begun to provide direction in the field of wellness coaching is Wellcoaches at www.wellcoaches.com. This organization has partnered with the American College of Sports Medicine (ACSM) to create a fitness coach certification ("Fitness Coach Training Program," 2007). The program trains people who would like to become fitness coaches through several lessons in the exercise support process. Topics include behavior change and assessment, goal setting, developing a positive supportive relationship with the client, how to provide a fitness coaching session, challenges in fitness coaching, and techniques and interventions in fitness coaching.

Physical Activity Counselors

Physical activity counselors and consultants work with primary-care physicians to help patients become more physically active (Fortier, Tulloch, & Hogg, 2006). They focus on preventing rather than treating disease. Often physicians do not have time or are not trained in counseling to help their patients increase and maintain physical activity. Thus, physical activity counselors as part of multidisciplinary teams working directly with primary-care physicians can help patients live healthy, physically active lives, which may help improve the health of society overall.

Physical activity counselors have university degrees and have received training in the exercise sciences; they support patients in maintaining their exercise programs. They also help patients maintain a positive outlook on the importance of staying active (Fortier, Tulloch, & Hogg, 2006; "Role of Physical Activity Counsellors," 2008).

As part of its primary-care practice, the West Carleton Family Health Team in Canada employs a physical activity counselor, who works with patients at the clinic. The physical activity counselor helps patients stay motivated and set exercise goals ("Physical Activity Counsellor," 2008).

Individuals have begun their own physical activity counseling businesses. One business focused on physical activity counseling is Vancouver Island Physical Activity Counseling. Clients use goal setting and journal writing as tools to help them achieve their goals of healthier eating, weight loss, and overall wellness. They also attend workshops, take courses, read books, and watch DVDs ("Services," 2008).

In the UK an exercise referral system has been put in place to help people increase their physical activity. Through this system they may be referred to physical activity advisors (also known as active lifestyle advisors) within their cities. Physical activity advisors then provide support in face-to-face situations, which can help people become more motivated to exercise and understand the benefits of physical activity ("Physical Activity Advisors," 2008).

Physical activity counselors also provide exercise counseling as part of research projects funded by government agencies through nonprofit organizations or universities. The counselor may be part of a research team that analyzes the effects of cognitive-behavioral intervention on increasing physical activity in a certain population. Programs have been developed to provide physical activity counseling for people with type 2 diabetes, geriatric populations, and cancer patients.

One emerging area of research that may provide applied opportunities for students in the area of physical activity counseling is physical activity counseling for new mothers. Recent research has found physical activity counseling to be effective in increasing physical activity of new mothers (Cramp & Brawley, 2006).

> *The area of applied exercise psychology has explosive potential for private practitioners.*
>
> **Mark Anshel** (2006, p. 180)

Physical Activity Consultants for Communities

Physical activity consultants are hired by government or nonprofit agencies to promote physical activity in the community. This job has developed out of the need to help people become more physically active. In the United States, this type of position is often as a state physical activity coordinator. Recently the Centers for Disease Control in the United States has recommended that each state have a full-time school physical activity coordinator in order to promote physical activity ("Healthy Youth," 2006).

In New Zealand, an organization devoted to increasing physical activity is Sport Southland, which is part of 17 regional centers throughout New Zealand ("Health and Physical Activity," 2008). This organization has numerous physical activity managers and consultants who focus on helping people in the region become more physically active.

Directors of Physical Activity Promotion Programs

As nonprofit, state, and government organizations have begun to focus on program development related to physical activity promotion, individuals have been hired to direct these programs. A program director at a university might manage a physical activity intervention with a school district to help increase students' physical activity. Senior Services is a nonprofit agency that has a coordinator who directs a program focused on increasing physical activity of older adults. The program is called Physical Activity for a Lifetime of Success (PALS). The program director coordinates volunteers who are recruited to provide telephone support to older adults beginning a physical activity program. The volunteers focus on helping the exercisers set goals ("PALS," 2008).

Researchers in Psychology of Physical Activity

Another job area related to exercise psychology is research. As more projects obtain grant funding to analyze how people can be helped to become more active, university and nonprofit organizations are hiring individuals to be part of research staffs. An example of this type of position might be a person hired by a research center at a university that provides a physical activity program to the community. That person would coordinate the implementation of the program and collect, analyze, and evaluate data about the program.

The Short of It

- Individuals with training in sport and exercise psychology can help people increase their daily physical activity and become healthier through the use of research-based interventions, such as goal setting, social support, and coaching.
- Programs focused on helping people become more physically active are found in a variety of settings: fitness centers, employee worksites, government agencies, and private organizations.
- Students can apply their knowledge of exercise psychology in jobs such as wellness coach, physical activity counselor, physical activity advisor, physical activity program coordinator, and physical activity researcher.

The Future of Sport and Exercise Psychology

The field of sport and exercise psychology has come a long way since I was a graduate student at Michigan State University from 1991 to 1993. During my first year of graduate school, I was asked about my future plans. At that point I did not have a clear vision of what I could do. An administrative assistant told me that it would all turn out okay and that everyone in our field eventually ended up becoming a professor. Although that comment was meant as encouragement, I was not sure that I wanted to teach. At that time, there really was not much talk of all the related jobs that a master's degree in sport psychology could provide. Luckily, I found that my passion was to study, research, and teach in the field of sport psychology. Notice I did not say sport and *exercise* psychology. At that time there was not really much discussion of exercise psychology, and I cannot recall much discussion of the jobs of wellness coach, physical activity advisor, or physical activity counselor. I eventually realized that there really is a crucial field of applied exercise psychology. Throughout this book you've discovered interventions that you may decide to use one day as you help people improve their adherence to exercise. You may decide to pursue a career related to exercise psychology and help society benefit from increased physical activity.

When I left Michigan State in the summer of 1993 and moved to Morgantown, West Virginia, to pursue my doctorate, I still did not have a clear vision of how my career would progress. At West Virginia University I started to develop a clearer understanding of the training involved in becoming a professor in sport psychology through the mentoring of my professors, who challenged me to think about where our field was and where we were going. As a student, I listened to my mentors and asked questions about the field and the status of the field. Dr. Andy Ostrow inspired me to move beyond asking questions about why things were the way they were and instead work to find solutions to the problems that are in front of us. My mentors challenged me to think about the professional issues related to proper training in sport psychology and job opportunities. My hope is that this book will inspire you to pursue a career in sport and exercise psychology and to find answers to your questions.

During my doctoral program, my colleagues and I met on Friday mornings to discuss the profession of sport psychology. I remember feeling that our profession was not yet focused on addressing job opportunities (or lack thereof) in the field.

But through this book you now have information about these jobs and the theories and practical applications that support these jobs.

I hope that you can continue to advance the field of sport and exercise psychology and provide services to athletes, coaches, sport organizations, and exercisers. I hope also that you are encouraged by all the possibilities that are emerging in the field. Clearly, this field has much to offer athletes, coaches, sport organizations, and, probably most important, the general population.

As you have learned in reading this book, sport psychologists and mental training consultants play important roles in helping athletes and teams perform better. Sport psychologists teach mental training skills such as goal setting, imagery, relaxation, concentration, and self-talk, which help enhance the performance of athletes. Sport psychologists work with coaches and teams on team building and creating positive sport environments. Some sport psychologists counsel athletes during recovery from injury, and others are specially trained to deal with clinical issues in the athlete population, such as eating disorders or depression.

You might become interested in teaching life skills through sports, counseling athletes, providing performance lifestyle advising to athletes, or providing physical activity counseling to the general public. As a graduate student, you might want to take courses in the theoretical aspects of exercise psychology as well as course work dealing with applied exercise psychology. You might want to pursue course work involving life skills training and performance lifestyle services for athletes. By making these areas an integral part of your training, you will have opened up more job opportunities for yourself.

As more students seek training in these areas, research in life skills training for athletes and the applied aspects of exercise psychology will continue. As more applied job opportunities for students in sport and exercise psychology emerge, you can add to the knowledge base of the field by focusing graduate research studies on ways to provide exercise counseling to help the general population increase their levels of physical activity. These types of jobs will only become more important as technology becomes an even more prominent part of our daily lives.

People worldwide need to know about the great things that our field has to offer. This has already begun over the past four decades, but there is still much more work to be done. If you decide to practice in the field, undoubtedly a major focus of your work will be on building relationships with youth, high school, university, professional, and elite sport organizations so that they can understand how useful your consulting work can be.

As you have learned about the various interventions and the theories that support the interventions, you may be thinking about how you can find employment that allows you to provide these services. As you pursue your studies in this exciting field, you may find yourself building relationships with professional and university sport organizations in order to apply sport and exercise psychology interventions. As a student, keep in mind the importance of appropriate qualifications in the field. Sport and exercise psychology organizations in many nations have made great progress in dealing with professional issues. If you decide to continue your training in the field at the graduate level, you may want to pursue a degree that is multidisciplinary in nature.

The Internet has been instrumental in the advancement of our profession; it allows us to understand ideas from sport psychology practitioners throughout the world. Excellent sources of information can be found through the Web sites of professional sport psychology organizations. You may be interested in professional networking sites such as linkedin.com that sport psychology professionals worldwide are currently using. The sport psychology listserv (see Appendix A, p. 137) was developed in 1987 by Professor Michael Sachs of Temple University. During my time in graduate school it became influential in students' understanding of the professional issues presented in this book and, in some ways, the same professional issues are still being discussed today.

The use of technology will continue to grow in the field. Laptop computers are a common tool among practitioners. In the future of sport and exercise psychology consultation, videoconferencing and telephone consulting will probably become more common. Also, many more athletes, coaches, exercisers, and sport psychology professionals will have cell phones that have access to the Internet. This will invariably change the profession of sport and exercise psychology by increasing the demand for Web-based support and consulting.

I hope this book has helped you begin your journey of finding out more about the field of sport and exercise psychology. Good luck in your career pursuits.

Appendix A

Learn More About Sport and Exercise Psychology

Books

▶ Burke, K.L., Sachs, M.L., Fry, A., & Schweighardt, S. (2008). *Directory of graduate programs in applied sport psychology* (9th ed.). Morgantown, WV: Fitness Information Technology.

A resource for graduate students and practitioners. It lists graduate programs, internships, and career opportunities. It also discusses certification and licensure requirements and other concerns in the field.

▶ Lox, C.L., Martin Ginis, K.A., & Petruzzello, S.J. (2006). *The psychology of exercise: Integrating theory and practice* (2nd ed.). Scottsdale, AZ: Holcomb Hathaway.

An introduction to the field of exercise psychology.

▶ Silva, J.M., Metzler, J.N., & Lerner, B.S. (2007). *Training professionals in the practice of sport psychology.* Morgantown, WV: Fitness Information Technology.

A resource with information about the various professional issues in the field of sport psychology.

▶ United States Olympic Committee Sport Psychology Staff. (2002). *Sport psychology mental training manual.* Colorado Springs, CO: United States Olympic Committee.

An overview of various mental training techniques. It contains many examples and exercises in mental training.

▶ Weinberg, R.S., & Gould, D. (2007). *Foundations of sport and exercise psychology* (4th ed.). Champaign, IL: Human Kinetics.

An excellent introduction to the theory and practice of sport and exercise psychology.

▶ Williams, J.M. (Ed.). (2006). *Applied sport psychology: Personal growth to peak performance* (6th ed.). Boston: McGraw-Hill.

A practical guide to help graduate students and practitioners learn about the applied aspects of sport and exercise psychology.

▶ Wooden, J., & Jamison, S. (2007). *The essential Wooden: A lifetime of lessons on leaders and leadership.* New York: McGraw-Hill.

An overview of former UCLA basketball coach John Wooden's approaches to leadership, motivation, and team building.

Journal Articles

▶ Bennett, G. (2007). The role of a clinical psychologist in a Division I athletic program. *Journal of Clinical Sport Psychology, 1,* 261-269.

Information for students on working as a sport psychologist in a Division I athletic program.

▶ Fletcher, D., & Bisig, T.B. (2006). Mental conditioning at the world's toughest playground. *Sport and Exercise Scientist, 8,* 22-23.

A description of an applied sport psychology internship at the IMG Academies.

▶ Morris, T., Alfermann, D., Lintunen, T., & Hall, H. (2003). Training and selection of sport psychologists: An international review. *International Journal of Sport and Exercise Psychology, 1,* 139-154.

A review of information related to the training of sport psychologists throughout the world.

▶ Taylor, J. (2008). Prepare to succeed: Private consulting in applied sport psychology. *Journal of Clinical Sport Psychology, 2,* 160-177.

Information about starting a private practice in sport psychology.

▶ Williams, J.M., & Scherzer, C.B. (2003). Tracking the training and careers of graduates of advanced degree programs in sport psychology, 1994 to 1999. *Journal of Applied Sport Psychology, 15,* 335-353.

An overview of where graduate students in the field of sport and exercise psychology are working.

Web Sites

▶ English Institute of Sport Performance Lifestyle Section
www.eis2win.co.uk/pages/wha_pri_ace_01_home.aspx

Information about the role of the Performance Lifestyle support service at the English Institute of Sport.

▶ International Society of Sport Psychology
www.issponline.org

Information about the main international organization in the field of sport psychology.

▶ North American Society for the Psychology of Sport and Physical Activity
www.naspspa.org

Information about the professional activities of this organization.

▶ Sport and Exercise Science New Zealand
www.sesnz.org.nz

Information about accreditation for sport psychology and mental skills training in New Zealand.

▶ SportPsychology.com
http://sportpsychology.com

Information about the field of sport psychology.

Listservs

▶ APA Division 47 Listserv
www.apa47.org/aboutListserv.php

Information about the field of sport psychology.

▶ SportPsy Listserv
www.lsoft.com/scripts/wl.exe?SL1=SPORTPSY&H=LISTSERV.TEMPLE.EDU

Information and a discussion board about the field of sport psychology.

Appendix B

Implementing Sport and Exercise Psychology in the Real World

Academic Athletic Counselor

☐ How can sport psychology be helpful for athletic counselors? There are many ways in which sport psychology ideas can be helpful for those working with high school and college student-athletes. Communicating positively with the student-athletes you are working with is crucial. Let them know that you understand and can empathize with the stress they may be experiencing. Help them remain positive and focused. Teach them how to set daily and weekly academic goals.

☐ Help the athletes that you are working with develop their own personal vision and mission for where they want to go and explore the wide variety of career options available to them. Help them avoid a foreclosed identity or an overly exclusive athletic identity. Allow them to make their own decisions and to take responsibility for their decisions. Focus on helping the student-athletes you work with develop an internal locus of control.

☐ While working with student-athletes, it is likely that you will hear about their personal issues, career concerns, and academic concerns. It is important for you to be aware of any mental health issues that student-athletes may be dealing with and refer them to a campus mental health professional if necessary. You will be more prepared to make necessary referrals if you develop an excellent working relationship with a local sport psychologist or other psychologists and counselors.

☐ Make sure to focus your work not only on making sure the athletes that you are working with stay eligible to compete in their sport, but on teaching them important life skills.

Athlete

☐ Do you want to reach your highest level of athletic performance? Do you dream of becoming an all-star or a champion? Mental training is an important part of the process of becoming a champion. It is important not only to train technically, tactically, and physically for your sport, but also to train mentally.

☐ To train mentally, use a psychological skills training approach. Determine where you are athletically, where you want to go, and how you are going to achieve your goals.

☐ Use goal setting after you have assessed your technical, tactical, physical, and mental abilities. It is important to set daily short-term goals. This will allow you to focus on getting better each day. When setting goals, try to use performance and process goals (see chapter 3). Outcome goals, such as setting a goal to win a game, are not as effective because they are not under your control.

☐ Once you have assessed your skills and identified your goals, incorporate the use of mental skills into your routine to help achieve a high level of performance.

☐ With the use of goal setting, develop a plan to improve technically, tactically, physically, and mentally in your sport. Focus on putting in the effort day in and day out to achieve your goals.

☐ In practice begin to develop and use both physical and mental routines. Try to develop these routines in practice so that in competition, when you are faced with distractions, your routines can help you stay focused on the process of performance.

☐ After learning mental skills in practice, try to use skills such as visualization, self-talk, concentration, and relaxation in competition.

☐ Continue to self-monitor your goals and practice incorporating mental training along with your physical, technical, and tactical training throughout your athletic career.

Athletic Coach

☐ Do you struggle to build team cohesion among your athletes? Do you yell at athletes when they make a mistake? A better way to work with athletes is to use a cooperative approach in which you build trust.

☐ Try the compliment sandwich approach to instructing athletes. Let your athletes know what they did well, let them know what they can do next time to improve their performance, then provide a motivational statement to keep the athletes practicing and focused on improving their athletic performance.

☐ Help athletes focus on the process of performance rather than the outcome and on reaching their own potential. Help them set regular goals focused on improving their own technical, tactical, physical, and mental performance. This way your athletes will strive to reach their potential whatever that potential may ultimately be.

☐ Develop a positive atmosphere where you value athletes' thoughts and concerns.

☐ Teach your athletes keep winning in perspective and to strive to win, but not at all costs (Martens, 2004). Remember that you are a role model to your athletes and it is important that you behave in a proper way regardless of the outcome of competition.

☐ Appreciate the unique academic, personal, and career concerns of athletes. Encourage your athletes to excel in areas outside of the athletic environment. Let them know that you care about them as more than just athletes.

☐ Help athletes lessen their anxiety by reducing the uncertainty that they face, and by changing the way they view success (Martens, 2004). Help them view success as putting in the effort day in and day out to become as good as they can be.

☐ As a coach it is important to remember that you can also benefit from the same mental skills that you are teaching your athletes. Educate yourself about how you can improve your coaching performance by setting performance and process goals and by learning the skills of visualization, positive self-talk, concentration, and relaxation.

☐ Practice using these skills before, during, and after coaching athletes in practice, as well as in preparation for competitions and during competitions. Use the skills that you are learning to stay emotionally calm before, during, and after competitive events and to manage daily stress.

Athletic Trainer

☐ As an athletic trainer it is important to understand the relationship between life stress and athletic injury. Since high levels of stress can increase the risk of athletic injury, the athletic training professional can help prevent injuries by helping athletes manage their stress. Provide social support to your athletes. Let them know that you care about their concerns. Discuss ways to manage stress with the athletes you work with.

☐ Do you often get upset when your athletes are not making progress toward their rehabilitation goals? Have you tried to motivate athletes to focus on their rehabilitation by using a negative approach? Try to motivate injured athletes by emphasizing the good progress they are making and helping them stay focused on things they can control in their own rehabilitation.

☐ While an athlete is going through the process of rehabilitation remember to listen to the athlete's concerns and be encouraging. Provide the athlete with social support and talk to counselors or psychologists about the possibility of providing support groups for the injured athletes that you work with.

☐ While listening to your athletes' concerns, it is important to understand the ways athletes often experience athletic injury. Remember that injured athletes will often deny that they are injured, and sometimes experience anger and depression.

☐ Be aware of any issues that may require a referral to a licensed mental health professional. Develop close relationships with mental health professionals on your campus or in your community.

☐ Help the athletes that you are working with incorporate mental skills training into their rehabilitation, including concentration, relaxation, goal setting, and visualization. Not only can these skills help in rehabilitation from injury, but they will help athletes in their life outside of athletics and help them improve their athletic skills.

Clinical and Counseling Psychologist and School Psychologist

☐ How can the information in this text be helpful for clinical psychologists? You can implement information about sport and exercise psychology into your private practice or within the school environment, especially when working with athletes. This text provides insights on the issues that athletes deal with on and off the field. By reading the information in this book you have taken an excellent step in familiarizing yourself with the field of sport psychology.

☐ Become familiar with sport psychology organizations in your country. Specifically, if you are a practicing psychologist in the United States, I suggest that you find out about the excellent resources that the Association for Applied Sport Psychology and the American Psychological Association Division 47 have to offer.

☐ If you plan to work with athletes as part of your practice, consider pursuing training in sport psychology. Certifications in nations throughout the world exist to help guide you as you are looking to make sport psychology and mental training for athletes a part of your practice. A specific example is the certification offered by the Association for Applied Sport Psychology (AASP). Training for this certification includes specific sport psychology and sport science course work in addition to completing supervised hours working on mental training for athletes and adherence to physical activity and exercise for nonathletes.

☐ Become familiar with how sport and exercise psychology is being used to help the general population increase their adherence to daily physical activity. Through understanding exercise psychology, psychologists and other mental health professionals can contribute a great deal to society by helping people become more physically active.

Fitness Professional

☐ Do you often see the fitness facility that you work for become very crowded at the beginning of a new year? After a few months is the facility a lot less crowded? Have many of the individuals not renewed their memberships? Ideas from sport and exercise psychology can help people incorporate daily physical activity into their lives.

☐ Apply the stages of change theory in your work with exercisers. Determine what stage of change your client is in and try to match the interventions that you are using to that stage.

☐ Help the clients that you are working with set realistic goals. Keep them focused on daily and weekly goals that emphasize the process of making physical activity a fun and enjoyable daily habit.

☐ Emphasize the importance of fun. Help your clients find activities that they enjoy.

☐ While working with your clients, provide social support and help them overcome barriers to daily exercise. Provide support to your clients to help them change their behavior. Help them understand how to manage their time in order to incorporate daily physical activity.

Physical Education Teacher

☐ Do you control your students' behavior with intimidation and fear? Or are you a submissive physical education teacher who uses a roll-out-the-ball approach to teaching and lets your students do what they want? A cooperative style of leadership, in which you focus on developing a positive relationship with your students, will provide better results. Students may have a more positive outlook about your class if you use a positive leadership style, and in turn you may encourage them to have a more positive view of lifelong physical activity.

☐ Listen to your students and allow them to make decisions related to class. This will allow you to develop a positive classroom environment.

☐ Provide students with instruction that gives them confidence in the physical education classroom. Introduce, demonstrate, and explain sport skills using the IDEA approach to teaching. Focus on providing positive feedback to your students every day. Catch them doing something good and let them know what they are doing well both technically and tactically. Provide students with positive feedback for good behavior in your classroom.

☐ Your physical education students will progress more if they are involved in setting their own goals. Help your students set process and performance goals, because physical education students will have more control over these goals than they have over goals which are outcome based (such as winning a relay or scrimmage). Process goals are goals your physical education students should focus on while performing a sport skill, such as aiming for the backboard shooting square when attempting basketball free throws. A related performance goal would be to improve from making 1 out of 10 free throws to making 4 out of 10 free throws.

Public Health Professional

☐ How can sport and exercise psychology be helpful to you as a public health professional? Knowledge gained from sport and exercise psychology can help lead nations throughout the world toward developing more physically active lifestyles.

☐ You may be very concerned about the sedentary behaviors that many children throughout the world seem to be adopting. We need to make sport and physical activity a fun experience for youth. Sport and exercise psychology can help you understand how to do this by creating positive sport and exercise environments for youth (see chapters 5 and 9).

☐ Create coaching education programs based on sport and exercise psychology knowledge so that more of the world's children can have positive sport experiences. As a result, more children will continue being involved in physical activity and sport throughout their lifetimes.

☐ As a public health professional, you know about the problems of obesity throughout the world. The sport and exercise psychology profession is focused on ways to help individuals throughout the world change their behavior to become more physically active. You may consider helping your states and nation become more physically active by locally promoting campaigns to increase physical activity (such as the Pan-Canadian Physical Activity Strategy, A Healthy and Active Australia, and Sport England).

☐ You can help improve the physical activity level of your nation by incorporating physical activity counselors and wellness coaches into the medical and fitness professions. Excellent examples and models can be seen in the suggestions of Fortier, Tulloch, and Hogg (2006) and the YMCA Coach Approach developed by James Annesi (see chapter 9).

Strength and Conditioning
and Performance Coach

☐ Do you often have athletes that are not motivated at a level that you think they should be? You can motivate athletes to achieve at high levels by stressing confidence and developing a positive relationship with the athletes that you are working with.

☐ Let the athletes you are working with know that you believe they can improve their physical performance. Be a positive strength and conditioning coach by letting athletes know what they are doing well. While coaching your athletes physically, introduce, demonstrate, and explain the skills that you would like them to perform. Say positive things to your athletes so they have a positive mindset when training.

☐ Help your athletes set goals for physical performance. Assess where they are physically and what physical training goals they want to achieve, then work with your athletes to create a training program that will help them try to reach their performance goals. Make sure that while your athletes are improving their physical skills they are focused on what they are trying to achieve and not comparing themselves to other athletes that they may be competing with in terms of strength, speed, or power.

☐ Stress to your athletes the importance of using imagery and positive self-talk in the training process. Also make sure to remind your athletes of the importance of not overtraining and burning out.

☐ Develop close working relationships with athletic coaches and discuss the goals that have been developed for the athletes that you are working with.

☐ Remember that the athletes you are training may have other concerns in their lives in addition to training physically for their sport. Listen to the athletes that you are working with and let them know you care about them.

☐ Watch for signs of substance abuse related to an athlete trying to enhance physical performance (e.g., use of anabolic steroids). Additionally, watch for signs of eating disorders or other issues related to eating correctly while training.

☐ Develop close relationships with mental health professionals and refer athletes appropriately if you recognize issues that you believe may be clinical in nature or may be improved through the help of a mental health professional.

Sport Management and Business Professional

☐ Have you ever been on an athletic team that was not enjoyable to be a part of? If so, what type of environment did the coach of the team create? Have you ever been on an athletic team that was fun to be on? How did the enjoyable experience differ from the experience that was not enjoyable? Most often the reason an athletic team is not enjoyable is the leadership style used by the coach.

☐ Like coaches in an athletic environment, sport management and business professionals can provide an intrinsically motivating and enjoyable work environment. Your leadership approach can make a huge difference in the motivation of your employees. Adopt a style of leadership similar to those of well-known successful coaches like Jim Tressel, Phil Jackson, John Wooden, and Dean Smith (see chapter 5).

☐ Let your employees know how much you care about them and catch them doing good work. When an employee working for you makes a mistake, use it as part of a learning process. Help the individual you are working with analyze the mistake and determine how he or she can improve. Continue to provide encouragement to the individuals under your supervision.

☐ Incorporate team building into your management style. Help build positive task and social cohesion among your employees and colleagues (see chapter 4). Be a teacher and try to find ways to keep the work environment positive.

References

2006 sports medicine sport psychology survey. (2006). Retrieved September 17, 2007, from www.sportsmed.org/secure/reveal/admin/uploads/documents/2006%20Sport%20Psychology%20FINAL%20REPORT%202%2017%2006.pdf.

2007 post draft press conference. (n.d.). Philadelphia 76ers. Retrieved October 14, 2008, from www.nba.com/sixers/draft/2007_draft_press_070630.html.

Abbott, H. (2006, December 18). True Hoop: Phil Jackson Coaching Stories. Retrieved October 14, 2008, from http://myespn.go.com/blogs/truehoop/0-19-65/Phil-Jackson-Coaching-Stories.html.

About applied sport and exercise psychology. (2008). Association for Applied Sport Psychology. Retrieved October 17, 2008, from http://appliedsportpsych.org/about/about-applied-sport-psych.

About ASEP. (2008). Retrieved September 15, 2008, from www.asep.com/about.cfm.

About PCA. (2008). Positive Coaching Alliance. Retrieved October 18, 2008, from www.positivecoach.org/subcontent.aspx?SecID=95.

About performance lifestyle. (2008). Welsh Rugby Union. Retrieved July 19, 2008, from www.wru.co.uk/13674_13681.php.

"Academic coaches" to help student-athletes to score in the classroom. (2008). HISD Connect. Retrieved July 18, 2008, from www.houstonisd.org/HISDConnectDS/v/index.jsp?vgnextoid=dc335c781cf29110VgnVCM10000028147fa6RCRD&vgnextfmt=default.

Adams, B. (2002, January 16). Sports psychologist Joel Fish helps main line athletes think like winners. *Main Line Times*. Retrieved October 18, 2008, from www.zwire.com/site/news.cfm?BRD=1676&dept_id=43829&newsid=3002663&PAG=461&rfi=9.

AFL coach accreditation courses. (2008). Australian Football League. Retrieved September 14, 2008, from www.afl.com.au/News/NEWSARTICLE/tabid/208/Default.aspx?newsId=55403.

Aided freshman athletes: Columbia reveals study experiment during football season. (1930, November 16). *New York Times*, N4.

American College of Sports Medicine (ACSM). (2006). Psychological issues related to injury in athletes and the team physician: A consensus statement. *Medicine and Science in Sports and Exercise, 38*, 2030-2033.

Andersen, M. (2002). Foreword. In J.M. Silva & D.E. Stevens (Eds.), *Psychological foundations of sport* (pp. xiii-xiv). Boston: Allyn & Bacon.

Andersen, M.B. (2002). Helping college student-athletes in and out of sport. In J.L. Van Raalte and B.W. Brewer (Eds.), *Exploring sport and exercise psychology* (2nd ed.) (pp. 373-393). Washington, D.C: American Psychological Association.

Andersen, M.B., Williams, J.M., Aldridge, T., & Taylor, J. (1997). Tracking the training and careers of graduates of advanced degree programs in sport psychology, 1989-1994. *The Sport Psychologist, 11*, 326-344.

Anderson, A., Vogel, P., & Albrecht, R. (1999). The effect of instructional self-talk on the overhand throw. *Physical Educator, 56*, 215-221.

Anderson, R.J. (2004). Down and out. *Training and Conditioning*. Retrieved September 21, 2008, from www.momentummedia.com/articles/tc/tc1408/downout.htm.

Annesi, J.J. (2003). Effects of a cognitive behavioral treatment package on exercise attendance and dropout in fitness centers. *European Journal of Sport Science, 3*, 1-16.

Annesi, J.J., & Unruh, J.L. (2004). Effects of a cognitive behavioral treatment protocol on the dropout rates of exercise participants in 17 YMCA facilities of six cities. *Psychological Reports, 95*, 250-256.

Anshel, M.A. (2006). *Applied exercise psychology: A practitioner's guide to improving client health and fitness*. New York: Springer.

APS college of sport psychologists: About us. (2008). Australian Psychological Society. Retrieved October 12, 2008, from www.groups.psychology.org.au/csp/about_us/.

The art of the free throw: Gilbert Arenas, Washington Wizards. (2007). Retrieved September 15, 2007, from www.nba.com/wizards/news/art_of_the_free_throw.html.

AT&T Classic: Zach Johnson. (2007, May 20). ASAP Sports. Retrieved September 15, 2007, from www.asapsports.com/show_interview.php?id=42996.

Athletic performance: Sport psychology: Helping student-athletes in all aspects of their lives. (2007). Virginia Tech Media Guide. Retrieved September 14, 2008, from www.hokiesports.com/football/2007MG/support.pdf.

Aussie swim coach charges Russian athletes hypnotized. (1957, September 15). *Pacific Stars and Stripes*, p. 20.

Bacon, V.L., Lerner, B.S., Trembley, D., & Seestedt, M. (2005). Substance abuse. In J. Taylor and G. Wilson (Eds.), *Applying sport psychology: Four perspectives* (pp. 229-247). Champaign, IL: Human Kinetics.

Barnhart, T. (2007, July 22). College football: Smart program lifts high school players. *Atlanta Journal Constitution*, 14E.

Batik, O., Phelan, E.A., Walwick, J.A., Wang, G., & LoGerfo, J.P. (2008). Translating a community-based motivational support program to increase physical activity among older adults with diabetes at community clinics: A pilot study of physical activity for a lifetime of success (PALS). *Preventing Chronic Disease*. Retrieved July 21, 2008, from www.cdc.gov/PCD/issues/2008/jan/pdf/07_0142.pdf.

Baugh, F.G., & Benjamin, L.T., Jr. (2006). Walter Miles, Pop Warner, B.C. Graves, and the psychology of football. *Journal of the History of the Behavioral Sciences, 42*, 3-18.

Bauman, J. (2008, August). Sport psychology at the Olympics. DIV47NEWS: Exericse and Sport Psychology Newsletter, *21*(2). Retrieved October 11, 2008, from www.apa47.org/pdfs/summer08newsletter.pdf

Bean, C.H. (1927). Job-analyzing athletics. *Journal of Applied Psychology*, 11, 369-380.

Beckmann, J., & Kellmann, M. (2003). Procedures and principles of sport psychological assessment. *The Sport Psychologist, 17*, 338-350.

Become a certified consultant. (2007). Association for Applied Sport Psychology. Retrieved August 30, 2008, from www.aaasponline.org/consultants/become-certified.

Bennett, G.T. (2007). The role of a clinical psychologist in a Division I athletic program. *Journal of Clinical Sport Psychology, 1*, 261-269.

Berra, Y., & Kaplan, D. (2001). *When you come to a fork in the road: Take it*. New York: Hyperion.

Big athletes alert, speedy as small men, coach proves. (1931, January 9). *Charleston Gazette*, p. 2.

Blair, S.N., Applegate, W.B., Dunn, A.L., Ettinger, W.H., Haskell, W.L., King, A.C., Morgan, T.M., Shih, J.H., & Simons-Morton, D.G. (1998). Activity counseling trial (ACT): Rationale, design, and methods. *Medicine and Science in Sports and Exercise, 30*, 1097-1106.

Bloom, G., & Stevens, D.E. (2002). Case study: A team-building mental skills training program with an intercollegiate equestrian team. *Athletic Insight, 4*(1). Retrieved September 15, 2007, from www.athleticinsight.com/Vol4Iss1/EquestrianTeamBuilding.htm.

Brannon, E.W. (1913, December 14). The psychology of football: Dr. Wolfe of the University of Nebraska illustrates his new theory using three 1913 Cornhuskers stars to prove it. *Lincoln Daily Star*, p. 14.

Breckon, J.D., Johnston, L.H., & Hutchinson, A. (2008). Physical activity counseling content and competency: A systematic review. *Journal of Physical Activity and Health, 5*, 398-417.

Brewer, B.W. (1998). Psychological applications in clinical sports medicine: Current status and future directions. *Journal of Clinical Psychology in Medical Settings, 5*, 91-102.

Brewer, B.W. (2000). Doing sport psychology in the coaching role. In M.B. Anderson (Ed.), *Doing sport psychology* (pp. 237-247). Champaign, IL: Human Kinetics.

Brewer, B.W., & Petitpas, A.J. (2005). Returning to self: The anxieties of coming back after injury. In M.B. Andersen (Ed.), *Sport psychology in practice* (pp. 93-108). Champaign, IL: Human Kinetics.

Brewer, B.W., & Petrie, T.A. (2002). Psychopathology in sport and exercise. In J.L. Van Raalte and B.W. Brewer (Eds.), *Exploring sport and exercise psychology* (2nd ed.) (pp. 307-323). Washington, D.C.: American Psychological Association.

Broughton, E., & Neyer, M. (2001). Advising and counseling student-athletes. *New Directions for Student Services, 93*, 47-53.

Brown, C. (2005). Injuries: The psychology of recovery and rehab. In. S. Murphy (Ed.), *The sport psych handbook* (pp. 215-235). Champaign, IL: Human Kinetics.

BU Athletic Enhancement Center. (2007). Retrieved September 14, 2007, from www.bu.edu/aec.

Buckworth, J., & Dishman, R.K. (2002). *Exercise psychology*. Champaign, IL: Human Kinetics.

Burke, K.L., Sachs, M.L., Fry, A., & Schweighardt, S. (2008). *Directory of graduate programs in applied sport psychology* (9th ed.). Morgantown, WV: Fitness Information Technology.

Burton, D., & Raedeke, T.D. (2008). *Sport psychology for coaches*. Champaign, IL: Human Kinetics.

Campbell, B. Jr. (1930, March 1). Help! Aid! Also, assistance! Grizzlies are going to pick quarter thru psychology. *Helena and Daily Independent*, p. 8.

Campbell, E., & Ruane, J. (1999). *The Earl Campbell story: A football great's battle with panic disorder*. Toronto: ECW Press.

Canada's Sports Hall of Fame. (n.d.). Honoured members: Lloyd Percival. Retrieved October 14, 2008, from www.cshof.ca/accessible/hm_profile.php?i=386.

Career counseling for elite performers. (2008). Victoria University. Retrieved July 19, 2008, from www.staff.vu.edu.au/cc4ep/source/FlyerFinal.pdf.

Career development program. (2008). National Basketball Players Assocation. Retrieved October 18, 2008, from www.nbpa.com/nbpanbaed_pub.php.

Careers and education. (2008). Australian Sports Commission. Retrieved July 19, 2008, from www.ausport.gov.au/participating/athletes/career_and_education.

Carodine, K., Almond, K.F., & Gratto, K.K. (2001). College student-athlete success both in out of the classroom. *New Directions for Student Service, 93*, 19-33.

Carr, C. (2007, Fall). Growing pains. *Division 47: Exercise and Sport Psychology Newsletter, 20*(3), 1. Retrieved November 8, 2008, from www.apa47.org/pdfs/2007%20Fall%20ESPNews.pdf.

Carron, A.V., Colman, M.M., Wheeler, J., & Stevens, D. (2002). Cohesion and performance in sport: A meta analysis. *Journal of Sport and Exercise Psychology, 24*, 168-188.

Carron, A.V., & Dennis, P.W. (1998). The sport team as an effective group. In J.M. Williams (Ed.). *Applied sport psychology: Personal growth to peak performance* (pp. 127-141). Mountain View, CA: Mayfield Publishing.

Carron, A.V., Spink, K.S., & Prappevessis, H. (1997). Team building and cohesiveness in the sport and exercise setting: Use of indirect interventions. *Journal of Applied Sport Psychology, 9*, 61-72.

Carron, A.V., Widmeyer, W.N., & Brawley, L.R. (1985). The development of an instrument to assess cohesion in sport teams: The group environment questionnaire. *Journal of Sport Psychology, 7*, 244-266.

Carter, J.E. (2005). Sport psychology: Locker room confessions. In R.D. Morgan, T.L. Kuther, & C.J. Habben (Eds.), *Life after graduate school in psychology: Insider's advice from new psychologists* (pp. 275-287). New York: Psychology Press.

CHAMPS/Life Skills: Frequently Asked Questions. (n.d.). National Collegiate Athletic Association. Retrieved October 16, 2008, from www.ncaa.org/wps/ncaa?ContentID=32329.

Chappell, M. (2006, February 27). Combine prospects also subject to psychological testing. *USA Today*. Retrieved September 16, 2007, from www.usatoday.com/sports/football/draft/2006-02-27-psych-testing_x.htm.

Chelladurai, P., & Saleh, S.D. (1980). Dimensions of leader behavior in sports: Development of a leadership scale. *Journal of Sport Psychology, 2*, 34-45.

Cogan, K.D. (2005). Eating disorders: When rations become irrational. In S.M. Murphy (Ed.), *The sport psych handbook* (pp. 237-253). Champaign, IL: Human Kinetics.

Consultant Finder. (2008). British Association of Sport and Exercise Sciences. Retrieved October 17, 2008, from www.bases.org.uk/consfinder.asp?a=list&dbtAccredCategory=&dbtSpecialisation=Sport+Psychologist&dbtSpecialistPopulation=&dbtSports=&dbtArea=.

Cornelius, A. (2002). Psychological interventions for the injured athlete. In J.M. Silva & D.E. Stevens (Eds.), *Psychological foundations of sport* (pp. 224-246). Boston: Allyn and Bacon.

Cox, R.H. (2007). *Sport psychology: Concepts and applications* (6th ed.). New York: McGraw-Hill.

Cramp, A.G., & Brawley, L.R. (2006). Moms in motion: A group-mediated cognitive-behavioral physical activity intervention. *International Journal of Behaviorial Nutrition and Physical Activity, 3*, 23.

Curry, J. (2005, April 14). Steinbrenner hires a motivational coach (no laughing). *New York Times*, D2.

Dale, G. (2003). *Coach's guide to teambuilding* [DVD]. Ames, IA: Championship Productions.

Dale, G., & Conant, S. (2005). *101 teambuilding activities: Ideas every coach can use to enhance teamwork, communication, and trust.* Durham, NC: Excellence in Performance.

Deaner, H., & Silva, J.M. (2002). Personality and sport performance. In J.M. Silva & D.E. Stevens (Eds.), *Psychological foundations of sport* (pp. 48-65). Boston: Allyn & Bacon.

DiCicco, T., Hacker, C., & Salzberg, C. (2002). *Catch them being good: Everything you need to know to successfully coach girls.* New York: Viking.

Dishman, R.K., & Buckworth, J. (2006). Exercise psychology. In J.M. Williams (Ed.), *Applied sport psychology: Personal growth to peak performance* (pp. 616-647). Boston: McGraw-Hill.

Dorfman, H.A. (2003). *Coaching the mental game: Leadership philosophies and strategies for peak performance in sports and everyday life.* New York: Taylor.

Dorfman, H.A., & Kuehl, K. (1995). *The mental game of baseball: A guide to peak performance* (2nd ed.). South Bend, IN: Diamond Communications.

Doss-Antoun, J. (2006, September 28). Visualizations key for Bronco cross country. *The Santa Clara*. Retrieved September 15, 2007, from http://media.www.thesantaclara.com/media/storage/paper946/news/2006/09/28/Sports/Visualizations.Key.For.Bronco.Cross.Country-2314036.shtml?norewrite200610170553&sourcedomain=www.thesantaclara.com.

Driediger, M., Hall, C., & Callow, N. (2006). Imagery use by injured athletes: A qualitative analysis. *Journal of Sport Sciences, 24*, 261-272.

Durand, V.M., & Barlow, D.H. (2006). *Essentials of abnormal psychology* (4th ed.). Belmont, CA: Thomson Wadsworth.

Ellis, A. (1962). *Reason and emotion in psychotherapy.* New York: Lyle Stuart.

Ellis, A. (1994). The sport of avoiding sports and exercise. A rational emotive behavior therapy perspective. *The Sport Psychologist, 8,* 248-261.

Equivalence. (n.d.). Sport and Exercise Science New Zealand. Retrieved September 2, 2008, from www.sesnz.org.nz/sess/equivalence.html.

Esfarjani, B. (2006, May 22). Coaches focus on academics. *USA Today.* Retrieved October 16, 2008, from www.usatoday.com/sports/college/other/2006-05-21-play-it-smart_x.htm?loc=interstitialskip.

Etzel, E.F., Watson, J.C., Visek, A.J., & Maniar, S.D. (2006). Understanding and promoting college student-athlete health: Essential issues for student affairs professionals. *NASPA Journal, 43,* 518-546.

Ewing, M.E., & Seefeldt, V. (1989). *Participation and attrition patterns in American agency-sponsored and interscholastic sports: An executive summary.* North Palm Beach, FL: Sporting Goods Manafacturer's Association.

Exercise (physical activity) counseling. (2007). Retrieved September 20, 2007, from www.american-heart.org/presenter.jhtml?identifier=4534.

Fales, E.D. (1952, July 20). A good athlete? Today? Science may pry the secret from your eyes. *Parade,* 7.

Ferrante, A.P, Etzel, E.F., & Lantz, C. (1996). Counseling college student-athletes: The problem, the need. In E.F. Etzel, A.P. Ferrante, & J.W. Pinkney (Eds.). *Counseling college student-athletes: Issues and interventions* (2nd ed.) (pp. 3-24). Morgantown, WV: Fitness Information Technology.

Find a certified consultant. (2008). Association of Applied Sport Psychology. Retrieved October 17, 2008, from http://appliedsportpsych.org/consultants/find-a-consultant.

Fitness coach training program. (2007). Retrieved September 27, 2007, from www.wellcoach.com/index.cfm?t=44222c233f55303f2b493d2b593250403f3e3c4c213540423e37255a595d482a5a434836394440494e5d583d3853332f5f0a.

Fletcher, D., & Bisig, T.B. (2006). Mental conditioning at the world's toughest playground. *Sport and Exercise Scientist, 8,* 22-23.

Floeckher, P. (2007, February 7). Sport psychologists and graduate students help prospects prepare for NFL Combine. Retrieved October 14, 2008, from http://news.georgiasouthern.edu/viewArticle.php?id=265.

Fortier, M., Tulloch, H., & Hogg, W. (2006). A good fit: Integrating physical activity counselors into family practice. *Canadian Family Physician.* Retrieved October 16, 2008, from www.pubmedcentral.nih.gov/picrender.fcgi?artid=1781505&blobtype=pdf.

Fuchs, A.H. (1998). Psychology and the Babe. *Journal of the History of the Behaviorial Sciences, 34,* 153-165.

Fullerton, H.S. (1921). Why Babe Ruth is greatest home-run hitter. *Popular Science Monthly, 99*(4), 19-21, 110. Retrieved September 16, 2007, from http://psychclassics.yorku.ca/Fullerton.

Gardiner, A. (2006). Surfacing from depression. *USA Today.* Retrieved from www.usatoday.com/news/health/2006-02-05-womens-health-depression_x.htm.

Gardner, F.L. (2007). Introduction to the special issue: Clinical sport psychology in American intercollegiate athletics. *Journal of Clinical Sport Psychology, 1,* 207-209.

Gardner, F., & Moore, Z. (2006). *Clinical sport psychology.* Champaign, IL: Human Kinetics.

Generalized anxiety disorder (GAD). (2008). National Institute of Mental Health. Retrieved July 20 2008, from www.nimh.nih.gov/health/topics/generalized-anxiety-disorder-gad/index.shtml.

Gleeson-Kreig, J.M. (2006). Self-monitoring of physical activity: Effects on self-efficacy and behavior in people with type 2 diabetes. *The Diabetes Educator, 32,* 69-77.

Goddard, M. (2004). An assessment of the effectiveness of the CHAMPS/Life Skills program at the University of North Texas. *Dissertation Abstracts International, 65*(03), 776.

Gould, D. (2002). Moving beyond the psychology of athletic excellence. *Journal of Applied Sport Psychology, 14*, 247-248.

Gould,D., Guinan, D., Greenleaf, C., Medbery, R., & Peterson, K. (1999). Factors affecting Olympic performance: Perceptions of athletes and coaches from more and less successful teams. *The Sport Psychologist, 13*, 371-394.

Gould, D., & Pick, S. (1995). Sport psychology: The Griffith era, 1920-1940. *The Sport Psychologist, 9*, 391-405.

Gould, D., & Udry, E. (1994). Psychological skills for enhancing performance: Arousal regulation strategies. *Medicine and Science in Sports and Exercise, 26*, 478-485.

Grabmeier, J. (2002, August 23). About 15 percent of major college athletes may have symptoms of eating disorders, study suggests. Retrieved September 18, 2007, from http://researchnews.osu.edu/archive/athlteat.htm.

Grant, E. (2005, December 4). Inside Scott Boras Corporation. *Dallas Morning News*. Retrieved September 14, 2007, from www.dallasnews.com/sharedcontent/dws/spt/baseball/rangers/stories/120405dnspoborastrinkets.259f7ba.html.

Green, C.D. (2003). Psychology strikes out: Coleman Griffith and the Chicago Cubs. *History of Psychology, 6*, 267-283.

Greenspan, M.J., & Andersen, M.B. (1995). Providing psychological services to student-athletes: A developmental psychology approach. In S.M. Murphy (Ed.). *Sport psychology interventions* (pp. 177-191). Champaign, IL: Human Kinetics.

Greenspan, M., & Feltz, D.L. (1989). Psychological interventions with athletes in competitive situations: A review. *The Sport Psychologist, 3*, 219-236.

Hack, B. (2005). Qualifications: Education and experience. In S. Murphy (Ed.), *The sport psych handbook* (pp. 293-304). Champaign, IL: Human Kinetics.

Hack, B. (2007). The development and delivery of sport psychology services within a university sports medicine department. *Journal of Clinical Sport Psychology, 1*, 247-260.

Hacker, C. (2000a). Sports psych: Team building 101. Retrieved September 15, 2007, from http://eteamz.active.com/soccer/instruction/psych/article.cfm?article=tb101.

Hacker, C. (2000b). Sports psych: Team building—article 1. Retrieved September 15, 2007, from http://eteamz.active.com/soccer/instruction/psych/article.cfm?article=tb0400.

Hacker, C.M. (2001a). Women's World Cup: Performance enhancement through mental skills training. *Professional Psychology: Research and Practice, 31*, 363-364.

Hacker, C.M. (2001b). The quest for gold: Applied psychological skills training in the 1996 Olympic Games. *Journal of Excellence, 4*, 5-20.

Hall, C.R., Rodgers, W.M., & Barr, K.A. (1990). The use of imagery by athletes in selected sports. *The Sport Psychologist, 4*, 1-10.

Hamson-Utley, J.J., Martin, S., & Walters, J. (2008). Athletic trainers' and physical therapists perceptions of the effectiveness of psychological skills within sport injury rehabilitation programs. *Journal of Athletic Training, 43*, 258-264.

Handling the pressure: Four NBA greats dish out advice on dealing with the finals spotlight for the first time. (2007). NBA Encyclopedia: Playoff Edition. Retrieved September 15, 2007, from www.nba.com/encyclopedia/finals/Handling_Pressure.html.

Harding, T. (2006, June 1). Draft a study in preparation: Many future draftees surprised by level of team preparation. Retrieved September 17, 2008, from http://mlb.mlb.com/news/article.jsp?ymd=20060601&content_id=1483531&vkey=news_mlb&fext=.jsp&c_id=mlb.

Harding, T. (2007, April 26). Seeing success, and achieving it: Visualization methods help rookie pitcher Hirsh. Retrieved October 17, 2008, from http://colorado.rockies.mlb.com/news/article.jsp?ymd=20070426&content_id=1931524&vkey=news_col&fext=.jsp&c_id=col.

Harr, E. (2003, May). Working fun into your fitness: If you want to eat right and exercise for a lifetime, you must get some pleasure out of it. Here's how to create a diet and exercise plan you'll actually enjoy—Get motivated. *Shape*. Retrieved from http://findarticles.com/p/articles/mi_m0846/is_9_22/ai_100106597.

Harris, D. (2006a, July 2). NCAA athletes slowly accepting mental wellness' role in careers. *Dayton Daily News*, A6. Retrieved September 26, 2008, from www.redorbit.com/news/health/558647/ncaa_athletes_slowly_accepting_mental_wellness_role_in_careers/index.html.

Harris, D. (2006b, July 2). More OSU athletes seeking help from sport psychologists. *Dayton Daily News*, A1.

Harwood, C. (2008). Developmental consulting in a professional football academy: The 5 Cs coaching efficacy program. *The Sport Psychologist, 22*, 109-133.

Health and physical activity. (2008). Sport Southland. Retrieved July 22, 2008, from http://sportsouthland.co.nz/index.cfm/programmes/health___physical_activity.

Healthy youth. (2006). Centers for Disease Control. Retrieved October 19, 2008, from www.cdc.gov/healthyYouth/PhysicalActivity/promoting_health/strategies/school.htm.

Heaney, C.A. (2006). Recommendations for successfully integrating sport psychology into athletic therapy. *Athletic Therapy Today, 11*, 60-62.

Hellmich, N. (2006, February 5). Athletes' hunger to win fuels eating disorders. *USA Today*. Retrieved from www.usatoday.com/news/health/2006-02-05-women-health-cover_x.htm.

Hill, C.E. Jr. (2001, February 22). Cowboys notes. *Fort Worth Star-Telegram*, p. 5.

Holmes, J. (2007, May 20). Mental toughness secures Johnson's place in the big time. Retrieved September 15, 2007, from www.pgatour.com/2007/r/05/20/zjohnson.sider/index.html.

Holt, N.L., & Dunn, J.G.H. (2006). Guidelines for delivering personal-disclosure mutual-sharing teambuilding interventions. *The Sport Psychologist, 20*, 348-367.

Hosick, M. B. (2005a, March 14). Psychology of sport more than performance enhancement. *NCAA News Online*. Retrieved October 14, 2008, from www1.ncaa.org/membership/ed_outreach/health-safety/psychologyofsport.pdf.

Hosick, M.B. (2005b, February 28). Forum places psychological focus on mental-health issues. *NCAA News*. Retrieved from www1.ncaa.org/membership/ed_outreach/health-safety/forummentalhealthpdf.pdf.

Howden, S. (2006, April 14). The science behind the commonwealth triumphs. *Edinburgh Evening News*. Retrieved July 25, 2008, from http://sport.scotsman.com/commonwealthgames/The-science-behind-the-Commonwealth.2764494.jp.

Hu, J. (2006, June 21). NBA Finals: Miami—Nice! MVP Wade leads the Heat to first championship. *San Francisco Chronicle*. Retrieved July 18, 2007, from www.sfgate.com/cgi-bin/article.cgi?f=/c/a/2006/06/21/SPG8JJHNPS1.DTL.

Hudgens, M. (2008, May 18). Unity council will prove crucial to Huskers' success. Retrieved September 24, 2008, from www.realfootball365.com/index.php/articles/nebraska/11257.

Intermediate coaching general principles. (2008). Australian Sports Commission. Retrieved September 14, 2008, from www.ausport.gov.au/__data/assets/pdf_file/0006/181698/Intermediate_GP_fact_sheet_low_res.pdf.

Jackson, P., & Delehanty, H. (1995). *Sacred hoops: Spiritual lessons of a hardwood warrior*. New York: Hyperion.

Janssen Peak Performance. (2005). Retrieved November 22, 2006, from www.jeffjanssen.com.

Janssen Peak Performance. (2007). Retrieved September 16, 2007, from www.jeffjanssen.com/coaching/about.html.

Janssen, J. (2002). *Championship team building: What every coach needs to know to build a motivated, committed, and cohesive team*. Cary, NC: Winning the Mental Game.

Joel H. Fish, PhD, Director. (n.d.). Center for Sport Psychology. Retrieved September 16, 2008, from www.psychologyofsport.com/index.html.

Jones, G. (2002). Performance excellence: A personal perspective on the link between sport and business. *Journal of Applied Sport Psychology, 4*, 268-281.

Jones, T. (2007, February 27). Teams go to great lengths to scout players' character. *Columbus Dispatch*. Retrieved September 16, 2007, from www.dispatch.com/dispatch/contentbe/dispatch/2007/02/27/20070227-E1-02.html.

Jordan, M. (1998). *For the love of the game*. New York: Crown.

Kegley, S. (2007, June 27). Rookies put through NFL crash course. Retrieved October 12, 2008, from www.sf49ers.com/pressbox/news_detail.php?PRKey=3130&section=PR%20News.

Kelly, P., & Hickey, C. (2004). Focault goes to footy: Professionalism, performance, prudentialism, and Playstations in the life of AFL footballers. Retrieved October 18, 2008, from www.tasa.org.au/conferencepapers04/docs/LEISURE/KELLY_HICKEY.pdf.

Kerkhoff, B. (2007, February 9). Helping athletes the smart way. *Kansas City Star*, D4.

Kirschenbaum, D. (1997). *Mind matters: Seven steps to smarter sport performance*. Carmel, IN: Cooper.

Klemash, C. (2006). *How to succeed in the game of life: 34 interviews with the world's greatest coaches*. Kansas City: Andrews McMeel.

Kornspan, A.S. (2006). Applying psychology to football in the 1930s and 1940s. *Applied Research in Coaching and Athletics Annual, 21*, 83-99.

Kornspan, A.S. (2007a). E.W. Scripture and the Yale Psychology Laboratory: Studies related to athletes and physical activity. *The Sport Psychologist, 21*, 152-169.

Kornspan, A.S. (2007b). The early years of sport psychology: The work and influence of Pierre de Coubertin. *Journal of Sport Behavior, 30*, 77-93.

Kornspan, A.S., & Duve, M.A. (2006). A niche and a need: A summary for the need for sport psychology consultants. *Annals of the American Psychotherapy Association, 9*(1), 19-25.

Kornspan, A.S., & Etzel, E.F. (2003). What do we know about the career maturity of college student-athletes: A brief review and suggestions for career development work with student-athletes. *Academic Athletic Journal, 17*, 15-33.

Kornspan, A. S., & Lerner, B.S. (2005). Graduate education in applied sport psychology: Suggestions for the training of sport psychology consultants. *Annals of the American Psychotherapy Association, 8*(3), 18-24.

Kornspan, A.S., & MacCracken, M.J. (2001). Psychology applied to sport in the 1940s: The work of Dorothy Hazeltine Yates. *The Sport Psychologist, 15*, 342-345.

Kornspan, A.S., & MacCracken, M.J. (2003). The use of psychology in professional baseball: The pioneering work of David F. Tracy. *Nine: A Journal of Baseball History and Culture, 11*, 36-43.

Kornspan, A.S., Shimokawa, K., Duve, M.A., Pinheiro, V. (2007, October). Sport psychology service provision: A content analysis of NCAA Division IA athletic department websites. Poster presentation at the annual meeting of the Association for Applied Sport Psychology, Louisville, Kentucky.

Krzyzewski, M., & Spatola, J.K. (2006). *Beyond basketball: Coach K's keywords for success*. New York: Warner.

Kuharsky, P. (2007, July 18). Pacman Jones has hope for camp. Retrieved October 12, 2008, from http://m.tennessean.com/detail.jsp?key=59556&full=1.

Lanning, W. (1982). The privileged few: Special counseling needs of athletes. *Journal of Sport Psychology, 4*, 19-23.

Lasser, E.S., Borden, F., & Edwards, J. (2006). *Sport psychology library: Bowling: The handbook of bowling psychology*. Morgantown, WV: Fitness Information Technology.

Laurila, D. (2007, March 5). Prospectus Q&A—Bob Tewksbury. *Baseball Prospectus.* Retrieved September 14, 2007, from www.baseballprospectus.com/article.php?articleid=5931&mode=print.

Lawson, J.H. (1928). Report of the medical officer. American Olympic Committee's report of the American Olympic Committee: Ninth Olympic Games, Amsterdam, 1928, second Olympic Winter Sports, St. Moritz, 1928 (pp. 39-41). New York: American Olympic Committee.

Leffingwell, T.R., Durand-Bush, N., Wurzberger, D., & Cada, P. (2005). Psychological assessment. In J. Taylor & G. Wilson (Eds.), *Applying sport psychology: Four perspectives* (pp. 85-100). Champaign, IL: Human Kinetics.

Leith, L.M. (2003). *The psychology of coaching team sports: A self-help guide.* Toronto: Sport Books.

Lesyk, J.J. (1998). *Developing sport psychology within your clinical practice: A practical guide for mental health professionals.* San Francisco: Jossey-Bass.

Life services. (2008). Canadian Sport Centre Ontario. Retrieved July 19, 2008, from www.cscontario. ca/web_page/life_services.php.

Linn, V. (2004, November 2). UPMC counselor helps athletes with the mental aspect of the game. *Pittsburgh Post-Gazette.* Retrieved September 14, 2007, from www.post-gazette.com/pg/04307/405140.stm.

Littlejohn, R. (2005). *Careers in fitness and personal training.* New York: Rosen.

Loucks, A.B., & Nattiv, A. (2005). The female athlete triad. *The Lancet, 366,* S49-S50.

Lox, C.L., Martin Ginis, K.A., & Petruzzello, S.J. (2006). *The psychology of exercise: Integrating theory and practice* (2nd ed.). Scottsdale, AZ: Holcomb Hathaway.

The Magglingen Declaration. (2008). International Council for Coach Education. Retrieved October 12, 2008, from www.icce.ws/priorities/magglingen.htm.

Marshall, E. (1910, November 13). The psychology of baseball: Discussed by A.G. Spalding. *New York Times,* SM 13.

Martens, R. (1987). *Coaches guide to sport psychology.* Champaign, IL: Human Kinetics.

Martens, R. (2004). *Successful coaching.* Champaign, IL: Human Kinetics.

Mason, A. (2006, July 8). From the field to the lanes: Final camp practice replaced by bowling outing. Retrieved September 15, 2007, from www.denverbroncos.com/page.php?id=334&storyID=5739.

McCann, S.C. (2000). Doing sport psychology at the really big show. In M.B. Andersen (Ed.), *Doing sport psychology* (pp. 209-222). Champaign, IL: Human Kinetics.

McCann, S.C. (2005). Roles: The sport psychologist. In S.M. Murphy (Ed.), *The sport psych handbook* (pp. 279-291). Champaign, IL: Human Kinetics.

McCann, S.C. (2006). Coaching in the last few minutes: Ten things to remember. *USOC Olympic Coach E-Magazine.* Retrieved January 20, 2008, from http://coaching.usolympicteam.com/coaching/kpub.nsf/v/5dec06.

McCann, S.C. (2007, August). Preparing for major competitions: Team-building. *USOC Olympic Coach E-Magazine.* Retrieved September 16, 2007, from http://coaching.usolympicteam.com/coaching/kpub.nsf/v/4aug07.

McCann, S.C., Jowdy, D.P., & Van Raalte, J.L. (2002). Assessment in sport and exercise psychology. In J.L. Van Raalte & B.W. Brewer (Eds.), *Exploring sport and exercise psychology* (2nd ed.) (pp. 291-305). Washington, DC: American Psychological Association.

McCloy, C.H. (1958). What is sports medicine? *Journal of Health, Physical Education, and Recreation, 29*(1) , 45-48.

McClurg, J. (2006, June). Organizational profile: United States Military Academy's Center for Enhanced Performance. *PEM Newsletter, 3*(1). Retrieved from http://appliedsportpsych.org/files/file/pem/jun06.pdf .

McNair, D.M., Lorr, M., & Droppelman, L.F. (1971). *Manual for the profile of mood states.* San Diego: Educational and Industrial Testing Service.

Meet our experts. (2008). Scottish Institute of Sport. Retrieved July 25, 2008, from www.sisport.com/sisport/2000.html.

Meet the coaches. (2007). University of Miami Medical Wellness Center. Retrieved September 20, 2007, from http://wellness.med.miami.edu/x113.xml.

Mental and physical training. (2008). Hank Haney International Junior Golf Academy. Retrieved August 30, 2008, from www.ijga.com/golf_mental.asp.

Mental conditioning: Coaches. (2008). IMG Academies. Retrieved September 14, 2008, from www.imgacademies.com/teams/default.sps?iTeamID=1050.

Metzler, J. (2002). Applying motivational principles to individual athletes. In J.M. Silva & D. Stevens (Eds.), *Psychological foundations of sport* (pp. 80-106). Boston: Allyn & Bacon.

Meyer, S.K. (2005). NCAA academic reforms: Maintaining the balance between academics and athletics. *Phi Kappa Phi Forum, 85*(3), 15-18.

Mihoces, G. (2007, June 19). Neurological tests will be mandatory. *USA Today,* p. 2C.

Miller, G.M., & Wooten, R.H. Jr. (1995). Sports counseling: A new counseling specialty area. *Journal of Counseling and Development, 74,* 172-173.

Miller, P.S., & Kerr, G.A. (2003). Role experimentation of intercollegiate student-athletes. *The Sport Psychologist, 17,* 197-200.

Molinari, D. (2004, May 29). NHL Combine: Effective tool, but not original idea. *Pittsburgh Post-Gazette.* Retrieved September 16, 2007, from www.post-gazette.com/pg/04150/323871.stm.

Moore, T. (2007, June 21). Fish-ing for players. Retrieved September 15, 2007, from www.phillyburbs.com/pb-dyn/news/100-06212007-1366529.html.

Moran, A.P. (2004). *Sport and exercise psychology: A critical introduction.* London: Routledge.

Morris, T., Alfermann, D., Lintunen, T., & Hall, H. (2003). Training and selection of sport psychologists: An international review. *International Journal of Sport and Exercise Psychology, 1,* 139-154.

Morse, E. (2008). What a sport psychiatrist does. . . . *Journal of Clinical Sport Psychology, 2,* 202-203.

Moshak, J. (2003). The team enhance program. *Athletic Therapy Today, 8*(2), 9-16.

Mullen, M. (2007, March 29). Tewksbury gets in their heads. *Nashua Telegraph.* Retrieved September 15, 2007, from www.nashuatelegraph.com/apps/pbcs.dll/article?AID=/20070329/SPORTS/203290377/-1/sports).

Munsey, C. (2007, July/August). Getting ahead of the game. *Monitor on Psychology, 38*(7). Retrieved September 15, 2007, from www.apa.org/monitor/julaug07/gettingahead.html.

Münsterberg, H. (1914). *Psychology, general and applied.* New York: Appleton.

Murphy, B. (2006, August 9). College athletes look for mental edge. Retrieved September 15, 2007, from http://sports.espn.go.com/ncaa/news/story?id=2543474.

Naismith, J. (1941). *Basket ball: Its origin and development.* New York: Association Press.

Narducci, M. (2007, June 17). It takes more than basketball skills: Joel Fish, the Sixers team psychologist, also evaluates players at predraft workouts, on and off the court. *Philadelphia Inquirer,* p. E12.

NCAA (National Collegiate Athletic Association). (2007). *2007-2008 NCAA sports medicine handbook.* Retrieved December 20, 2007, from www.ncaapublications.com/Uploads/PDF/2007-08_sports_medicine_handbook6786d571-ad07-492e-85cc-075cb4c74e51.pdf.

NCACE domain specific review. (2008). National Association for Sport and Physical Education. Retrieved October 17, 2008, from www.aahperd.org/naspe/template.cfm?template=ncace_domain_review.html.

Newin, J., Bloom, G.A., & Loughead, T.M. (2008). Youth ice hockey coaches perceptions of a team-building intervention program. *The Sport Psychologist, 22*, 54-72.

Nideffer, R.M. (1976). Test of attentional and interpersonal style. *Journal of Personality and Social Psychology, 34*, 394-404.

Nideffer, R.M., & Sagal, M. (2001). *Assessment in sport psychology*. Morgantown, WV: Fitness Information Technology.

Niven, A., & Owens, A. (2007). Qualifications and training routes to becoming a practising sport and exercise psychologist in the UK. (2007). *The Sport and Exercise Scientist*, (11). Retrieved July 17, 2008, from www.bases.org.uk/newsite/pdf/SESMarch07PsychTgRoutes.pdf.

O'Connor, E.A. Jr. (2004). Which questionnaire? Assessment practices of sport psychology consultants. *The Sport Psychologist, 18*, 464-468.

O'Connor, E.A. Jr. (2007). Recognition and referral of psychological issues in sports medicine. Retrieved September 18, 2007, from www.grsportscenter.com/sportstalk.html#recognition.

O'Connor, J., & Kapsidelis, T. (2006, April 2). Notes. *Richmond Times Dispatch*, C14.

Orlick, T. (2000). *In pursuit of excellence* (3rd ed.). Champaign, IL: Human Kinetics.

Orlick, T. (2008). *In pursuit of excellence: How to win in sport and life through mental training*. Champaign, IL: Human Kinetics.

Orlick, T., & Partington, J. (1988). Mental links to excellence. *The Sport Psychologist, 2*, 105-130.

Orsega-Smith, E.M., Payne, L.L., Mowen, A.J., Ho, C.H., & Godbey, G.C. (2007). The role of social support and self-efficacy in shaping the leisure time physical activity of older adults. *Journal of Leisure Research, 39*, 705-727.

Overview of graduate sport psychology training. (2007). University of North Texas. Retrieved September 13, 2007, from www.sportpsych.unt.edu/edandtraining/study_container.htm.

Packers player development. (2007). Retrieved September 14, 2007, from www.packers.com/team/player_development.

Paivio, A. (1985). Cognitive and motivational functions of imagery in human performance. *Canadian Journal of Applied Sport Sciences, 10*, 22S-28S.

PALS. (2008). Senior Services: Promoting the well-being of older adults. Retrieved October 19, 2008, from www.seniorservices.org/pals/index.htm.

Pannaccio, T. (2006, October 2). Flyers spend weekend looking for chemistry. *Philadelphia Inquirer*, F3.

Pasquarelli, L. (2007, February 27). Character studied closely at combine. Retrieved December 20, 2007, from http://sports.espn.go.com/nfl/draft07/columns/story?columnist=pasquarelli_len&id=2781672.

Performance enhancement and applied sport psychology. (2007). Kansas State University. Retrieved September 14, 2007, from www.k-state.edu/counseling/student/sports.htm.

Performance lifestyle. (2008). Scottish Institute of Sport. Retrieved July 25, 2008, from www.sisport.com/sisport/510.html.

Peterson, K. (2005). Overtraining: Balancing practice and performance. In S. Murphy (Ed.), *The sport psych handbook* (pp. 49-70). Champaign, IL: Human Kinetics.

Petitpas, A.J., & Buntrock, C.L. (1995). Counseling athletes: A new specialty in counselor education. *Counselor Education and Supervision, 34*, 212-219.

Petitpas, A.J., Cornelius, A.E., Van Raalte, J.L., & Jones, T. (2005). A framework for planning youth sport programs that foster psychosocial development. *The Sport Psychologist, 19*, 63-80.

Petitpas, A.J., Van Raalte, J.L., Cornelius, A.E., & Presbrey, J. (2004). A life skills development program for high school student-athletes. *Journal of Primary Prevention, 24*, 325-334.

Physical activity advisors. (2008). Get Moving Nottingham. Retrieved July 24, 2008, from www.getmovingnottingham.nhs.uk/ymca-active-4-life/physical-activity-advisors.

Physical activity counsellor. (2008). West Carleton Family Health Team. Retrieved July 22, 2008, from www.wcfht.ca/services/physical_activity.htm.

Physical inactivity: A global public health problem. (2008). World Health Organization. Retrieved September 27, 2008, from www.who.int/dietphysicalactivity/factsheet_inactivity/en/index. html.

Player development at the clubs. (2007). National Football League. Retrieved September 18, 2007, from www.nfl.com/playerdevelopment/clubs.

Player development. (2007). National Football League. Retrieved September 18, 2007, from www. nfl.com/playerdevelopment/overview.

Player development. (2008). National Football League. Retrieved October 16, 2008, from www.nfl. com/playerdevelopment/overview.

Player programs. (2008). National Basketball Players Association. Retrieved October 16, 2008, from www.nbpa.com/playerprograms_pub.php.

Porentas, J. (2006). Buckeye head-coach. Retrieved from www.the-ozone.net/misc/2006/head-coach. htm.

Position description. (2008). Government of South Australia. Retrieved July 19, 2008, from www. recsport.sa.gov.au/pdf/ACE%20Psych.pdf.

Post-doctoral fellowship program in college mental health. (2007). University of Southern California. Retrieved August 31, 2008, from www.usc.edu/student-affairs/Health_Center/cs.postdoctoral. shtml.

Proper, K.I., Hildenbrandt, V.H., Van der Beek, A.J., Twisk, J.W., & Van Mechelen, W. (2003). Effect of individual counseling on physical activity fitness and health: A randomized controlled trial in a workplace setting. *American Journal of Preventive Medicine, 24,* 218-226.

Psychologist to aid selection of Illini athletes. (1922, March 23). *Wisconsin Rapids Daily Tribune,* p. 8.

Rabasca, L. (1999, November). They give athletes a kick in the confidence. *APA Monitor Online, 30*(10). Retrieved September 15, 2007, from www.apa.org/monitor/nov99/in2.html.

Ragni, P. (1989). Athletes psychoanalysed. *Olympic Review, 265,* 501-505.

Ramsay, H.M. (2005). State licensing board requirements defined: An examination of several pre and post doctoral training requirements leading to licensure. Retrieved July 16, 2008, from www.appic.org/downloads/UNH_Licensure_Project_8-3-05.doc.

Ravizza, K., & Osborne, T. (1991). Nebraska's 3R's: One-play-at-a-time preperformance routine for collegiate football. *The Sport Psychologist, 5,* 256-265.

Registration. (2006). New Zealand Psychologist Society. Retrieved August 31, 2008, from www. psychology.org.nz/psychinnz/registration.html.

Report of the surgeon general: Adults. (2007). Centers for Disease Control. Retrieved September 20, 2007, from www.cdc.gov/nccdphp/sgr/pdf/adults.pdf.

Research and development. (2007). Metro Atlanta YMCA. Retrieved September 27, 2008, from www.ymcaatlanta.org/Membership/default.asp?id=1099#Jim_Annesi,_Ph.D._Bio.

Rice, D. (2007, January 9). Buckeyes discuss disappointing defeat. Retrieved January 19, 2008, from http://ohiostate.scout.com/2/607968.html.

Rice, G. (1935, March 21). Tension and relaxing. *Syracuse Herald,* p. 32.

Riley, B.G. (1943). Boxing and psychology. *Physical Educator, 3,* 95-96.

Roarke, S.P. (2006, June 1). Prospects being put the test. Retrieved December 20, 2008 from www. lethbridgehurricanes.com/index.php?p=144&newsID=2650.

Robbins, L. (2006, March 30). Cinderfella has a shrink: Dr. Bob told George Mason you gotta believe. *New York Post,* p. 97.

Role of physical activity counsellors (PAC). (2008). The PAC Project. Retrieved July 23, 2008, from www.health.uottawa.ca/pac/index.php?page=pacrole&lang=an.

Ross, S. (2006, January 29). Mind over matter in knee surgery. *Pittsburgh Tribune Review*. Retrieved September 17, 2007, from http://knee-surgery-info.net/Knee-Surgery-News/2006/01/29/knee-surgery-or-injury-recovery-is-mind-over-matter.

Rushall, B.S., Hall, M., Roux, L., Sasseville, J., & Rushall, A.C. (1988). Effects of three types of thought content instructions on skiing performance. *The Sport Psychologist, 2*, 283-297.

Russia eyes hypnotism in sport, Aussie says. (1957, September 15). *New York Times,* p. S11.

Rutgers University Sport Psychology Program. (2007). Retrieved September 28, 2007, from www.scarletknights.com/sportsmed/sp-program/page4.htm.

Sachs, M.L., Burke, K.L., & Salitsky, P.B. (Eds.). (1992). *Directory of graduate programs in applied sport psychology* (3rd ed.). Boise, ID: Association for the Advancement of Applied Sport Psychology.

Samuelson, P. (2003). An investigation into the perception of student-athletes regarding the academic component of the NCAA CHAMPS/Life Skills program. *Dissertation Abstracts International, 65*(02), 433.

Sarnataro, B.R. (2005, August 25). A new approach to fitness coaching: Gyms focus on building better habits. Retrieved October 18, 2008, from http://www.webmd.com/fitness-exercise/features/a-new-approach-to-fitness-coaching.

Schools & academic coaches. (2008). Play It Smart. Retrieved October 12, 2008, from www.playitsmart.org/Play_schools.php.

Senecal, J., Loughead, T.M., & Bloom, G.A. (2008). A season-long team-building intervention: Examining the effect of team goal setting on cohesion. *Journal of Sport and Exercise Psychology, 30*, 186-199.

Services. (2008). Vancouver Island Physical Activity Counselling. Retrieved September 28, 2008, from www.vipac.ca/services.php.

Sheridan, C. (2006, August 11). Great motives elevate champs. Retrieved October 14, 2008, from http://sports.espn.go.com/nba/dailydime?page=dailydime-060621.

Shilts, M.K., Horowitz, M., & Townsend, M. (2004). Goal setting as a strategy for dietary and physical activity behavior change: A review of literature. *American Journal of Health Promotion, 19*, 81-93.

Shipley, A. (1999, June 29). A successful science project. *Washington Post*, D1. Retrieved September 15, 2007, from www.washingtonpost.com/wp-srv/sports/soccer/longterm/worldcup99/articles/psych29.htm.

Shipley, A. (2006, October 4). The Heat's title brings perks and expectations. *Washington Post*, E1.

Shulte, T. (2002, October 2). Psychologist aids football team. *Daily Nebraskan*. Retrieved September 15, 2007, from http://media.www.dailynebraskan.com/media/storage/paper857/news/2002/10/02/SportsfirstDown/Psychologist.Aids.Football.Team-1724284.shtml.

Silva, J.M. (1994). Sport performance phobias. *International Journal of Sport Psychology, 25*, 100-118.

Silva, J.M. (2002). The evolution of sport psychology. In J.M. Silva & D.E. Stevens (Eds.), *Psychological foundations of sport* (pp. 1-26). Boston: Allyn & Bacon.

Silva, J.M., & Stevens, D.E. (2002). *Psychological foundations of sport*. Boston: Allyn & Bacon.

Singer, R.N. (1988). Psychological testing: What value to coaches and athletes. *International Journal of Sport Psychology, 19*, 87-106.

Skolnick, E. (2007, February 1). Learning to cope after the game is over: Players struggle with a new life after football. *South Florida Sun Sentinel*, C10.

Slinger, J. (2007, March 20). Mental floss for the untidy minds. *The Star.* Retrieved October 11, 2008, from www.thestar.com/comment/columnists/article/193819.

Smith, A. (2007, December 15). Mental test for future stars. *Hobart Mercury*, p. 85.

Smith, D., Bell, G.D., & Kilgo, J. (2004). *The Carolina way: Leadership lessons from a life in coaching.* New York: Penguin Press.

Smith, L. (2005). Mind over matter: Focus, concentration, control . . . the latest trend in winning programs is mental skills training. Here's how to implement it at any level of play. *Athletic Management, 17.03.* Retrieved December 20, 2008, from www.athleticmanagement.com/2007/02/mind_over_matter.html.

Smoll, F.L., & Smith, R.E. (2006). Development and implementation of coach-training programs: Cognitive-behavioral principles and techniques. In J.M. Williams (Ed.), *Applied sport psychology: Personal growth to peak performance* (5th ed.) (pp. 458-480). Boston: McGraw-Hill.

Special feature: Dr. Rich Gordin's golf tips. (2007). Retrieved September 15, 2007, from www.mikeweir.sympatico.msn.ca/news/fullstory.sps?iNewsid=298585&itype=6655&iCategoryID=665?id=298585&itype=6655&pageno=9#6.

Sport consulting and psychological counseling for student athletes. (2007). Retrieved September 14, 2007, from http://caps.ucdavis.edu/consultationoutreach/sport/index.htm.

Sport Psychology Conference for Coaches. (2007). Coaches Association of British Columbia. Retrieved September 15, 2008, from www.coaches.bc.ca/coaches%20week/sport_psychology.html.

Sport psychology: Getting focused. (2007). Retrieved September 14, 2007, from www.mascsa.psu.edu/psychology.html.

Sport Psychology Staff: United States Olympic Committee. (2008). *Sport psychology mental training manual* (9th printing). Colorado Springs, CO: United States Olympic Committee.

Staff directory. (2008). The official site of the University of Tennessee Women's Athletic Department. Retrieved September 14, 2008, from www.utladyvols.com/inside-ut/staff-directory.html.

Stansbury Fitness and Wellness Center. (2007). Retrieved September 20, 2007, from www.wvu.edu/~physed/stansfit.

Steinberg, D. (2006, April 1). How to win games and influence people. *Washington Post,* E1.

Stinson, T. (2006, November 9). Falcons at Ravens: Plenty of kick left; Andersen, 46, still legging it for greatness. *Atlanta Journal Constitution,* F1.

Stotlar, D.K., & Wonders, A. (2006). Developing elite athletes. A content analysis of U.S. national governing body systems. *International Journal of Applied Sports Sciences, 18,* 121-144.

Suinn, R.M. (1972). Behavior rehearsal training for ski racers. *Behavior Therapy, 3,* 519-520.

Taylor, J. (2008). Prepare to succeed: Private consulting in applied sport psychology. *Journal of Clinical Sport Psychology, 2,* 160-177.

Teachers—Postsecondary. (2007). *U.S. Department of Labor Bureau of Labor Statistics Occupational outlook handbook, 2008-09 edition.* Retrieved July 16, 2008, from www.bls.gov/oco/ocos066.htm.

Terry, P. (2005). Tribute to Jeffrey Bond. *The Sporting Mind: The Newsletter of the APS College of Sport Psychologists, 4*(2). Retrieved October 11, 2008, from www.groups.psychology.org.au/Assets/Files/the_sporting_mind2_2005.pdf.

Thelwell, R.C., Weston, N.J.V., Greenless, I.A., & Hutchings, N.V. (2008). A qualitative exploration of psychological skills use in coaches. *The Sport Psychologist, 22,* 38-53.

Thomas, B. (2003, August 11). FSU united in search to avoid repeat of last year. *Florida Times Union.* Retrieved September 11, 2008, from www.jacksonville.com/tu-online/stories/081103/col_13245480.html.

Thomas, J., & Fox, D. (2007, March 2). Draft diary: Strong Combine for Joe Thomas. Retrieved September 16, 2007, from http://nfldraft.rivals.com/content.asp?CID=648005.

Thompson, R.A., & Sherman, R.T. (2007). *Managing student-athletes' mental health issues.* Retrieved December 20, 2008, from www.princeton.edu/uhs/pdfs/NCAA%20Managing%20Student-Athletes'%20Mental%20Health%20Issues.pdf.

Tigers in major development boost. (2007, December 12). Richmond Football Club. Retrieved October 12, 2008, from www.richmondfc.com.au/Season2007/News/NewsArticle/tabid/6301/Default.aspx?newsId=54232

Tony DiLeo speaks with Sixers.com. (2007). Retrieved September 16, 2007, from www.nba.com/sixers/draft/dileo_070521.html.

Tracy, D.F. (1951). *Psychologist at bat.* New York: Sterling.

Transcript, Giants General Manager Jerry Reese. (2007, April 19). Retrieved September 16, 2007, from www.giants.com/news/transcripts/story.asp?story_id=25084.

Triplett, N. (1898). The dynamogenic factors in pacemaking and competition. *American Journal of Psychology, 9,* 507-533.

Tuckman, B.W. (1965). Developmental sequence in small groups. *Psychological Bulletin, 63,* 384-399.

Tulloch, H., Fortier, M., & Hogg, W. (2006). Physical activity counseling in primary care: Who has and who should be counseling. *Patient Education and Counseling, 64*(1-3), 6-20.

Udry, E., Gould, D., Bridges, D., & Beck, L. (1997). Down but not out: Athlete responses to season-ending ski injuries. *Journal of Sport and Exercise Psychology, 19,* 229-248.

United States Olympic Committee. (2002). *Sport psychology: Mental training manual.* Colorado Springs: Author.

UPMC Sports Center Hires "Mental Trainer." (2004, October 12). *Pittsburgh Business Times.* Retrieved November 8, 2008, from www.bizjournals.com/pittsburgh/stories/2004/10/11/daily5.html.

USOC athlete career program. (2008). U.S. Olympic Committee. Retrieved September 21, 2008, from http://teamusa.org/content/index/883.

USOC performance enhancement team. (2008). The Women's Mat. Retrieved October 18, 2008, from www.thewomensmat.com/usastaff/performance.asp.

USOC sport psychology services. (2008). Retrieved October 18, 2008, from www.usoc.org/content/index/948.

Vallance, J.K.H., Dunn, J.G.H., & Causgrove Dunn, J.L. (2006). Perfectionism, anger, and situation criticality in competitive youth ice hockey. *Journal of Sport and Exercise Psychology, 28,* 383-406.

Van Raalte, J.L., & Andersen, M.B. (2007). When sport psychology consulting is a means to an end(ing): Roles and agendas when helping athletes leave their sports. *The Sport Psychologist, 21,* 227-242.

Van Raalte, J.L., & Williams, J.M. (1994). American Psychological Association: Division 47. *Graduate training and career possibilities in exercise and sport psychology.* Retrieved September 18, 2007, from www.apa.org/divisions/div47/APA%20Div%2047%20(3)/Sport%20Psych%20a%20Guide/gradtrain.htm.

Vargas-Tonsing, T.M. (2006). Relaxation training. In R. Bartlett, C. Gratton, & C.G. Rolf (Eds.), *Encyclopedia of International Sport Studies* (vol. 3) (pp. 1134-1135). Abingdon, Oxford, UK: Taylor and Francis Group.

Vealey, R.S. (1994). Current status and prominent issues in sport psychology interventions. *Medicine and Science in Sport and Exercise, 26,* 495-502.

Vinella, S. (2003, September 23). The game plan: Steps to success. Cleveland Indians system maps road to improvement. *Cleveland Plain Dealer.* Retrieved September 16, 2007, from www.cleveland.com/gameplan/index.ssf?/gameplan/more/part3.html.

Voight, M., & Callaghan, J. (2001). A team building intervention program: Application and evaluation with two university soccer teams. *Journal of Sport Behavior, 24,* 420-431.

Wadyka, S. (2007, January 4). Free the mind and fewer injuries may follow. *New York Times*. Retrieved October 16, 2008, from www.nytimes.com/2007/01/04/fashion/04fitness.html?ex=1190174400&en=55544c72f46f0f19&ei=5070.

Wankel, L.M., & Thompson, C. (2006). Motivating people to be physically active: Self-persuasion vs. balanced decision making. *Journal of Applied Social Psychology, 7*, 332-340.

Weinberg, R.S., & Comar, W. (1994). The effectiveness of psychological interventions in competitive sport. *Sports Medicine, 18*, 406-418.

Weinberg, R.S., & Gould, D. (2007). *Foundations of sport and exercise psychology* (4th ed.). Champaign, IL: Human Kinetics.

Weinberg, R.S., Smith, J., Jackson, A., & Gould, D. (1984). Effect of association, dissociation, and positive self-talk strategies on endurance performance. *Canadian Journal of Applied Sport Sciences, 9*, 25-32.

Welcome. (2008). International Society for Sport Psychiatry. Retrieved September 2, 2008, from www.theissp.com.

Welcome to the NCAA CHAMPS/Life skills program. (2008). National Collegiate Athletic Association. Retrieved October 12, 2008, from www.ncaa.org/wps/ncaa?ContentID=13 .

What is the N4A? (2007). National Association of Academic Advisors for Athletics. Retrieved September 17, 2007, from http://nfoura.org/about.

What we do. (2007). Get Psyched Sports. Retrieved September 14, 2007, from http://getpsyched sports.org.

Where are they now? (2008). Association for Applied Sport Psychology. Retrieved July 25, 2008, from http://appliedsportpsych.org/students/where.

Why see a regulated professional? (2008). Canadian Psychological Association. Retrieved August 31, 2008, from www.cpa.ca/public/##3.

Williams, J.M., & Scherzer, C.B. (2003). Tracking the training and careers of graduates of advanced degree programs in sport psychology, 1994 to 1999. *Journal of Applied Sport Psychology, 15*, 335-353.

Williams, J.M., & Scherzer, C. (2006). Injury risk and rehabilitation: Psychological considerations. In J.M. Williams (Ed.), *Applied sport psychology: Personal growth to peak performance* (5th ed.) (pp. 565-594). Boston: McGraw-Hill.

Williams, J.M., & Straub, W.F. (2006). Sport psychology: Past, present, future. In J.M. Williams (Ed.), *Applied sport psychology: Personal growth to peak performance* (5th ed.) (pp. 1-14). Boston: McGraw-Hill.

Williams, J.M., & Widmeyer, W.N. (1991). The cohesion-performance outcome relationship in a coacting sport. *Journal of Sport and Exercise Psychology, 13*, 364-371.

Willis, J.D., & Campbell, L.F. (1992). *Exercise psychology*. Champaign, IL: Human Kinetics.

Winerman, L. (2005). Psychology in the stadium: Psychologist and former track star Nicki Moore helps the University of Oklahoma athletics department better serve its student-athletes. *Monitor on Psychology, (36)*. Retrieved October 12, 2008, from www.apa.org/monitor/apr05/stadium.html.

Winter, B. (1981). *Relax and win*. San Diego: Barnes.

Winthrop's sports medicine program. (2004). Winthrop's sports medicine program adds psychological element to enhance treatment. *Cornerstone, 14*(3). Retrieved September 17, 2007, from www.winthrop.org/newsroom/publications/vol14_no3_2004/page15.cfm.

Wood, S. (2005, June 29). Blue Jays' Halladay back on the ball. *USA Today*. Retrieved September 21, 2008, from www.usatoday.com/sports/baseball/al/bluejays/2005-06-29-halladay-resurgence_x.htm.

Wooden, J., & Jamison, S. (2004). *My personal best: Life lessons from an All-American journey*. New York: McGraw-Hill.

Wooden, J., & Jamison, S. (2007). *The essential Wooden: A lifetime of lessons on leaders and leadership.* New York: McGraw-Hill.

Working as a psychologist. (2008). Australian Psychological Society. Retrieved July 16, 2008, from www.psychology.org.au/study/working.

Wormald, H., Waters, H., Sleap, M., & Ingle, L. (2006). Participants' perceptions of a lifestyle approach to promoting physical activity: Targeting deprived communities in Kingston-Upon-Hull. BMC Public Health. Retrieved July 24, 2008, from www.pubmedcentral.nih.gov/articlerender.fcgi?artid=1560127.

Wrisberg, C.A., & Fisher, L.A. (2005). Mental rehearsal during rehabilitation. *Athletic Therapy Today, 10*(6), 58-59.

Writing Group for the Activity Counseling Trial Research Group. (2001). Effects of physical activity counseling in primary care: The activity counseling trial: A randomized controlled trial. *The Journal of the American Medical Association, 286,* 677-687.

Wyshynski, G. (2007, May 15). Sigmund Freud, Red Wings coach. Retrieved October 12, 2008, from http://nhl.fanhouse.com/2007/05/15/sigmund-freud-red-wings-coach/#cont.

Yates, D.H. (1943). A practical method of using set. *Journal of Applied Psychology, 27,* 512-519.

YMCA helps all family members to adopt healthy behaviors. (2007, January 9). Retrieved September 28, 2007, from www.hometowncherokee.com/living/health/ymca-helps-all-family-mem.shtml.

YMCAs offer customized workout programs: Scientifically-developed method cuts dropout rates. (2005, June 27). Retrieved September 20, 2007, from www.msnbc.msn.com/id/8373791.

Zaichkowsky, L.D. (2006). Industry challenges facing sport psychology. *Athletic Insight, 8*(3). Retrieved September 18, 2007, from www.athleticinsight.com/Vol8Iss3/IndustryChallenges.htm.

Ziegler, S.G. (1987). Negative thought stopping: A key to performance enhancement. *Journal of Physical Education, Recreation, and Dance, 58*(4), 66-69.

Zimmerman, B. (2007, March 10). Mental approach part of UF's plan. *Gainesville Sun.* Retrieved September 15, 2007, from www.gainesville.com/apps/pbcs.dll/article?AID=/20070310/GATORS07/703110308/-1/sports.

Author Index

Note: The italicized *f* following page numbers refers to figures.

A

Abbott, H. 71
Adams, B. 87
Albrecht, R. 51
Aldridge, T. 11
Alfermann, D. 17, 25
Almond, K.F. 104, 105
Andersen, M. 42, 101
Andersen, M.B. 11, 93, 101
Anderson, A. 51
Anderson, R.J. 99
Annesi, J.J. 126, 128
Anshel, M.A. 123, 130

B

Bacon, V.L. 116, 119
Barlow, D.H. 117
Barnhart, T. 103
Barr, K.A. 46
Batik, O. 128
Baugh, F.G. 7
Bauman, J. 16
Bean, C.H. 7
Beck, L. 95
Beckmann, J. 83
Bell, G.D. 57, 58, 74
Benjamin, L.T., Jr. 7
Bennett, G.T. 110, 114, 116
Berra, Y. 30, 44
Bisig, T.B. 26
Blair, S.N. 128
Bloom, G. 60, 63
Bloom, G.A. 63
Borden, F. 62, 63
Brannon, E.W. 7, 83
Brawley, L.R. 57, 130
Breckon, J.D. 128
Brewer, B.W. 34-35, 53, 97, 99, 116, 117
Bridges, D. 95
Broughton, E. 103
Brown, C. 95, 97
Buckworth, J. 125, 126, 127
Buntrock, C.L. 33, 100
Burke, K.L. 100
Burton, D. 53

C

Cada, P. 70, 82, 87
Callaghan, J. 63
Callow, N. 46
Campbell, B., Jr. 7
Campbell, E. 117
Campbell, L.F. 14
Carodine, K. 104, 105
Carr, C. 20
Carron, A.V. 57, 60, 61
Carter, J.E. 27, 112
Causgrove Dunn, J.L. 51
Chappell, M. 82, 84
Chelladurai, P. 70
Cogan, K.D. 115, 116
Colman, M.M. 57
Comar, W. 52
Conant, S. 62
Cornelius, A. 95, 97, 98
Cornelius, A.E. 34, 103
Cox, R.H. 21, 61, 84, 111
Cramp, A.G. 130
Curry, J. 30

D

Dale, G. 62
Deaner, H. 43
Delehanty, H. 47, 58
Dennis, P.W. 60
DiCicco, T. 62
Dishman, R.K. 125, 126, 127
Dorfman, H.A. 49, 50, 71, 78
Doss-Antoun, J. 46
Driediger, M. 46
Droppelman, L.F., 84
Dunn, J.G.H. 51, 63
Durand, V.M. 117
Durand-Bush, N. 70, 82, 87
Duve, M.A. 27, 28-29, 42, 52

E

Edwards, J. 62, 63
Ellis, A. 41
Esfarjani, B. 92
Etzel, E.F. 100, 101, 115, 116
Ewing, M.E. 69

F

Fales, E.D. 9
Feltz, D.L. 51-52
Ferrante, A.P. 101
Fisher, L.A. 98
Fletcher, D. 26
Floeckher, P. 47
Fortier, M. 33, 125, 129, 148
Fox, D. 85
Fry, A. 18, 119
Fuchs, A.H. 83
Fullerton, H.S. 83

G

Gardiner, A. 110
Gardner, F. 14, 52, 114
Gardner, F.L. 112
Gleeson-Kreig, J.M. 127
Godbey, G.C. 126
Goddard, M. 108
Gould, D. 4, 7, 16, 17, 45, 48, 49f, 51, 61, 72,
    74, 75f, 76, 88, 94f, 95-96, 97, 98f, 111,
    115, 125f
Grabmeier, J. 115
Grant, E. 32
Gratto, K.K. 104, 105
Green, C.D. 83
Greenleaf, C. 51
Greenless, I.A. 47
Greenspan, M. 51-52
Greenspan, M.J. 101
Guinan, D. 51

H

Hack, B. 110, 114
Hacker, C. 61, 62
Hacker, C.M. 56, 61
Hall, C. 46
Hall, C.R. 46
Hall, H. 17, 25
Hall, M. 51
Hamson-Utley, J.J. 99
Harding, T. 46, 86
Harr, E. 122
Harris, D. 111, 112
Harwood, C. 26
Heaney, C.A. 96
Hellmich, N. 115
Hickey, C. 85
Hildenbrandt, V.H. 128
Hill, C.E., Jr. 85
Ho, C.H. 126
Hogg, W. 33, 125, 129, 148
Holmes, J. 40
Holt, N.L. 63
Horowitz, M. 126
Hosick, M.B. 13, 110

Howden, S. 107
Hu, J. 60
Hudgens, M. 59
Hutchings, N.V. 47
Hutchinson, A. 128

I

Ingle, L. 128

J

Jackson, A. 51
Jackson, P. 47, 58
Jamison, S. 47, 58-59, 68
Janssen, J. 56, 58, 61-62
Johnston, L.H. 128
Jones, G. 72
Jones, T. 34, 85
Jordan, M. 45
Jowdy, D.P. 84, 88

K

Kaplan, D. 30, 44
Kapsidelis, T. 68
Kegley, S. 33
Kellmann, M. 83
Kelly, P. 85
Kerkhoff, B. 103
Kerr, G.A. 104
Kirschenbaum, D. 45, 127
Klemash, C. 75
Kornspan, A.S. 5, 6, 7, 8, 9, 10, 13, 27, 28-29, 52,
    56, 82, 83, 100, 119
Krzyzewski, M. 60
Kuehl, K. 49
Kuharsky, P. 33

L

Lanning, W. 101
Lantz, C. 101
Lasser, E.S. 62, 63
Laurila, D. 31
Lawson, J.H. 47
Leffingwell, T.R. 70, 82, 87, 89
Leith, L.M. 44, 50, 57, 60
Lerner, B.S. 13, 116, 119
Lesyk, J.J. 32
Linn, V. 30
Lintunen, T. 17, 25
Littlejohn, R. 124
Lorr, M. 84
Loucks, A.B. 115
Loughead, T.M. 63
Lox, C.L. 14

M

MacCracken, M.J. 8, 9, 10
Maniar, S.D. 115

Marshall, E. 7
Martens, R. 43, 47, 50, 70, 74, 75, 77, 143
Martin, S. 99
Martin Ginis, K.A. 14
Mason, A. 63
McCann, S.C. 53, 60, 73-74, 84, 85, 88, 111
McClurg, J. 34
McNair, D.M. 84
Medbery, R. 51
Metzler, J. 74
Meyer, S.K. 105
Mihoces, G. 87
Miller, G.M. 100
Miller, P.S. 104
Moore, T. 87
Moore, Z. 14, 52, 114
Moran, A.P. 59
Morris, T. 17, 25
Morse, E. 35
Moshak, J. 88
Mowen, A.J. 126
Mullen, M. 53
Munsey, C. 52
Murphy, B. 16, 28, 43

N

Naismith, J. 5
Narducci, M. 87
Nattiv, A. 115
Newin, J. 63
Neyer, M. 103
Nideffer, R.M. 49, 84, 89
Niven, A. 30

O

O'Connor, E.A. 83, 112
O'Connor, J. 68
Orlick, T. 51, 84, 92
Orsega-Smith, E.M. 126
Osborne, T. 50
Owens, A. 30

P

Paivio, A. 45
Pannaccio, T. 59
Partington, J. 51
Pasquarelli, L. 86
Payne, L.L. 126
Peterson, K. 48, 51
Petitpas, A.J. 33, 34, 97, 100, 103, 108
Petrie, T.A. 116, 117
Petruzello, S.J. 14
Pick, S. 7
Pinheiro, V. 28-29, 52
Porentas, J. 111, 119
Prappevessis, H. 60, 61

Presbrey, J. 103
Proper, K.I. 128

R

Rabasca, L. 44
Raedeke, T.D. 53
Ragni, P. 10
Ramsay, H.M. 25
Ravizza, K. 50
Rice, D. 71
Rice, G. 48
Riley, B.G. 10
Roarke, S.P. 85
Robbins, L. 68
Rodgers, W.M. 46
Ross, S. 96, 97
Roux, L. 51
Ruane, J. 117
Rushall, A.C. 51
Rushall, B.S. 51

S

Sachs, M.L. 18, 100, 119
Sagal, M. 89
Saleh, S.D. 70
Salitsky, P.B. 100
Salzberg, C. 62
Samuelson, P. 108
Sarnataro, B.R. 33, 122, 125
Sasseville, J. 51
Scherzer, C. 97, 98
Scherzer, C.B. 21
Schweighardt, S. 18, 119
Seefeldt, V. 69
Seestedt, M. 116
Senecal, J. 63
Sheridan, C. 60
Sherman, R.T. 14, 112, 114
Shilts, M.K. 126
Shimokawa, K. 28-29, 52
Shipley, A. 56, 59
Shulte, T. 59
Silva, J.M. 9, 11, 42, 43, 117
Singer, R.N. 88
Skolnick, E. 108
Sleap, M. 128
Slinger, J. 4
Smith, A. 85
Smith, D. 57, 58, 74
Smith, J. 51
Smith, L. 68, 78
Smith, R.E. 70, 75, 76, 77
Smoll, F.L. 70, 75, 76, 77
Spatola, J.K. 60
Spink, K.S. 60, 61
Steinberg, D. 68
Stevens, D. 57

Stevens, D.E. 42, 60, 63
Stinson, T. 42
Stotlar. D.K. 53
Straub, W.F. 16, 21, 34
Suinn, R.M. 46

T

Taylor, J. 11, 32
Terry, P. 31
Thelwell, R.C. 47
Thomas, B. 59
Thomas J. 85
Thompson, C. 127
Thompson, R.A. 14, 112, 114
Townsend, M. 126
Tracy, D.F. 9, 50
Trembley, D. 116
Triplett, N. 6
Tuckman, B.W. 57
Tulloch, H. 33, 125, 129, 148
Twisk, J.W. 128

U

Udry, E. 48, 95
Unruh, J.L. 128

V

Vallance, J.K.H. 51
Van der Beek, A.J. 128
Van Mechelen, W. 128
Van Raalte, J.L. 34, 76, 84, 88, 101, 104
Vargas-Tonsing, T.M. 48
Vinella, S. 87

Visek, A.J. 115
Vogel, P. 51
Voight, M. 63

W

Wadyka, S. 93
Walters, J. 99
Wankel, L.M. 127
Waters, H. 128
Watson, J.C. 115
Weinberg, R.S. 4, 16, 17, 45, 48, 49f, 51, 52, 61, 74, 75f, 76, 88, 94f, 95-96, 97, 98f, 111, 115, 125f
Weston, N.J.V. 47
Wheeler, J. 57
Widmeyer, W.N. 57
Williams, J.M. 11, 16, 21, 34, 57, 76, 93, 97, 98
Willis, J.D. 14
Winerman, L. 27, 111, 112, 117
Winter, B. 8, 10
Wonders, A. 53
Wood, S. 4
Wooden, J. 47, 58-59, 68
Wooten, R.H., Jr. 100
Wormald, H. 128
Wrisberg, C.A. 98
Wurzberger, D. 70, 82, 87
Wyshynski, G. 34

Z

Zaichkowsky, L.D. 119
Ziegler, S.D. 51
Zimmerman, B. 43

Subject Index

Note: The italicized *f* and *t* following page numbers refer to figures and tables, respectively.

A

ABC model 41*f*
academic athletic counselor 141
academic concerns 101
academic success coach 33
ACE Cricket Academy 26
American College of Sports Medicine 93, 96, 129
American Heart Association 122
American Psychological Association (APA) 14-15
Andersen, Morten 42
Anderson, William G. 5
Annesi, Jim 125, 127, 148
anorexia nervosa 115
anxiety 47, 116-117
Arenas, Gilbert 50
assessment
 about 82-83
 in clinical sport psychology 114
 of psychological characteristics 83
 research support 89
 sport managers' opinions 86
 sport psychology use 84-88
 types of 83-84
 venues 84
Association for Applied Sport Psychology (AASP)
 about 14-15
 certification 11, 17, 25, 123, 145
 educating coaches and parents 69
 foundation by Silva 42
 Performance Excellence Movement 34
 student participation 16
athlete developmental concerns
 academic concerns 101
 career concerns 100
 college athletic departments 103-105
 high school athletic departments 103
 personal development 101
 professional sport leagues and teams 105-106

programs for elite athletes 106-108
 providers 101-108
 research support 108
athlete interviews 85-86
athlete mental skills
 postselection assessment 86-88
 preselection assessment 84-86
 research support 51-52
 using 142
athlete training 142
athletic centers 30
athletic coach 143
athletic trainer 144
Auerbach, Red 75
Australian Psychology Accreditation Council 25

B

Babcock, Mike 34
Bean, Charles Homer 7
behavioral change 125-126
Belkeir, Kelly 122
Bennett, Gary 27
Berra, Yogi 30, 44
biofeedback 48
Blair, Steven 128
Bloom, Gordon 34
body rehearsal 97
Bohling, Chad 30
Bond, Jeff 31
Bonello, Frank 86
Boston University Athletic Enhancement Center 30
Bowden, Bobby 59
breathing techniques 48
Briles-Hinton, Jill 43
British Association of Sport and Exercise Sciences 25
British Psychological Society 25
Brooks, Carla 122
Brown, Paul 7
bulimia 115

C

cardiac rehabilitation 124-125
Carr, Chris 20
CHAMPS/Life Skills coordinators 33, 104, 105
clinical and counseling issues 13-14
clinical and counseling psychologist 145
clinical assessment screenings 88
clinical sport psychology
    about 111
    common work duties 113f
    mental health issues treated by 114
    nature of counseling 112, 114
    psychologist responsibilities 112
    research support 117
    service providers 118-119
    venues 112
Coach Approach 122, 125, 127, 128, 129, 148
coaching
    athletic coach 143
    coaches on team building 58-60
    education programs 34, 72-73, 76-78
    mental skills training 53
    motivation 74-75
    philosophies 73-74, 78
    positive environment 69, 70-71, 72-73
    styles 71
cognitive-behavioral skills 40, 126
cognitive-behavioral sport consultation 41-43
command style of coaching 71
community physical activity consultants 130
compliment sandwich approach 75, 143
concentration 49-50
consulting
    clinical and counseling issues 13-14
    cognitive-behavioral sport consultation 41-43
    consultant certification 17
    employment opportunities 22
    at high school level 52
    independent consulting 23
    mental training vs. clinical sport psychology
        12t
    methods for teaching coaches 73-75
    at Olympic and national team levels 53
    and physical activity advising 32-33
    positive leadership 70
    positive sport environment for coaches 78
    at professional level 53
    for sports agencies 32
    team-building services 64
    at university level 52-53
cooperative style of coaching 71
coping imagery 97
Coubertin, Pierre de 6, 8
counseling 22, 29-30, 33, 104-105, 110-111
Czech, Dan 47

D

decision balance 126-127
depression 114-115
DiCicco, Tony 56
DiLeo, Tony 86
Dorfman, Harvey 4, 49, 50, 71
drug testing 116

E

eating disorders 115-116
Ellis, Albert 41
Elms, Susie 107
emotive imagery 97
Erikson, Sven Goran 59
Espenschade, Anna 9
European Federation of Psychologists' Associations 25
exercise programs, dropout rates 126f
exercise psychology
    about 4-5, 123-124
    careers 23, 133-135
    focus on, 14
    interventions in exercise process 126-128
    providers 128-131
    research support 128
    services provided 125-126
    vs. sport psychology 124t
    venues 124-125
external locus of control 100
extrinsic motivation 74

F

Ferguson, Alex 59
Ferraro, Thomas 96
First Tee program 34
Fish, Joel 86, 87
fitness coach certification 129
fitness professional 146
Fitz, G.W. 5-6
flow state 42
Frontiera, Joe 52

G

generalized anxiety disorder 116-117
Gentry, Mike 27
Get Psyched for Sports 34
goal setting 44-45, 97, 126, 147, 149
Griffith, Coleman 7, 83
group development, linear theory of 57
Gulick, Luther 5

H

Hacker, Colleen 56, 61
Halladay, Roy 4
Hamm, Mia 56
Harris, Dorothy 10

Henderson, Robert 7
Henry, Franklin 9
Hewlett, Lan 103
Hirsh, Jason 46
Hitchcock, Ken 59
Holmes, Joseph 83
hypnosis 8-9

I

IDEA approach 75, 147
imagery 45-47, 97-98, 149
injury
    athletes' responses to 94-95
    counseling services providers 99-100
    group counseling 99
    high school sport-related injuries 93f
    psychology of rehabilitation 92-94
    referrals to sport psychologists 95-96
    rehabilitation interventions 96-99, 144
    research support for counseling 99
    stress contribution to 93-94, 144
intelligence testing 7, 82, 85
International Junior Golf Academy 26
Internet. See Web sites
internship opportunities 26
interventions 8-9
intrinsic motivation 74-75

J

Jackson, Phil 48, 58, 70-71, 150
Jacobson, Edmund 8, 48, 98
James, Lebron 12
James, William 5
Janssen, Jeff 64
Jarrett, Dwayne 92
Johanson, Albert 83
Johnson, Warren 9
Johnson, Zach 40, 41

K

Kalkstein, Don 31
Kimball, Aimee 40, 96, 97
King, Billy 86
Krzyzewski, Mike 60
Kübler-Ross, Elisabeth 94
Kuehl, Karl 49
Kulbacki, Kellen 43

L

Larranaga, Jim 68
Lawther, John 7
leadership style 70, 147
Leidl, Dan 52
licensed counselors 119
licensed psychologists 118
life skills, through youth sport 34

M

Magglingen Declaration 72
Major League Baseball
    mental skills evaluations 87-88
    mental training consultants 32
    performance-enhancement services 53
    psychological testing 86, 90
    rookie career development program 106
    sport psychology jobs 30-31
Maniar, Sam 28, 111, 119
Martens, Rainer 77
Martin, Kristin 99
mastery imagery 97
Maxwell, John C. 71
McCloy, Charles H. 8
McElrathbey, Ray 103
McKay, Rich 82, 86
McKenzie, Iona 93
meditation 48
mental health issues 114
mental imagery 45-47, 97-98, 149
mental skills. See athlete mental skills
mental training 12-13, 40, 43-51, 56
Metzler, Jonathan 47
Miles, Walter 7, 83
Moore, Nicki 27, 112
motivation 74-75, 149
motivational highlight videos 47
Move for Health 122-123
multidisciplinary training 20
Mumford, George 48
Munsterberg, Hugo 83
Murphy, Shane 20

N

Naismith, James 5
National Association of Academic Advisors
    for Athletics 104
National Basketball Association 87, 90, 106
National Collegiate Athletic Association (NCAA)
    CHAMPS/Life Skills program 104, 105, 108
    mental health issues focus 13, 111, 112
National Football Foundation 103
National Football League
    athlete assessments 84
    counseling for athletes 13
    development programs 105-106
    intelligence testing 7, 82, 85
    neuropsychological assessment 88
    player development specialists 33
    Play It Smart program 33
    psychological testing services 90
neuropsychological assessment 88
new psychology 6
Nideffer's concentration model 49f

North American Society for the Psychology of Sport and Physical Activity 10

O

obesity 123
objective goals 44
obsessive-compulsive disorder 117
Olympic athletes
    career programs 108
    clinical issues 112
    consultants to 53
    relaxation 47
    and sport psychology 10
    team building 60
Osborne, Tom 74
Ostrow, Andy 133
outcome goals 44

P

panic attacks 117
Pelini, Bo 59
performance coach 149
performance development 114
performance dysfunction 114
performance enhancement 12, 52-53
performance-enhancing substances 116
Performance Excellence Movement 34
performance goals 44
performance impairment 114
performance termination 114
personal development 13, 101
personality tests 85
Peterson, Kirsten 118
Philippe, Jean 6
phobias 117
physical activity 123-124, 148
physical activity counselors 129-130
Physical Activity for a Lifetime of Success 128, 131
physical activity promotion program directors 130-131
physical education teacher 147
Pickens, Morris 40
Play It Smart 33, 92, 103
Polian, Bill 82
Portus, Marc 85
positive self-talk 50-51, 98, 127, 149
positive sport environment 69-70, 72-73, 76-78
postdoctoral training 29
practice drills 62
process goals 44
professional sports jobs 30-32
Profile of Mood States 84
progressive relaxation 48
psychological interventions 8-9

psychological skills training 41
psychological testing 88, 89-90
psychology licensure laws 25
public health professional 148

R

Ravizza, Ken 68
relaxation 9, 10, 47-48, 98
reliability, defined 89
research 24, 131
Rice, Grantland 48
Richmond Football Club 31
Riley, Pat 59-60
Rini, Richard 29
Rotella, Bob 68
Royal, Darrell 103
Ruth, Babe 83

S

Sachs, Michael 135
school psychologist 145
Scottish Institute of Sport 107
Scripture, E.W. 5, 82
self-monitoring 127
self-talk 50-51, 98, 127, 149
self-worth issues 101
Shanahan, Mike 63
Silva, John M. 42
SMART goals acronym 45
Smith, Dean 57, 58, 74, 150
social cohesion 57
social workers 119
Spalding, A.G. 6-7
sport academy careers 26
sport and exercise psychology
    about 4-5
    academic positions 23
    athlete development careers 23
    career paths 22, 23, 24-32, 32-35, 133-135
    current status of field 11-15
    exercise psychology careers 23
    future of field 16, 133-135
    history 6-8, 8-10, 10-11
    implementing in real world 141-150
    origins 5-6
    professional practice issues 17-18
    roles of sport and exercise psychologists 21f
    training 20-22, 24
sport management and business professional 150
sport psychiatry 35
sport psychology
    about 4-5
    application to other industries 34-35
    assessment use in 84-88

career paths 22, 24, 133-135
   vs. exercise psychology 124*t*
   graduate training 17-18
   history 6-8, 8-10, 10-11
   injury counseling services 99-100
   injury referrals 95-96
   multidisciplinary training 119
   predoctoral and postdoctoral training 29
   professional organizations 14-16
sports medicine 8, 35
sports medicine clinic 95
stages of change theory 125-126
Stagner, Ross 7
Stark, Jack 59
stork stand 50
strength and conditioning coach 149
stress, contribution to injury 93-94, 144
student-athletes 26
subjective goals 44
submissive style of coaching 71
substance abuse 116, 149
success stories
   Bud Winter 10
   Jeff Bond 31
   Jeff Janssen 64
   Jim Annesi 127
   Joel Fish 87
   John M. Silva 42
   Kirsten Peterson 118
   Rainer Martens 77
   Susie Elms 107
Suinn, Richard 10
support groups 99
Sutton Tennis Academy 26

T
Talented Athlete Scholarship Scheme 26
Tarkanian, Jerry 76
task cohesion 57
task goals 58
team activities 63
team-bonding sessions 63
team building
   about 57
   activities for athletes 62-63
   approaches 60-61, 61-62
   benefits 57-58
   consultant services to athletes 64
   in management style 150
   as mental training 56
   research support 63
   successful coaches on 58-60
Team Enhance 99, 115
team meetings 62-63
tenure-track position 22, 24
Test of Attention and Interpersonal Style 84

Tewksbury, Bob 31, 53
Thomas, Isiah 46
Thomas, Joe 85
Thompson, Jim 77
thought-stopping technique 51
Torre, Joe 75
Tracy, David F. 9, 50
Tressel, Jim 70-71, 150
Triplett, Norman 6
Troutwine Athletic Profile 82, 84, 85

U
United States Military Academy 34
university athletic department jobs 27-29
university counseling centers 29-30
university sports jobs 27-30
Unruh, Jennifer 125

V
validity, defined 89
visualization techniques 45. *See also* mental
   imagery

W
Wafer, Ken 103
Walsh, Bill 75
Warner, Pop 7
Web sites
   coaching instructor certification 77
   postdoctoral opportunities 29
   predoctoral opportunities 29
   Sport Psychiatry Web 35
   sport psychology and mental training ser-
     vices 73
   wellness coaching 129
   youth sport development organizations
     102
wellness coaches 129
Winter, Bud 8, 10
Winter, Tex 71
Wolfe, Harry K. 7, 83
Wonderlic Personnel Test 7, 82, 84
Wooden, John 58-59, 75, 76, 150
Wright, Steven 31
Wundt, Wilhelm 5
Wurzberger, Dean 87

Y
Yates, Dorothy 8, 10, 50
YMCA approach 125
youth sport development organizations 102
Yukelson, Dave 20, 28, 99

Z
Zaichkowsky, Leonard 119
Zinser, Nate 59
Zuppke, Bob 7, 83

About the Author

Alan S. Kornspan, EdD, is an associate professor at the University of Akron in Akron, Ohio. He has taught sport psychology since 1997. His research has focused on historical issues related to sport and exercise psychology, and his articles have been published in such journals as *The Sport Psychologist, Journal of Sport Behavior,* and *Journal of Mental Imagery.*

Kornspan is an active member of the Association for Applied Sport Psychology (AASP), serves as the associate editor of its newsletter, was a member of the AASP graduate training committee, and is currently a member of the AASP organizational outreach committee. He earned his EdD in sport behavior in 1997 from West Virginia University.